Journal of Semitic Studies Su

STUDIES IN JEWISH PRAYER

Edited by

Robert Hayward and Brad Embry

Published by Oxford University Press
on behalf of the University of Manchester
2005

OXFORD
UNIVERSITY PRESS

Great Clarendon Street, Oxford OX2 6DP

Oxford University Press is a department of the University of Oxford.
It furthers the University's objective of excellence in research, scholarship,
and education by publishing worldwide in

Oxford New York

Athens Auckland Bangkok Bogotá Buenos Aires Cape Town
Chennai Dar es Salaam Delhi Florence Hong Kong Istanbul Karachi
Kolkata Kuala Lumpur Madrid Melbourne Mexico City Mumbai Nairobi
Paris São Paulo Shanghai Singapore Taipei Tokyo Toronto Warsaw

with associated companies in Berlin Ibadan

Oxford is a registered trade mark of Oxford University Press
in the UK and in certain other countries

Published in the United Kingdom
by Oxford University Press, Oxford

ISSN 0022-4480
ISBN 0-19-929641-3
ISBN 978-0-19-929641-5

Subscription information for the *Journal of Semitic Studies* is available at the journal website:
jss.oupjournals.org

Printed in Great Britain by Bell & Bain Ltd, Glasgow

Table of Contents

Robert Hayward
Preface   iv

Crispin H.T. Fletcher-Louis
The Aqedah and the Book of Watchers (1 Enoch 1–36)   1

Siam Bhayro
'... *and you know everything before it happens* ...': A Complaint Against
the Inaction of the Most High in 1Enoch 9   33

L.T. Stuckenbruck
Pleas for Deliverance from the Demonic in Early Jewish Texts   55

Archie T. Wright
Prayer and Incantation in the Dead Sea Scrolls   75

Bradley J. Embry
Prayer in Psalms of Solomon *Or* The Temple, Covenantal Fidelity, and Hope   89

Niclas Förster
The Prayer of Choni in Josephus Antiquities XIV 24   101

Gillian Greenberg
The Faith of the Translator of the Peshitta: Some Indications in P-Isaiah   117

Stefan C. Reif
Approaches to Sacrifices in Early Jewish Prayer   135

Robert Hayward
The Temple as a Place of Prayer in the Pentateuchal Targumim   151

Dan Levene
Jewish Liturgy and Magic Bowls   163

Jeremy Schonfield
The Four-fold Structure of the Passover Haggadah   185

Naftali Loewenthal
'From the Source of *Raḥamim*': Graveside Prayer of Habad Hasidism   207

Preface

The essays collected in this volume represent the final, revised forms of papers delivered to the annual Conference of the British Association for Jewish Studies, meeting at Hatfield College, Durham from 15th–17th July 2003. The theme of the conference was Jewish Prayer throughout the ages: the contributions reflected the wide interest in this topic not only as a fitting subject for critical academic study in the traditional manner, but also as a matter impinging on vital aspects of Jewish life and practice in modern society, with its self-declared interest in spirituality and the interior life.

As is sometimes the case with Conferences of this kind, some contributors decided to present detailed reports of 'work in progress', which is part of a larger project destined for publication at some later date. The preferred option of such scholars is often to wait until the whole project is complete, before setting out their results, on the not unreasonable grounds that only when research is complete is a balanced and objective conclusion available for their work. The Durham Conference was no exception to this state of affairs. Joanna Weinberg and Piet van Boxel, presenting a joint paper entitled '*What's Wrong with the Maḥzor? Christian Censorship in the Sixteenth Century*', offered the delegates a fascinating insight into the minds of the Christian censors, indicating their motives and ambitions, and illustrating from manuscript material how they set about their work, their attitudes to Jews and to Jewish Scholarship and their ultimate aims. Their paper was designed to give a fresh insight into the procedure that governed Christian handling of, or rather tampering with, the Roman Mahzor printed in Bologna in 1540. Their re-evaluation was based on a hitherto unknown manuscript in the Vatican Library, containing excerpts from the Roman Mahzor (*Maḥzor Romi*) in Latin and Italian translation, accompanied by marginal comments. On investigation, it transpired that although the passages reflect conventional Christian criticism of Jewish texts, the purpose of the undertaking was to propagate information about the prayer-book and Jewish liturgical tradition without any ostensible polemic objective. It was suggested that these notes were to be used as a resource for Christians when engaged in debate with Jews.

The papers published here treat particularly (not surprisingly, perhaps) of three main areas. The first, chronologically speaking, is prayer as it stands revealed in the Qumran texts and in writings dubbed Apocrypha and Pseudepigrapha. With the more or less complete publication of the Qumran documents, research into what these texts from Second Temple times might have to tell us about Jewish prayer began to surge; and there is evidently no sign of any lessening of interest in this matter. Likewise, after years of comparative neglect, Jewish apocryphal and pseudepigraphical writings have begun to claim the scholarly attention they deserve. It goes without saying that important historical material can be unearthed from these sources: equally important are the insights to be gleaned from the specific concerns articulated in prayers or prayer-like material preserved in these works, which in many instances turn out to have remained (in one way or another) within the broad stream of the Jewish liturgical tradition, sometimes prominently so, sometimes in a minor key, sometimes in greatly modified forms. Modern study of prayer in Qumran texts and in Apocrypha and Pseudepigrapha thus finds a place in this volume, along with an analysis of 'charismatic' prayer as understood by the historian Josephus.

Secondly, some rabbinic perspectives find their place here, from two different, but complementary directions. Aramaic magic bowls, exotic, mysterious, and often difficult to read and interpret, offer a wealth of information on prayer and liturgy 'applied', as it were, to everyday life. These artefacts introduce us directly to a world which the Sages of Talmudic and later times were undoubtedly aware of; but it was a world about which they were often reticent, sometimes embarrassed, and not infrequently critical. It is therefore instructive to compare rabbinic texts: results of study of some of the bowls are given in this volume, showing how 'popular' and 'official' attitudes to prayer, so to speak, were closely inter-related and in dialogue with one another. Two papers consider the significance of the Temple and its service (a matter of no little concern to those who produced the magic bowls) in relation to formal prayer of the Jewish community after the destruction of the Temple, especially the prayer of the synagogue service, and rabbinic comments about its relationship to the service of the Temple. These comments turn out to be much more varied and nuanced than is sometimes supposed, the Temple's significance as a place for prayer and as a central focus for prayer being matters for debate and discussion throughout the rabbinic period.

Finally, the modern Western world poses familiar problems and questions for those who would pray: some of these problems arise directly from a single antipathy towards traditional ways and lead to the rejection or radical modification of those traditions, for whatever reason; others come about as the result of philosophical challenges, the modern intellectual climate being generally umsympathetic to prayer as traditionally understood. At the same time, so fragmented is this Western society of ours that, paradoxically, tradition may still make itself heard, and even find itself being re-asserted with fresh vigour. This volume includes essays which critically analyse the effects of modernity on the tradition of Jewish prayer, and at the same time open to our eyes the constant dialogue and interaction between today's Jewish prayer and the praises and petitions of earlier generations of Jews. Not least do the essays on prayer in the modern period illustrate the continuing vigour, creativity, and relevance of those who, to all eternity, accept their obligation to declare the greatness, the holiness, and the praise of the Creator and King of the Universe.

Robert Hayward   Brad Embry

The Aqedah and the Book of Watchers (1 Enoch 1–36)

Crispin H.T. Fletcher-Louis

In this paper I bring together a text (the Book of Watchers) and a tradition (the Aqedah) which have not, hitherto, been related to one another in modern scholarship. Both contain important material on the subject of prayer. Both the text and the tradition have problems which, I suggest, are loosened through an appreciation of the role each plays in the formation of the other. Along the way, the manner in which scriptures were interwoven in the creation of some pseudepigraphical texts will, I hope, be better understood.

The story of God's testing of Abraham through the command to sacrifice his son Isaac in Genesis 22 is much developed in post-biblical literature where in rabbinic tradition it is called the Aqedah, 'the *binding* (of Isaac)'. Where the biblical text centres attention on Abraham's act of fidelity, rabbinic and targumic traditions highlight equally the active, not passive, role of Isaac who is a knowing, adult and willing victim of the intended sacrifice. There is no one, single, complete, haggadic account of the Aqedah and there are important differences between the picture in the Targums and rabbinic texts.[1] A variety of additions to the biblical text appear across a diverse body of literature: Isaac asks to be bound so that his sacrifice is perfect; he has a vision of the angels and of heaven; Abraham prays that his and Isaac's obedience would be remembered on behalf of Isaac's children; all this takes place on the Mountain that will become the site of Solomon's temple. Despite the fact that Isaac is *not* sacrificed in Genesis 22, some texts nevertheless claim his blood was shed or, even that he was offered as a holocaust — leaving 'the ashes of Isaac' as a memorial — before he was resurrected. Isaac's willingness to be sacrificed — if not his actual sacrifice — is then a meritorious act, in view of which, in subsequent salvation history God acts to save his people Israel.

The fully sacrificial benefits of Isaac's action are also tied to the Spring and Autumn New Year festivals. Today the Aqedah is remembered in the Musaph prayer

---

1   For recent surveys see S. Spiegel, *The Last Trial* (New York 1967); J.D. Levenson, *The Death and Resurrection of the Beloved Son: The Transformation of Child Sacrifice in Judaism and Christianity* (New Haven 1993), 173–99.

1

for the Rosh ha-Shanah service; a liturgical association attested in Talmudic tradition (b. Meg. 31a; b. Rosh ha-Shana 16a; Gen. Rab. 56:9; Lev. Rab. 29:9). On the other hand, the second century BCE pseudepigraphon Jubilees dates the event to the 14th of Nisan, the day of Passover.[2] That association is natural, given that on both days the firstborn is spared through the substituted sacrifice of a lamb or ram.[3] Already in Philo of Alexandria the story is related to the daily slaughter of the lambs of Tamid.[4]

How old and how faithful to the biblical text is this tradition? Almost half a century ago G. Vermes gave fresh impetus to the study of the Aqedah in a study that argued for an early, pre-Christian dating of its core.[5] Vermes relied on the evidence of the targums that he dated early, along with material in Jubilees and the late first century CE writings of Josephus and Pseudo-Philo's Biblical Antiquities.[6] In the late seventies and early eighties Bruce Chilton and Philip Davies argued in several publications against the early dating.[7] In their view, Josephus and Pseudo-Philo do not provide reliably pre-Christian material (both write after 70 CE), the targumic evidence is also late and sacrificial elaborations of the biblical story are best explained as a polemical response to the Christian understanding of the atoning work of Christ's death, in the new world deprived of temple sacrifices. On this showing the Aqedah is a radical transformation of Genesis 22 itself.

---

2   Jubilees 17:15 says the command to sacrifice came on the twelfth of Nisan. This means the sacrifice was made 'on the third day' (Gen. 22:4), that is the fourteenth of Nisan, followed by the three further days of the return journey before the Sabbath's rest (see J.C. VanderKam, 'The *Aqedah*, *Jubilees*, and PseudoJubilees', in C.A. Evans and S. Talmon (eds), *The Quest for Context and Meaning: Studies in Biblical Intertextuality in Honor of James A. Sanders* [Leiden 1997], 241–61 [246–7]).

3   For the Passover connection see the Targums to Exod 12:42; Mekhilta de R. Ishmael §7, lines 78–9; Exod. Rab. 15:11. And see Pseudo-Philo's Biblical Antiquties 40:8 for the 14th of the (unnamed) month as a memorial to an *Aqedah*-like event (discussed below).

4   Philo, De Abr. 198. Cf. m. Tamid 4:1; Lev. Rab. 2:11.

5   G. Vermes, *Scripture and Tradition in Judaism: Haggadic Studies* (Studia postBiblica 4, Leiden 1961), 193–227. Cf. R. Le Déaut, *La nuit pascale* (Analecta biblica 22, Rome 1963), 131–212.

6   Vermes suggests the origin of the *Aqedah* in its haggadic form is a reading of Genesis 22 through the suffering servant song of Isaiah 53 and the experience of the martyrs in the Maccabean crisis. This means it must be dated to that crisis or sometime after it (*Scripture* 202–4) and 'the martyrdom of the seven sons of a pious woman, recorded in II Maccabees vii, may have been the precise occasion' (203–4).

7   P.R. Davies and B.D. Chilton, 'The Aqedah: A Revised Tradition History', *Catholic Biblical Quarterly* 40 (1978), 514–46; P.R. Davies, 'Passover and the Dating of the Akedah', *Journal of Jewish Studies* 30 (1979), 59–67; B. Chilton, 'Isaac and the Second Night: A Consideration', *Biblica* 61 (1980), 78–88, cf. B. Chilton, 'Recent Discussion of the Aqedah', *Targumic Approaches to the Gospels. Essays in the Mutual Definition of Judaism and Christianity* (Lanham 1986), 39–49.

Whilst Davies and Chilton have rightly challenged scholarship to careful attention to the details of the textual evidence, not all have been persuaded by their principal theses. In particular, Robert Hayward, and, to a lesser extent, Alan F. Segal, have raised objections to their interpretation of the post-biblical evidence.[8] Indeed, two recent monographs dedicated to the interpretation of Genesis 22 have concluded that, in effect, the rabbinic sacrificial reading accords very well with biblical text's own intention. Jon D. Levenson and Walter Moberly read Genesis 22 — against the tide of modern scholarly opinion — as a foundational text for the sacrificial cult at Jerusalem.[9] Both have stressed linguistic and thematic indications that the mysterious 'land of Moriah' (22:2) looks forward to the location of Israel's cult in Jerusalem (Mount Moriah as it is called in 2 Chron. 3:1). And Levenson has highlighted the way in which, within its wider canonical context, the text functions not as an eradication of human sacrifice, but its transformation: Genesis 22 is a foundational narrative for the Jerusalem sacrificial cult where, in particular, God has ordained various substitutions for the life of the human firstborn that he otherwise claims (see Exod. 22:28–9; 34:19–20; Deut. 15:19–23; Exod. 12:21–3; 13:2, 12–15; Num. 3:11–13, 40–51; 8:14–19).

If Levenson and Moberly are right about the text's original intention, then the Aqedah does not need to be a response either to Christian atonement theology or to the loss of the temple: its main themes belong firmly within Second Temple reflection on the biblical story, and at crucial points it reflects the wider pattern of child sacrifice in Israel's pre-exilic Canaanite context.[10] In fact, some support for Vermes' dating has now come from the publication of a fragmentary Dead Sea Scroll text — 4Q225 — that retells the Genesis 22 story in ways that anticipate the later rabbinic complex.[11] In

---

8   C.T.R. Hayward, 'The Present State of Research into the Targumic Account of the Sacrifice of Isaac', *Journal of Jewish Studies* 32 (1981), 127–50 and 'The Sacrifice of Isaac and Jewish Polemic against Christianity', *Catholic Biblical Quarterly* 52 (1990), 292–306; A.F. Segal, '"He who did not spare His only Son…": Jesus, Paul, and the Aqedah', in P. Richardson (ed.), *From Jesus to Paul: Studies in Honour of Francis Wright Beare* (Waterloo, Ontario 1984), 169–84. See now also L.A. Huizenga, 'The Battle for Isaac: Exploring the Composition and Function of the *Aqedah* in the Book of *Jubilees*', *Journal for the Study of the Pseudepigrapha* 13 (2002), 33–59 for a critique of Davies' and Chilton's handling of the *Jubilees* evidence.

9   Levenson, *Beloved Son*; R.W.L. Moberly, *The Bible, Theology, and Faith. A Study of Abraham and Jesus* (Cambridge 2000).

10 For the continuities between the formative context of Genesis 22 and its later post-biblical (transformative) interpretations see esp. Levenson, *Beloved Son*, 173–99.

11 See G. Vermes, 'New Light on the Sacrifice of Isaac from 4Q225', *Journal of Jewish Studies* 47 (1995), 140–6; VanderKam, 'The *Aqedah*' and J.A. Fitzmyer, 'The Sacrifice of Isaac in Qumran

particular, the scene now includes 'angels of holiness standing weeping (מלאכי קודש עומדים בוכים) above' the place of Isaac's imminent slaughter (2 ii 5). This prefigures the tradition found in the Midrash Rabbah (Gen. Rab. 56:5, cf. 57:7) according to which 'the ministering angels wept (בכו מלאכי השרת)' as Isaac stretched out his hand to take the knife.[12]

Davies and Chilton had claimed that their thesis is 'most eloquently ... supported not by the few texts in which mention of Isaac's offering is made but by the many whose cumulative silence almost drowns the fashionable chorus for a pre-Christian Aqedah, namely the whole of the Qumran literature ... together with a host of apocryphal and pseudepigraphical works.'[13] The publication of 4Q225 now puts paid to their confident appeal to 'the whole of the Qumran literature'. And, one purpose of the rest of this essay is to suggest that a Jewish pseudepigraphon from the end of the fourth or early in the third century BCE — the Book of Watchers — contains some thinly veiled allusions to the story of Isaac's binding and aborted sacrifice.

The Book of Watchers is the first of the five books in the Enochic corpus now known as 1 Enoch. The Book of Watchers (1 Enoch 1–36) is largely taken up with a fuller version of the brief story in Gen. 6:1–4 in which sons of God descend to earth to have intercourse with the daughters of men. It is likely that the Book of Watchers relies on a longer and well-known story that is only paraphrased in Genesis, though in its current form the pseudepigraphical text is certainly younger than both Genesis and the version known to Genesis. Partly because of the discovery of second century BCE Aramaic fragments of the work at Qumran, but also because of the theological and political tone and content of the work, the majority now date it to the third century BCE or earlier. Whilst the book certainly contains older material from different contexts, Eibert J.C. Tigchelaar and the present writer have argued that in its final form the Book of Watchers is written from the perspective of Jerusalem as a polemic against the Samaritans who, (according to tradition) some time in the late fourth century BCE, like the watchers in primeval history, left the God-ordained site of the true temple and priestly service to form a heterodox cult.[14]

Literature', *Biblica* 83 (2002), 211–29. Palaeography dates the text to the turn of the eras (c. 30 BCE – 20 CE) (see DJD XIII, 140).

12 It is possible also that Isaac has a vision of these angels and that it is *his*, as much as Abraham's, faith which is being tested. As in Jubilees (17:16; 18:9ff) the archdemon Mastema (and his angels) also play a prominent part in the drama.

13 Davies and Chilton, 'Revised Tradition History', 518.

14 The watchers' illegitimate intercourse thus alludes typologically to the exogamous behaviour of Jerusalem priests who (so the story goes) founded the breakaway temple at Shechem (see Josephus

The story at the heart of the book (chs 6–15) — with which we are concerned — proceeds as follows. A group of two hundred angels sees the beautiful daughters of mankind and decides to choose wives to bear their children. They make a pact, swearing an oath to carry through their deed and they descend from heaven to earth at Mount Hermon. Through their intercourse they beget giants who take over the world, make humans their slaves and a satisfaction for their lust for blood. They also lead humanity astray by teaching them the making of weapons for war, ladies' beauty treatments and ornamentation, and occult sciences; the reading of the heavenly bodies and the cutting of roots. From all this chaos and bloodshed the earth cries out to heaven for help and the archangels carry the cry for justice to God enthroned in his palace.

In chapter 10, God decrees the imminent destruction of the earth and everything on it through the flood. He tells one of his angels to warn Noah ('the son of Lamech') of the coming deluge that he might hide himself and be spared (10:1–2). God further commissions the angels Raphael, Gabriel and Michael to punish and imprison (to bind) the fallen angels (the watchers); and to set about the destruction of their offspring. At this time Enoch is off stage. His dwelling and activities are with those watchers who had *not* abandoned their heavenly calling. These watchers now send Enoch to tell the sinful watchers of their imminent fate. The latter then ask him to intercede on their behalf (chs 12–13). He does so, repeating their prayers in mantra-like fashion at the waters of Dan at the southwest foot of Mount Hermon until he falls asleep. In his dream Enoch has revelations that include God's rejection of the watchers' prayer for forgiveness and a confirmation of the divine condemnation.

Although these chapters are central to the book they have some problems: they appear repetitive and disjointed. The story of the Flood is imperfectly introduced in 10:1–3 as the context for the judgement on the watchers that follows (10:4–15:12). Once the fact of the coming flood is stated it plays no further role in the story and it is not the means by which the watchers and their offspring are punished or destroyed.[15]

Ant. 11:306–12). See E.J.C. Tigchelaar, *Prophets of Old and the Day of the End. Zechariah, the Book of Watchers and Apocalyptic* (Oudtestamentische Studien 35, Leiden 1996), 198–203 and C.H.T. Fletcher-Louis, *All the Glory of Adam: Liturgical Anthropology in the Dead Sea Scrolls* (Studies on the Texts of the Deserts of Judah 42, Leiden 2002), 24–7.

15 Contrast 3 Macc. 2:4 and Job 26:5 LXX. The juxtaposition of Flood and punishment of the watchers may be explained by the close association of the Flood story and the Day of Atonement (on which see now R.S. Kawashima, 'The Jubilee Year and the Return of Cosmic Purity', *Catholic Biblical Quarterly* 65 [2003], 370–89). The punishment of the watchers has some connection to the proceedings of Yom Kippur (see below).

The chronological relationship between the flood and the destruction of the watchers is also unclear. Given the heinous crimes of the not-so-angelic children and their once-angelic fathers the reader wants a swift, merciless fulfilment of the divine decree. Instead, before the punishment is carried out there is a delay, during which Enoch intercedes for the watchers (chs 12–15). There is also the somewhat awkward sending of Enoch to announce the divine decree to the fallen watchers before the archangels Raphael, Gabriel and Michael carry out their commission. Given the Flood setting, the reader expects any part for a human protagonist to be played not by Enoch, but by Noah. But, after his introduction in 10:1–3, Noah plays no further role in the story.

A number of biblical texts, I suggest, contribute to the apparently untidy structure of 1 Enoch 10–14. Chief among these is Genesis 22 and its related biblical and post-biblical traditions. One effect of the additional account of Enoch's mission to the angels and intercession on their behalf is the repetition of material. It means that there are now three occasions on which it is said that besides the punishment of the watchers themselves, their *loved ones,* their children, will not be spared either:

To Michael God says of the watchers in 10:12: 'and when their sons perish and they see the destruction of their beloved ones (ὅταν ... ἴδωσιν τὴν ἀπώλειαν τῶν ἀγαπητῶν), bind them for seventy generations in the valleys of the earth.'

Enoch is informed in 12:6 of the fate of the watchers: 'And concerning their sons – in whom they rejoice – the slaughter of their beloved ones they will see (τὸν φόνον τῶν ἀγαπητῶν αὐτῶν ὄψονται); and over the destruction of their sons they will lament and make petition forever, and they will have no mercy or peace.'

In 14:6, after his vision, Enoch returns to deliver the divine reprimand to the watchers: 'And that before these things, you will see the destruction of your sons, your beloved ones (... ἴδητε τὴν ἀπώλειαν τῶν υἱῶν ὑμῶν τῶν ἀγαπητῶν)' (= 4Q204 vi 16 [חביבי]כ[ו]ן).

These three statements sound some suggestive echoes of the Genesis 22 story. Three times Isaac is called Abraham's only (יחיד) or beloved son (LXX has ἀγαπητός) (Gen. 22:2, 12, 16). The language is distinctive of that Genesis story, occurring nowhere else in the Pentateuch, and rarely outside it. The linguistic connection between the Book of Watchers and Genesis 22 is strongest for the Greek, where both refer to the respective children as ἀγαπητός.[16] The Aramaic evidently

---

16 Later Greek translations of Genesis 22 have τὸν μονογενῆ (Aquila) and τὸν μόνον σου (Symmachus) not ἀγαπητός. But the LXX almost certainly reflects the dominant Greek translation of the text in the third and second centuries BCE.

had not יחיד but חביב.[17] But the Greek translator's choice of ἀγαπητός indicates that an allusion to Genesis 22 was intended in the Aramaic. Although the later targums (Pseudo-Jonathan and Onqelos) do use יחיד in their versions of Genesis, the choice of the Aramaic חביב for the Hebrew יחיד is unsurprising. The use of ἀγαπητός in the LXX translation of Gen. 22:2, 12, 16 and related texts (Amos 8:10; Jer. 6:26; Judg. 11:34 A) shows that in this context יחיד was taken to mean, not just the 'only' child, but the one whom the parent dearly loves (cf. Gen. 22:2 אשר אהבת).[18] So the use of the Aramaic חביב for the only child of Genesis 22 accords entirely with the Septuagint's evidence for the understanding of the passage's linguistic nuances.

Secondly, in each of these three passages from the Book of Watchers it is expressly stated that the watchers 'will *see*' the destruction of their beloved children. A prominent verbal root in Genesis 22 is ראה, 'to *see*'. In 22:4 Abraham lifts his eyes and *sees* the place for the sacrifice that God provides for him. In 22:8 Abraham reassures his son that God will *see* to it and provide a victim to sacrifice and, sure enough, in 22:13 Abraham lifts his eyes and *sees* the ram caught in the bush. Finally, in 22:14 Abraham names the mountain-top spot, 'the LORD *sees*/provides (יהוה יראה, cf. LXX κύριος εἶδεν).' In Genesis 22 God sees and Abraham's son is spared. In the Book of Watchers there is no provision of forgiveness for the children of the watchers; but their fathers see them destroyed.

Thirdly, we are perhaps meant to hear an echo of the *binding* of Isaac in the *binding* of the watchers. Again the linguistic and conceptual parallels are not exact. In Genesis 22:9 the peculiar verb *'āqad* is used for the binding of Isaac's limbs as he is prepared for the altar. In 1 Enoch extant portions have instead the verb *'sr*. And whilst the beloved son is bound in Genesis 22, in 1 Enoch it is the parents, the watchers, not their children who are bound. But the Greek makes a closer linguistic connection between the two bindings. In the LXX of Genesis 22 the verb refers specifically to a binding of the feet — συμποδίζω. In 1 Enoch the watchers are similarly to be bound by their hands and feet (1 En. 10:4: (Panopolitanus) 'and he said to Raphael, Δῆσον τὸν Ἀζαὴλ ποσὶν καὶ χερσίν'; Syncellus has 'Go Raphael, and δῆσον τὸν Ἀζαὴλ χερσὶ καὶ ποσὶ συμπόδισον αὐτόν', cf. 10:11, 12; 13:1; 14:5). And we should note that although the verb *'āqad* later gave the story its distinctive rabbinic nomenclature — the Aqedah — the verb's significance in this regard is not attested in any of the

17 It is not absolutely certain that חביב was used at 10:12 and 12:6 since the Aramaic is not extant. And it is possible, though surely unlikely, that, since 4Q204 vi 16 is fragmentary, the Aramaic used יחיד after and in addition to חביביכון.

18 See Levenson, *Beloved Son,* 30–1.

primary sources prior to the Tannaitic material. And even then, when Targum Pseudo-Jonathan tells the story it quite happily does so without using the rare verb *'āqad* at all.

If there is a parallel between the two texts it is obviously asymmetrical: Abraham and *his* beloved — Isaac — are the model of pious obedience; the sinful watchers and their monstrous, but beloved, children manifest perverse disobedience. Where Isaac is bound because of his father's faithfulness to God's command, but ultimately his bonds are loosed, the watchers are bound because of their transgression and the chaos wrought by their children, and their sins are not forgiven. In the biblical text the father's piety achieves his child's release. In our pseudepigraphon the fathers' wickedness guarantees their childrens' destruction though the emphasis is placed on the watchers' own punishment, not that of their offspring.

Are these sufficient points of correspondence to establish an intended allusion to the biblical text in the Book of Watchers? Perhaps not, but further circumstantial evidence bolsters the case.

Enoch, Noah and Abraham: Parallels and Continuities

Abraham, Noah and Enoch have similar life stories and in antiquity there is evidence that Jews reflected deeply on the connections between them and between their historical contexts. Already, in Genesis they are singled out as those who 'walked with' God or the LORD (Gen. 5:22, 24; Gen. 6:9; Gen. 18:16, cf. 17:1; 24:40). Abraham and Noah are the first people with whom God makes a covenant (Gen. 6:18; 9:9–17 and 15:18; 17:2–21). There are ten generations from Adam to Noah (Genesis 5) and ten generations from Noah to Abraham (Gen. 11:10–26).[19] Enoch too takes a climactic position in the structure of primeval history, as the seventh from Adam (Gen. 5:18–24).

All three are also related to a destructive flood. After sending a flood to destroy all flesh God, of course, promised Noah that he would not repeat the act. But Abraham's generation suffers a similar, if more parochial fate. In Genesis 18–19 God sends a fiery conflagration on the wicked from which Abraham, his nephew Lot and Lot's family are spared. The parallels between the destruction of Sodom and the Flood have long been noted, both in Jewish antiquity, where the two stories often appear

---

19 This genealogical structure — the work of the Priestly compilers of the primeval history — was obvious to later readers (see e.g. m. Aboth 5:2–3; Josephus Ant. 1:79, 148).

together,[20] and by modern commentators.[21] They merit close attention: first, because they reflect the general interest in parallels and continuities between the lives of the primeval patriarchs and Abraham, secondly because of the possibility that the Sodom story has genetic parallels to the Book of Watchers' understanding of the events surrounding the Flood.

In both the Flood and Sodom stories divine wrath is directed at sexual perversion. In the former, angels have intercourse with women, in the latter men try to force themselves on angels. The Flood is sent to remove violence from the earth (Gen. 4:8; 6:4, 11–13; 1 En. 7:5; 8:1; 9:1). The Sodomites deal violently with strangers (Gen. 19:4–9). All the generation of the Flood, bar Noah and his immediate family, are destroyed. So too, 'the men of Sodom, both young and old, all the people to the last man' (Gen. 19:44), except Lot and his family, maltreat their guests and are destroyed. And, presumably if Abraham had not shown due hospitality he too would have suffered the divine wrath.[22] As it is, Abraham walks with the LORD in his threefold angelic form (Gen. 18:16), just as Enoch and Noah are said to have walked 'with *elohim',* 'with God', or, as later tradition takes, it 'with the gods, i.e. with the angels'. In its current form the emphasis is placed on the destruction of Sodom and Gomorrah by fire and brimstone. But Genesis says the LORD *rained down* (המטיר, ἔβρεξεν) fire and brimstone on the cities (Gen. 19:24, cf. 7:4); language that might evoke a torrential lightning storm. From Strabo (*Geog.* 16.2.44) and Josephus (War 4:484, cf. 5:566) we know this is the way the story was taken, at least by some ancient readers. The fact that Lot is to flee to the hills (19:16) perhaps assumes the valley below is to be flooded and Genesis itself suggests that, where there was once a fertile valley (Gen. 13:10; 14:3), the Dead Sea was then created by the fiery cataclysm.[23] In both stories, the hero's rescue is followed by his intoxication and shameful treatment by his children (Gen. 9:20–7; 19:30–8). And ancient parallels outside the Bible highlight the associations of the Sodom story with a *flood.*[24]

---

20 Sir. 16:8–9; Jub. 20:5–6; CD ii:14–3:12; Wis. 10:4–9; 3 Macc. 2:4–5; 2 Pet. 4–8; Jude 6–7; Josephus' War 5:566; T. Naph. 3:5–4:1; m. Sanh. 10:3; b. Sanh. 108a–109b; Memar Marqah 4:5, 12; 6:2.

21 For the parallels between the two stories see H. Gunkel, *Genesis* (Gottingen 1910), 77, 214; C. Westermann, *Genesis 12–36* (Minneapolis 1985), 297 and G.J. Wenham, *Genesis 16–50* (Dallas 1994), 40–3, 64.

22 The corporate solidarity between Abraham and those destroyed in Genesis 18–19 is emphasized by Josephus for whom the Sodomites are Abraham's 'friends' and 'neighbours' (Ant. 1:176).

23 Cf. Josephus Ant. 1:174, cf. War 5:81.

24 See Ovid *Metamorphoses* 8.618–724 and Joseph E. Fontenrose, *Philemon, Lot, and Lycaon* (Berkeley 1945). We should also note the intriguing statement in Josephus (Ant. 1:186) that the oak at which Abraham stays (in Gen. 13:18; 14:13 and 18:1) is not 'Mamre' but Ogyges (Ὠγύγη). This is the

Theatrically, the casting in Genesis 18–19 has a parallel to that in 1 Enoch 10–15.[25] Like Lot, Noah is in the midst of the generation that stands under judgement. Both Lot and Noah are rescued from imminent destruction because an angel warns them to flee (1 En. 10:1–3; Gen. 19:11–23). In the Book of Watchers, Enoch, Noah's great grandfather, is at this juncture off the earthly stage in the wings, 'with the watchers and the holy ones' (12:1–2).[26] This is an interpretation of the statement in Gen. 5:22, 24 that יתהלך חנוך את האלהים to the effect that 'Enoch walked with the angels'; taking *elohim* as a genuine plural ('gods'). It is these angels who tell Enoch of the coming fate of the fallen watchers, on behalf of whom Enoch then proceeds to offer prayers of intercession; in vain. Similarly, in Gen. 18:16–33 Abraham is some distance from Sodom when he 'walks with' the three angels of the LORD who disclose to him their intention to 'go down' to the city and destroy it. Abraham intercedes for the city. But for Lot and his family, his intercession is fruitless.

There are also intriguing connections between the role of the watchers, with their giant offspring, and the Abraham-Sodom story. In the Book of Watchers the angelic miscegenation is an outright transgression of the boundaries of creation. In Genesis, shortly before the fiery cataclysm that destroys Sodom and Gomorrah, Abraham's wife receives a divine visitation that leads to her conceiving the child of the promise, Isaac (Genesis 18). The LORD's own visitation provides legitimate transcendence of creation's 'laws' and so, in this respect, Sarah's son is the antipode to the watchers' demonic offspring. This anti-parallelism is especially noteworthy in the light of other Enochic literature where there is further speculation on a deliberate divine-human intercourse in the conception of the individual who survives the flood. In a tradition that was perhaps already known to the author of the Book of Watchers Noah is conceived ordinarily, but has the character at birth of an infant to divine parents (1 Enoch 106, 1QapGen 2, 5, cf. the birth of Melchizedek in *2 Enoch* 67–73).

---

name of a primeval Greek hero associated in Attic and Boeotian legend with stories of a flood. As his name might suggest he is also a giant ('Ωγύγη = ὁ γίγας?). On the possible function of Josephus' Ogyges, including its associations with the flood and giants, see Louis H. Feldman *Flavius Josephus: Judean Antiquities 1-4: Translation and Commentary* (3 vols, Leiden 2000), III, 70 n. 584 and *idem, Studies in Josephus' Rewritten Bible* (JSJSup 58, Leiden 1998), 20–1. And see further W. Fauth, 'Prähellenische Flutnamen: Og(es)-Ogen(os)-Ogygos', *Beiträge zur Namensforschung* 23 (1988), 361–79.

25 I am grateful to Siam Bhayro for alerting me to the parallels that follow.

26 G.W.E. Nickelsburg, *1 Enoch 1: A Commentary on the Book of 1 Enoch Chapters 1-36, 81-108* (Minneapolis 2001), 233 notes the contact with older Hellenistic tradition in the language of 1 En. 12:1–2.

In both the Flood/Book of Watchers story and in the Abraham material the narrative is driven by an expectation of the abundant growth of the human seed. This, of course, is a governing theme from the start of creation: humanity is to multiply and fill the earth (Gen. 1:28). But in the period between Adam and Noah a successful spread of human life is frustrated; a frustration caused by human violence (ch. 4) and the chaotic insurgence of the disobedient watchers (1 Enoch 6–9, see esp. 7:3), the 'sons of God' of Genesis 6. Humanity would have been wiped out were it not for a lineage for the righteous remnant through Enoch and Noah. In Noah a righteous 'seed [is] preserved for all generations' (1 En. 10:3), whilst the judgement of the watchers, and the destruction of their offspring removes the weeds that are choking the young shoots of a frail humanity.

In the Abraham cycle, the same theme dominates. Abraham is the one through whom the blessing on Adam will be fulfilled (12:2–3, cf. 17:2, 5–6; 28:3; 35:11). God promises Abraham that he will be the father of a multitude of nations (12:1–3; 15:5; 17:6, 16). But he is childless and Sarah is barren. And as they advance in age, desperate, but faithless measures, are taken to fulfil the promise (ch. 16). Narrative tension is first relieved when Sarah finally gives birth to Isaac. But it is not long before God tells Abraham to sacrifice this only son, the one through whom the promise is to be fulfilled. If Isaac is killed the promise surely falls. Through the sparing of the beloved, the seed is preserved and the promised reiterated (22:17–18); the tension is once again resolved.[27]

So, the Abraham cycle and the early pseudepigraphical material surrounding Enoch and Noah share a similar narrative structure:

Wondrous righteous child	→ *watery destruction of sinful generation*	→ *seed of righteous preserved*
Birth of Noah (1 Enoch 106 etc...)	→ Flood	→ seed of righteous preserved
Conception of Isaac	→ destruction of Sodom	→ seed of promise (through Abraham) preserved

Now, all these various parallels suggest that the account of the watchers' punishment was told with a conscious echo of the punishment of the inhabitants of Sodom and Gomorrah. It is not, therefore, surprising that in two passages in the Testaments of the

---

27 For the theme of raising up seed in the Sodom cycle see Gen. 19:32, 34.

Twelve Patriarchs Israel's patriarchs claim that the early Enochic material described the sin of the watchers in terms of the lawlessness of Sodom (T. Levi 14:1, 6 and T. Naph. 3:5–4:1). Did the development of the earlier tradition now extant in Genesis 6 later come under the influence of the Sodom story? Or do the parallels between the Sodom story and the Book of Watchers belie a much older common tradition that pre-dates the book of Genesis? We cannot tell. But, either way, the parallels help explain the disjointed structure of 1 Enoch 10–14. They also lend credence to our suspicion that the Book of Watchers has drawn on another passage from the Abraham cycle; the near sacrifice of Isaac.

Outside the Hebrew Bible, the Fall of the Watchers and Abraham stories are further linked by the belief of some that Abraham was himself of angelic-gigantic lineage. Pseudo-Eupolemus is probably a Samaritan work dating from the second century BCE or earlier. According to Pseudo-Eupolemus Abraham is of the lineage of the giants, some of whom escaped the Flood sent to destroy them for their impiety (Eusebius P.E. 9:17:2; 9:18:2). In Jewish tradition the giants of Greek and oriental myth are the sons of God of Gen. 6:1–4, the watchers whose sins are recounted in the Book of Watchers (e.g. Sir 16:7) or, in particular, they are those watchers' offspring (1 En. 7:2–5, cf. e.g. Jub. 5:1). Furthermore, Pseudo-Eupolemus says Abraham was a culture hero, teaching the Egyptians and the Phoenicians sciences and astrology. These he learnt from his ancestor Enoch who was himself a righteous giant, otherwise known to the Greeks by the name Atlas.

A genealogy that traces Abraham to the giants who survived a divine judgement on the sinful watchers should probably *not* be dismissed as idiosyncratically Samaritan and simply a reflection of un-Jewish syncretism with the mythology of Greece and Mesopotamia. The notion that Abraham's ancestors were giants might have been encouraged by the fact that one of Noah's sons — Japeth (Gen. 5:32; 6:10 and 10:1–5) — could be related to Iapetos, one of the giants of Greek myth.[28] The Genesis Apocryphon from Qumran perhaps thought of Noah in gigantic terms. Noah is born with a wondrous, angelic appearance that terrifies his father with the thought that his son was conceived by the promiscuous watchers (1QapGen cols. 2, 5, cf. 1 Enoch 106). Any grounds for this fear are rejected, but Noah's transcendent, divine identity is affirmed. Noah is, so-to-speak, a giant *not of the flesh but of the spirit* (cf. 1

---

28 For the identification (which is perhaps assumed in Sib. Or. 3:110–15) see John P. Brown, *Israel and Hellas* (3 vols, BZAW 299, Berlin, 2001), III, 82–3.

En. 106:17).[29] A little later in the Genesis Apocryphon God promises Noah: 'Do not be afraid, Noah, I am with you and with your sons, *who will be like you, forever.*' This continuity of identity between Noah and Abraham is then reflected in the addition of language to describe the life of the former from the life of the latter. According to the Genesis Apocryphon, after he leaves the ark Noah 'walked through the land, through its length and its breadth' (11:11). This is an addition to the biblical text that anticipates the way that in Gen. 13:17 Abraham will be told by God to 'Rise up, walk through the length and the breadth of the land,' that is to be given to him.[30] It is one more indication of the ways in which the Noah, Enoch and Flood stories were read in typological parallel to the Abraham stories.

The common idea that the righteous — Adam (Apoc. Abr. 23:5, 10, 14; 2 Enoch 30:13; Vita Adae et Evae 27:1); Moses(?) (Jewish Orphica 32–4); Enoch (3 Enoch 9); Jacob (Joseph and Aseneth 22:7); Judas Maccabeus (1 Macc 3:3) — are gigantic, shows that a tracing of Israel's lineage back to an antediluvian gigantic (but righteous) humanity that survived the flood was probably not unusual for the Judaism of antiquity. Language close to that in Pseudo-Eupolemus appears in the Jewish Orphica where 'a unique man, an offshoot from far back of the race of the Chaldeans' who has astronomical knowledge, 'is established in great heaven on a golden throne (where) he stands with his feet on the earth … (and) he stretches out his right hand to the ends of the ocean' (Long version 26–34). Because of the enthronement motif this could be Moses (cf. Ezekiel the Tragedian's Exagoge 68–82; Philo De Vita Mosis 1:155–8), though Chaldean lineage and astronomical knowledge would also fit Abraham.

All this means that a typological parallel between Abraham's near sacrifice of Isaac and the punishment of the watchers is natural. In the Book of Watchers Noah is a righteous human being who will be spared the Flood's coming destruction and cleansing of the chaos wrought by the fallen angels (1 En. 10:1–3). His seed survives because of the destruction of the watchers' beloved children and it continues, despite the temporary frustration, to grow and spread throughout the earth (1 En. 10:16–22), thereby fulfilling the original commanded to Noah in Gen. 9:1 ('God blessed Noah and his sons, and said to them, "Be fruitful and multiply, and fill the earth"'). In

---

29 See Fletcher-Louis, *Glory of Adam* 37–9. Here I disagree with John C. Reeves' view that the Birth of Noah is an outright polemic against the notion (attested in Pseudo-Eupolemus) that Noah and Abraham have a lineage back to the giants.

30 See M.J. Bernstein, 'Pentateuchal Interpretation at Qumran', in P.W. Flint and J.C. VanderKam (eds), *The Dead Sea Scrolls after Fifty Years* (Leiden 1998), 128–59 (146).

Abraham also the seed of the righteous, through the sparing of the beloved son, continues to multiply and fill the earth (Gen. 16:10; 17:6; 28:3; 35:11, cf. 12:1–3).

The Children of the Watchers and Jephthah's Vow

Further support for our claim that 1 Enoch 10–14 alludes to Genesis 22 comes from another biblical text that is closely related to the story of Isaac's near sacrifice. The distinctive language for the child to be sacrificed in Genesis 22 occurs in several other biblical passages. One of these is the story in Judges 11 of Jephthah's sacrifice of his daughter.

Jephthah the Gileadite vowed to sacrifice whoever greeted him on his return from defeating the Ammonites. His daughter, one who, like Isaac, is called his 'only, beloved' (רק היא יחידה, μονογενὴς αὐτῷ ἀγαπητή) child (Judg. 11:34), greeted him. Jephthah sacrifices her, as Abraham had intended to do to Isaac, as a burnt offering (עולה, Judg. 11:31, cf. Gen. 22:2, 3, 6–7, 13). The story is not just an inner-biblical parallel to Genesis 22; it is an important witness to Israel's pre-exilic contact with the Canaanite practice of child sacrifice (on which, see below) that stands behind the Abraham and Isaac story.

And, on close inspection, there are a number of intriguing parallels between the Jephthah story and the lives of the watchers in 1 Enoch. Jephthah binds himself with a vow. So do the watchers (1 En. 6:10). The fact is evidently an important one in the Book of Watchers since the watchers also descend at Hermon, the mountain of the oath or ban (חרמון, √חרם). Jephthah defeats Israel's enemies, partly, we are given to believe, because his vow has won him divine favour and military prowess. Perhaps a similar divine power is the expected effect of the watchers' vow. In any case, they are skilled in the arts of war (1 En. 8:1) and their bloodthirsty children wreak havoc amongst the human and animal populations (7:3–6, cf. 10:9, 12). Jephthah's beloved is consigned to death. The watchers' beloved are sentenced to death. According to Judg. 11:1–3 Jephthah is a bastard child of a prostitute. He is also a 'mighty warrior (גבור חיל)'. In Gen. 6:4 the angels of God have illegitimate intercourse with the daughters of men and produce גברים. For the Book of Watchers these גברים are the troublesome and bellicose giants (1 En. 7:2), the beloved, but now condemned, children of the watchers.

The relationships in Judges 11 are not an identical match to those of the watchers-giant story in 1 Enoch, but they are sufficiently similar that we can be confident a biblically literate author or reader of the Book of Watchers would hear an echo of the fate of Jephthah's daughter in the fate of the watchers and their children. And, as with echoes of Genesis 22, the intertextuality probably exhibits an asymmetry that furthers the polemic of the watchers' tale. In Judges 11 Jephthah goes willingly to death without so much as a whimper. In the Book of Watchers the watchers (including, we should probably assume, their second generation progeny, the giants) seek pardon with strenuous prayer — through Enoch their intercessor — and through lamentation (13:4–14:7). In Judges 11 the innocent suffers stoically, in the Book of Watchers the wicked resist their punishment wholeheartedly.

If the pattern by which the beloved child is sacrificed in Judges 11 *is* in mind in 1 Enoch 12–16 it obviously buttresses the allusion to Genesis 22, which, of these two 'death of the beloved' scriptural passages is by far the more prominent. But allusion to Judges 11 also helps explain a puzzling aspect of the narrative. It is not otherwise clear why there should be a period of delay between the announcing of the capital sentence on the watchers' children and its fulfilment. A delay that affords a period of weeping enables the author to describe the judgement of the watchers through the death of the beloved motif *as it is attested in Judges 11*. Before her death, Jephthah wanders for two months on the mountains and bewails her virginity with her companions (Judg. 11:37–9). Her lineage is cut off forever. Similarly, before the destruction of their beloved, and consequent end to their lineage, the watchers weep in the foothills of Mount Hermon (1 En. 13:9).

The Rationale for an Allusion to Genesis 22 in the Book of Watchers

If the Book of Watchers does allude to the later sparing of Abraham's beloved son what is the point of that allusion? And does an allusion to Genesis 22 in anyway help us trace the origins of the Aqedah — the post-biblical traditions surrounding Genesis 22? I suggest there are several reasons why the Book of Watchers has drawn on Genesis 22.

As our discussion has already intimated, the allusion makes the near-sacrifice of Isaac and the destruction of the watchers' children mutually illuminating. Abraham's faithfulness to the divine command is implicitly contrasted with the watchers' disobedience. Abraham did not weep over the imminent death of Isaac (a point stressed in Wis. 10:5), although according to the developing tradition (as attested in

4Q225) the angels *did* weep. The sinful watchers *do* weep for their fate and that of their children (1 En. 13:9).

But given the way in which the biblical text (Genesis 22) is brought into the extra-canonical text (1 Enoch), the primary point of the allusion is to allow the former to interpret the latter, rather than the other way around. And there are perhaps two ways that this is intended: (1) There is a polemic against pagan traditions of child sacrifice, that may have been associated particularly with Mount Hermon and (2) an allusion to an early form of the Aqedah supports the Book of Watchers' polemic against heterodox, non-Jerusalemite, cultic practice.

The Death of the Beloved at Hermon

In its original historical and canonical contexts Genesis 22 has to do with the biblical understanding of child sacrifice; a practice adopted by Israel's neighbours and some in her own (pre-exilic) community. This dimension of the story has been the particular focus of Levenson's important study.[31] Direct literary or archaeological evidence for child sacrifice in the Levant is meagre.[32] But indirect evidence from Phoenician sites in the western Mediterranean, especially Carthage, coupled with a credible body of literary evidence from classical and early Church authors, provides a compelling case that Israel's Canaanite neighbours took for granted the need, in various situations, to sacrifice children to appease or gain the power of their gods.[33] According to the biblical record the practice was well known (2 Kgs 3:26–7; 16:3, cf. Deut. 12:30–1; 18:10; Ps. 106:37–8) and, especially in the pre-exilic period, sometimes adopted by God's people (2 Kgs 16:3; 23:10; Isa. 57:5; Jer. 19:4–6; 7:31;

---

31 *Beloved Son*, esp. 18–35. In this regard Levenson takes up the work of Spiegel *Last Trial,* 53–62.

32 For a discussion of possible archaeological evidence see E. Lipiński, *Dieux et désses de l'univers phénicien et punique* (Leuven 1995), 438–40.

33 Besides Levenson's discussion (*Beloved Son*, 18–35) see S. Brown, *Late Carthaginian Child Sacrifice* (Sheffield 1991) and the survey of evidence in M.S. Smith, *The Early History of God* 2nd Edition (Grand Rapids 2002), 171–81. The classical sources are collected in J. Day, *Molech: A God of Human Sacrifice in the Old Testament* (Cambridge 1989), 86–91. And for Egyptian evidence for Canaanite child sacrifice see A. Spalinger, 'A Canaanite ritual found in Egyptian reliefs', *Journal for the Society for the Study of Egyptian Antiquities* 8 (1978), 47–60. Some have recently disputed the evidence for widespread infant sacrifice in the Phoenician world (e.g. M. Gras, P. Rouillard and J. Teixidor, 'The Phoenicians and Death', *Berytus* 39 (1991), 127–76 [150–73]). Even if the classical sources are largely symptomatic of anti-Punic/Phoenician defamatory propaganda — and, it must be said, the case for this is hardly compelling — then the Book of Watchers written, as it is, in the new Hellenistic world of ancient Judaism, could be viewed as one more witness to that propaganda.

32:35; Ezek. 16:20–1; 20:25–6; 23:37, 39, Ps. 106:37–8, 2 Chr. 33:6, cf. Lev. 20:2; 1 Kgs 16:34; Mic. 6:7).

The cremated remains of infants at Phoenician sites agree with literary accounts that victims were holocausts. Epigraphic evidence from these *tophets* (sacred precincts and crematoria) and the classical literary sources indicate that the sacrifice is sometimes made in fulfilment of a vow — as in Judges 11 — and as the result of a vision, a fact which correlates with the importance of the verb 'to see' in Genesis 22.[34] There is some important evidence that the practice was justified as an imitation of the behaviour of the gods themselves. Philo of Byblos says that according to Phoenician theology, during a plague the giant Kronos (alias El) offered his only son Ieoud ('Ιεοῦδ) to his father Ouranos, a fact which explains the behaviour of Phoenicians who, in times of crisis, sacrificed their most beloved children.[35] The name Ieoud reflects a Phoenician equivalent of the Hebrew יחיד.[36] And Diodorus Siculus confirms Philo's claim that child sacrifice was modelled after the behaviour of the gods themselves.[37] Furthermore, it may be that the Phoenician pattern is anticipated in the much earlier material from Ugarit. There, in the Baal Cycle, El famously loses his son Baal to the gods Yamm ('sea') and Mot ('death'). As Levenson comments, '[t]he Ugaritic material does not speak of a child sacrifice in the literal sense' but 'piecing together these texts, we can, with all due caution, speculate that they all reflect a pattern in which El in a moment of crisis, with disaster looming, handed over one of his divine offspring for enslavement or death.'[38]

The silence of the sources and the archaeology suggests that in the second half of the first millennium BCE child sacrifice waned in the Levant. However, it was vigorous, if not on the increase, in Carthaginian territory through the fourth and third

---

34 For the role of the vow in epigraphic evidence see Day, *Molech* 5, 7; Levenson, *Beloved Son* 22–3; Brown, *Child Sacrifice* 29–31, 33. For the literary evidence see Cleitarchus' (fourth century BCE) Scholia to Plato's Republic 337a (*FGrH* 137 F 9) and Silius Italicus, Punica IV.798. And note the possibility that Zeph. 1:5 refers to swearing oaths in association with the offering of Children to Molech (on which see Day, *Molech*, 69). Is a vow in view in the expression 'they sold themselves to do evil' immediately after the reference to child sacrifice in 2 Kgs 17:17? It cannot be a coincidence that Abraham is at Beersheba, 'the well of the *oath*' (so LXX), directly before (Gen. 21:31–3) and immediately after (22:19) the near sacrifice of his son, and that after Abraham has shown himself obedient God 'swears by himself' (22:16) that his promise to the patriarch will be fulfilled.

35 Frag. 3 (Eusebius P.E. 1.10.44 = 4.16.11). For the text see H.W. Attridge and R.A. Oden, *Philo of Byblos: The Phoenician History* (Catholic Biblical Quarterly Monograph Series 9, Washington 1981), 62–3. Instead of 'Ιεοῦδ other manuscripts have'Ιεδούδ, 'Ιερούδ and 'Ιρούδ.

36 The variant 'Ιεδούδ will then reflect the Hebrew *yādîd* 'beloved'.

37 Diodorus 20.14.4–7.

38 Levenson, *Death of the Beloved*, 33.

centuries BCE. It still persisted, even though suppressed by the Roman authorities, well into the first two or three centuries of the Christian era.[39] In the first century CE, Philo of Alexandria knows that Genesis 22 addresses the problem of pagan human sacrifice that remains a reality in his own day (Abr. 179–81, 84–7). And Curtius Rufus' account of Alexander the Great's siege of Tyre (332 BCE) shows that resorting to child sacrifice remained a realistic option for the Phoenician mother city in times of trouble in the fourth century BCE.[40]

With all due respect for the silence of the sources, we can suggest that this evidence for Canaanite cultic infanticide goes some way to explaining the location of the watchers story at Mount Hermon. Hermon was a site of considerable and long standing religious significance. Physically it dominates its surrounding territory and, with its snow-topped summit, fertile foothills from which the source of the river Jordan flows, it was revered as a cosmic Mountain. From the middle of the second millennium BC onwards it is one location of El's abode and the assembly of the gods.[41] It is the location of a Northern, and in Jerusalem's eyes 'heterodox', Israelite sanctuary (1 Kgs 12:29ff). It is now generally recognized that the Book of Watcher's account of the descent of the watchers at this spot is a thinly veiled polemic against the pagan veneration of the site: where El and his assembly once dwelt, there the Book of Watchers knows only the site of a condemned gathering of reprobate angels, whose memory lingers but whose destructive presence has been decisively dealt with in primeval history.

---

39 See esp. the testimony of Tertullian Apol. 9.2–4, but also Cicero, De Re Publica, III.9.15; Plutarch, On Superstition, 13 (Mor. 171C-D); Justin, Apol., II.12.5; Origen, Contra Celsum, V.27; Porphyry, De Abstinentia, II.27 (= Eusebeius P.E. IV.16.6); Minucius Felix, Octavius, XXX.3 and note the degree to which the much later Lamentations Rabbah (ad Lam. 1:9) still reflects some accurate knowledge of the practice (a text discussed recently by G. Bohak, 'Classica et Rabbinica', *Journal for the Study of Judaism* 31 (2000), 211–16).

40 Curtius Rufus 4.3.23. Curtius' statement is sometimes taken to mean that at Tyre in the fourth century infant sacrifice had ceased. But he only says that sacrifice of *freeborn* citizens of the city had discontinued, and a passage in Diodorus Siculus (20:14) may mean that this was because infant sacrifice continued through the immolation of a commoner, sons and daughters of slaves or foreigners.

41 For Hermon's mythological history see E. Lipiński, 'El's abode. Mythological traditions related to Mount Hermon and to the Mountains of Armenia', *Orientalia Lovaniensia Periodica* 2 (1971), 15–41. And for the role of these traditions in the formation of the Book of Watchers see C.H.T. Fletcher-Louis, 'The Revelation of the Sacral Son of Man: The Genre, History of Religions Context and the Meaning of the Transfiguration', in F. Avemarie and H. Lichtenberger (eds), *Auferstehung – Resurrection. The Fourth Durham-Tübingen-Symposium: Resurrection, Exaltation, and Transformation in Old Testament, Ancient Judaism, and Early Christianity* (WUNT 135, Tübingen 2001), 247–98 (267–71).

No text explicitly identifies the mountain as a site of child sacrifice. But circumstantial evidence points to this possibility. The Deuteronomist castigates the northern tribes in 2 Kings 17 because they 'made for themselves cast images of two calves; ... worshipped all the host of heaven, and served Baal. *They made their sons and their daughters pass through fire;* they used divination and augury' (vv. 16–17). This may mean the northern tribes' cult centres at Bethel and Dan (in the foothills of Hermon) were sites of child sacrifice. In this Jeroboam and his successors would rival the use made of the Hinnom valley outside Jerusalem by the kings of Judah, who used that place for infant holocausts (probably to a god called Molech — 1 Kgs 11:7; 2 Kgs 23:10; Jer. 7:31; 19:4–6; 32:35). The sacrificing of children in a valley is evidently connected to their intended destination in the underworld: the sacrifices are made 'among the oaks, under every green tree ... in the valleys, under the clefts of the rocks' and, thereby, the victims are 'sent far away, ... to Sheol' (Isa. 57:5, 9).[42] This describes the foot of Hermon as well as, if not better than, the Hinnom valley.[43] The cosmic mountain had at its base the access to the watery underworld, to Sheol (e.g. Ezek. 31, esp. vv. 14–17, cf. Isa. 14:13–15).

So many of the details of this background correspond to features of the Book of Watchers that now come into sharper relief. We should note at the outset the prominence given to the Hinnom Valley — the 'cursed valley' — in the tour of the cosmos in 1 Enoch 27. But Enoch does not dwell on that valley's sordid history since it is at Hermon, not Jerusalem, that demonic chaos enters the cosmos. According to 1 En. 7:3–5 the giants' behaviour goes well beyond that of ordinary warriors who demand sustenance from the economy of those they conquer; the giants devour even the blood of their subservient human underlings. Where Caananite religion and, in all probability, some in pre-exilic Israel accepted the need to satiate this divine hunger, to honour the vows made in respect of these cultic practices and to give credence to the visions granted in their fulfilment, the Book of Watchers castigates them at every

---

42 The importance of Sheol as the destination of the sacrifice is clear here whether or not Day (*Molech* 46–55; *Yahweh and the Gods of Canaan* [Sheffield 2000], 212–15 and G.C. Heider, *The Cult of Molek: A Reassessment* [JSOTS 43, Sheffield, 1986], 93–194) are right in their view that sacrifices are made to an underworld god called Molech. Some still maintain the alternative view that the Hebrew *mlk* refers originally to a particular type of sacrifice, not a god, e.g. K.A.D. Smelik, 'Moloch, Molech or Molk-Sacrifice? A Reassessment of the Evidence Concerning the Hebrew Term Molekh', *Scandinavian Journal of the Old Testament* 9 (1995), 133–92; M.S. Smith, *Early History* 171–81.

43 Note also that Asael is to be bound hand and foot and buried under 'sharp stones and jagged stones' (1 En. 10:5) in a way that recalls the language of Isa. 57:5–9.

point. The gods who demand human blood are demonic halflings.[44] Their own children have, indeed, been condemned to death, but any hoped for expiation and forgiveness is expressly denied (1 En. 10:12; 12:6; 14:6).[45] The purpose of the vow in child sacrifice is succinctly put by the near contemporary Cleitarchus who says of all those who followed Kronos that 'whenever they wished to succeed in any great enterprise, they would vow by one of their children if they achieved the things they longed for, to sacrifice him to the god'.[46] Given the watchers' vow when they first descend (in 1 En. 6:4, 6), our Jewish text insists they get their just deserts: their children *are* to die, but only because they are false gods whose cannibalistic behaviour must be eradicated. The sources make much of the weeping that attends child sacrifice. Parents do all they can to stop their children crying.[47] One text says that if a mother cries for her child the sacrifice is invalid, though it is carried through anyway.[48] This explains the satirical force of the account of the watchers' pathetic weeping in 1 En. 13:9.[49] Where the worshippers at the *tophets* of North Africa speak of their visions and Genesis 22 celebrates the vision of divine provision in the land of Moriah, the miserable watchers are no longer able to lift their eyes to heaven (1 En. 13:5) and it is Enoch, rather, who has the vision of God (1 En. 14:8–15:1).[50]

On this reading then, a number of features of the fall of the watchers story are carefully chosen to deride the religious practices of Israel's neighbours. That the events take place at Hermon both accords with the long tradition of Canaanite veneration of the mountain and the author's desire to condemn its adoption as a cultic centre by the northern tribes. The Book of Watchers' polemic fits not only the Deuteronomist's polemic against the northern tribes making 'their sons and their daughters pass through fire' but also, in the same context, their indulging in

---

44 Compare the language of child sacrifice in Ps. 106:37–8, 'They sacrificed their sons and their daughters to the *demons*; ... to the idols of Canaan'.

45 The expiatory power of child sacrifice is explicit at Mic. 6:7; Diodorus Siculus XIII.86.3; XX.144.4–7; Philo of Byblos' *Phoenician History*, frag. 3 (Eusebius, *P.E.* I.10.45 = IV.16.11) and Silius Italicus, *Punica*, IV.765–829.

46 Scholia on Plato's Republic 337a.

47 Minucius Felix, Octavius, XXX.3; Tertullian, Apol., IX.4.

48 Plutarch, De Superstitione, 13.

49 Does the two month period of weeping for Jephthah's daughter mean she is resigned to her fate, and free from tears, when it finally arrives?

50 This reading of the text may be supported by other indications that the characterisation of the watchers once had in mind especially the arrogance and sins of Phoenician culture. The watchers' revelation of the technique for the making of dye (1 En. 8:1) perhaps alludes to the famous Tyrian purple and their skill in metal craft, ornamentation and the working of precious stones accords well with the achievements of Phoenician culture (cf. e.g. Ezekiel 27).

'divination and augury' (2 Kgs 17:16–17). In the same breath 1 En. 7:1–5 says the giants devoured human beings and their parents taught humanity 'sorcery and charms, … the cutting of roots and plants.'[51]

And the way in which the destruction of the giants is portrayed, with echoes of the sacrifice of the beloved, has good precedent in Israel's prophetic tradition. In Ezekiel 38–9 the slaughter of Israel's enemy Gog is described in terms of the practice of child sacrifice that Israel so came to abhor. And, of course, Gog (גוג, Γωγ), was one of the giants (LXX Ezek. 39:18, 20: γίγας — Heb has גבור), who is related in important ways to the giants of priestly and Enochic tradition. In Gen. 10:2 he is one of the descendants of Japheth (יפת) whose name, along with that of the giant-like Jephthah (יפתח) of Judges 11, is probably a Semitic equivalent of the giant Iapetos of Greek tradition.[52] At the slaughter of the hordes of Gog there will be a feast for the birds and the wild animals that will 'eat the flesh of the [fallen] mighty (גבורים, γιγάντων) and drink their blood' (Ezek. 39:18–19). This is the inverse of 1 En. 7:4–5, where it is the giants themselves who kill men to devour them, sinning against the birds and beasts, eating flesh and drinking blood. As B.P. Irwin has convincingly shown, in Ezekiel 38–9 the immolation of Gog echoes the practices of the Jerusalem *tophet*.[53] Where Jerusalem's child holocausts are offered in the *gê' ben-hinnōm*, the 'valley of the Son of Hinnom', the bones of Gog and all his horde will be buried in the *gê' hᵃmôn gôg*, the 'valley of the multitude of Gog' (39:11, 15). They will be overcome by his 'blazing wrath (*'ēš 'eḇᵉrātî*)' (38:19, cf. 38:22 and 39:6). And, the other name of the place of burial is the 'valley of *hā'ōḇᵉrîm* ('those passing through', √ *'br*)' (39:11), which recalls the regular expression for human sacrifice in the Hinnom valley — 'to pass through (*lᵉha*ᵃ*ḇîr*) (fire/to Molech)' (Lev. 18:21; 2 Kgs 23:10; Jer. 32:35). So, from the priestly tradition represented by Ezekiel a description of God's judgement of his enemies, the

---

51 If the anti-Samaritan reading of the final form of the text is correct, then older material that dealt with the cultic practices of the northern tribes in the earlier, pre-exilic, period is preserved in the older material of 1 Enoch 7–8.

52 Gog comes from the land of Magog and he is numbered with Tubal (Ezek. 38:2, cf. Gen. 10:2 P). In the J material of Genesis 4 a certain Tubal-Cain is the first to make 'all kinds of bronze and iron tools'. As P.R. Davies has noted here Tubal-Cain's behaviour is reminiscent of the metal-working skills that the watchers reveal in 1 Enoch 8:1 ('Sons of Cain', in J.D. Martin and P.R. Davies (eds), *A Word in Season: Essays in Honour of William McKane* (Sheffield 1986), 35–56.

53 B.P. Irwin, 'Molek Imagery and the Slaughter of Gog in Ezekiel 38 and 39', *Journal for the Study of the Old Testament* 65 (1995), 93–112.

giants, in terms of child sacrifice would have been well-known to the fourth or third century author of the Book of Watchers.[54]

We have already had recourse to the evidence from the story of Jephthah's vow for the Book of Watchers' interest in child sacrifice. The retelling of that story in (the late first century BCE) Pseudo-Philo's Biblical Antiquities corroborates connections we have made between Hermon and child sacrifice. In Judges 11 Jephthah returns to meet his daughter at Mizpah over 150 km from Hermon. We are not told the location of the mountains on which she wanders weeping. Pseudo-Philo says she weeps at Hermon (40:3, 5–7).[55] Although it is not explicitly stated that she is then sacrificed at the mountain, and Pseudo-Philo may have had in mind the association between Jephthah's vow and the Hermon's linguistic affinity to 'the ban', it is as likely that he retains a memory of the fact that it was there that parents vowed their children to destruction. In fact, a tradition of lamentation, prayerful weeping, at Hermon is attested in the place name 'Abel-Maim' (Ara. Abel-Main, also known as Abel-Beth-Maacah; 1 Kgs 15:20; 2 Chr. 16:4) at the southern foot of Hermon long before it appears in either the Book of Watchers or the *Biblical Antiquities*.[56] And there is inscriptional evidence from the Greek and Roman periods that oaths were taken at the Mountain's sanctuaries.[57]

---

54 A Greek parallel to the flood stories of Noah and Lot — that of Lycaon — is variously associated both with the primeval battle of the giants and with the offensive practice of human sacrifice. See Fontenrose *Philemon* 29, 98, 106–8.

55 The Mountain is called 'Stelac' (40:4, 5) which must be Hermon, the mountain of snow (Heb *šlg*, Aram *tlg*). See *OTP* 2:353 n. h; H. Jacobson, *A Commentary on Pseudo-Philo's Liber Antiquitatum Biblicarum. With Latin Text and English Translation* (AGAJU 31, 2 vols, Leiden 1996), II, 965–6.

56 The root אבל meaning 'to mourn, lament'.

57 A bilingual inscription at Tel Dan reads 'to the god who is in Dan Zoilos made a vow (EYXHN, נדר).' A probably later, perhaps third century CE inscription reads 'according to the command of the greatest a[nd] holy god, those taking an oath (ὀμνύοντες) [proceed] from here'. For these two inscriptions and their relevance in interpreting the Book of Watchers see Nickelsburg, *1 Enoch 1: A Commentary* 244–7. The foot of Hermon is still a place for 'Phoenician' sacrifices in the third and fourth Christian centuries according to the testimony of Eusebius of Caesarea (Eccl. Hist. 7:17, cf. his Onamasticon s.v. Ἀερμών). With this background in mind, the place (Caesarea Philippi at the foot of Hermon) is a fitting place for Jesus to commit himself to a path of martyrdom (Mark 8:27, 31–7 and parallels) shortly before a mountain-top theophany when he is told that he is God's beloved son (ὁ υἱός μου ὁ ἀγαπητός, Mark 9:7).

(2) The Cultic Context of the Book of Watchers' Allusions to Genesis 22

Our understanding of the Book of Watchers has been greatly advanced in recent years by a new appreciation of its cultic context, details of which I here summarize.[58] In the literature of this period Enoch is a priest. His priestly credentials are explicit in Jubilees (4:25, cf. 21:10), 2 Enoch (22:8–10, cf. Ps. 133:2–3 and Zech. 3) and, I have argued, in Ben Sira (49:14).[59] In the Book of Watchers he intercedes for the fallen watchers at a cultic site. As he prays at the waters of Dan he has a dream vision (in 1 Enoch 14); he receives an incubation oracle, in which he is taken to the heavenly palace that is described in terms redolent of the tripartite Solomonic sanctuary.[60] He 'draws near' (Gk uses ἐγγίζω, Aramaic would have had קרב or נגש) to God in the way priests do (14:21–3). Indeed, his privileged access to God's inner sanctum is otherwise reserved for the high priest. His task is to deal with angels who have left their heavenly domain and who have had intercourse with the daughters of men. This recalls the issue of exagamy with which the priest and scribe Ezra dealt. Material in the Dead Sea Scrolls and related texts indicate that the behaviour of these angels was taken, at least typologically, to refer to the misbehaviour of priests surrendering their God-given vocation.[61]

Throughout the book the same priestly and cultic concerns are to the fore. The Book is introduced as Enoch's blessing (1:1), with language that anticipates Aaron's blessing in Num. 6:22–7 (1 En. 1:8). And at key moments thereafter, including the final verse of the book (36:4, cf 12:3, 22:14; 25:7), Enoch blesses. Chapters 2–5 contrast the orderly nature of the cosmos — the liturgical cycle ('festivals') of the sun and the moon — with the human transgression of natural law. In chapter 3 Enoch speaks of fourteen evergreen trees which, according to Jubilees 21, are the only trees to provide suitable wood for the altar. In his tours of the cosmos (chs 17–36), Enoch is shown the site of the future temple, in Jerusalem — the place of the tree of life (chs 25–7). And he is shown the places in the orient where the ingredients of the sacred incense and oil are obtained (chs 29–32).

---

58 See further M. Himmelfarb, *Ascent to Heaven in Jewish and Christian Apocalypses* (Oxford 1993), 25–46; C.H.T. Fletcher-Louis, *Glory of Adam* 21–7.

59 See Fletcher-Louis, *Glory of Adam* 25–7.

60 For similar incubation oracles at the Jerusalem sanctuary see Joel 1:13; Josephus *Ant.* 11:302–34.

61 See 4QLevi³ ar frags. 3 + 4 line 6–7; T. Levi 14–16, cf. CD 2:16–19.

The removal of the effects of the watchers' chaotic behaviour is described in cultic terms.[62] The angels are told to 'cleanse the earth from all impurity ...' (10:20). And the earliest interpreters relate the punishment of watchers to the Day of Atonement (Jubilees 5; 4QEnGiants[a] 7 i 6; 4Q180 1 7–8; Apoc. Abr. 13). The chief angel in chapter 10 is called Asael. This is taken to be an allusion to the Azazel of Leviticus 16 by the text's earliest interpreters. Asael is bound and banished to the desert at a place called Duda'el which may correspond to the sending of the scapegoat לעזאזל into the wilderness. Rabbinic tradition says the destination of the scapegoat was a placed called Beth Hiddudo/Hadudu (m. Yoma 6:8, cf. Tg. Ps-J on Lev. 16:21–2). In 1 En. 10:8 Raphael is told to 'write upon (Asael) all sin', in much the same way that sin is transferred to the goat in Leviticus 16. Commensurate with these Yom Kippur scapegoat allusions would be the fact that Enoch's ascent to heaven in chapter 14 gives him an experience otherwise reserved for the high priest on the 10th of *Tishri*.

Now, of course, amidst all this cultic furniture language that alludes to Isaac's near sacrifice and its wider interpretative context is very much at home. So we are brought to a point at the heart of the Aqedah tradition. From Josephus (Ant. 1:224, 226) onwards the Genesis 22 story is explicitly set at the site of Solomon's temple and, within the rabbinic material, this conceptually undergirds the meritorious and foundational nature of the binding of Isaac for all subsequent sacrifice in Jerusalem. Already the book of Chronicles identifies the land of Moriah in Gen. 22:2 with Zion — 'Mount Moriah' (2 Chr. 3:1) — and, as we have seen, some think that Genesis 22 itself intends that identification. And, if this identification is assumed in the third or fourth century BCE, further light is brought to the use of the death of the beloved motif in the Book of Watchers: *By denying a reprieve for the beloved of the watchers at Hermon, through an allusion to Genesis 22, the text denies that forgiveness is available outside of Jerusalem since it is Jerusalem where Isaac was spared* and it is Jerusalem where the Enochic priestly lineage would serve at the site of the future temple that Enoch is shown in 1 Enoch 25–7.[63] God's forgiveness is not available at the site of the pre-exilic northern sanctuary in Dan; the place were a primeval

---

62 For what follows, see most recently D. Stökl, 'Yom Kippur in the Apocalyptic imaginaire and the Roots of Jesus' High Priesthood', in J. Assman and G.G. Stroumsa (eds), *Transformations of the Inner Self in Ancient Religions* (Studies in the History of Religions 8, Leiden 1999), 349–66.

63 In 4Q225 the retelling of Genesis 22 (2 i 8 – ii 10a) is followed by a priestly genealogy: 'God blessed Isaac ... and he begat Jacob, and Jacob begat Levi ...' (2 ii 10b–12). The text is fragmentary, but it is possible that it contained both a priestly interpretation of Abraham's action in Genesis 22 and, through the genealogy, a conceptual connection from Abraham, through Levi, to Aaron, the Tabernacle and Temple.

outbreak of bloodthirsty demonic chaos started.[64] Neither is atonement available at Shechem, the post-exilic site in the north that rivals Jerusalem to the south.

In the much later Samaritan tradition it is claimed that Genesis 22 took place, not at Jerusalem, but at Shechem.[65] It is possible that the Book of Watchers is already responding to such claims. One detail of the text may be particularly important in articulating its pro-Jerusalem propaganda. Philo of Alexandria says the name Jerusalem means 'vision of peace' (*On Dreams* 2:250). Presumably, he or his tradition thinks the name is formed from the words *rō'eh* and *šālôm*. A better etymological explanation of the name is found in Gen. Rab. 56:10 where the language of vision in Genesis 22 is combined with the name Salem for the city in the Melchizedek story a few chapters earlier (at Genesis 14) to explain the name of Jerusalem as a '*Yireh Salem*' ('he will see peace'). As Levenson has pointed out, a word play on the roots *r'h* and *šlm* and the name Jerusalem is elsewhere attested already in Ps. 128:4–6 and may therefore be in view in Genesis 22 itself where the verbal root *r'h* occurs five times, each with the imperfect prefix *y* that is shared by the name *Yĕrûšālaim* (vv. 4, 8, 13, 14 [twice]).[66]

In fact, long before Genesis Rabbah in Jubilees we probably have a second century BCE witness to Jerusalem as the place of vision and of peace on the basis of Genesis 22. Jubilees is unusually economical in its interpretative additions to the biblical story when it relays the Genesis 22 account. Yet, two additions are striking. To the restatement of Gen. 22:14 — 'so Abraham called that place "The LORD has seen", so that it is said "in the mountain the LORD has seen"' — Jubilees adds the explanatory comment that, 'It is Mount Zion'. Without substantial deviation from the biblical text, Jubilees then repeats the words by which God reiterates his promise to Abraham in commendation for his faithfulness to the divine command (18:14–16, *par.* Gen. 22:15–18). This time the following is added to the biblical text: 'and I have

---

64 Is there any indication in the developed Enochic tradition that an allusion to Genesis 22 was well known and readily perceived by later readers of the Book of Watchers? Yes, perhaps. 2 Pet. 2:4 perhaps contains a verbal echo of Genesis 22: 'For if God did not spare (ἐφείσατο, cf. Gen. 22:12, 16 and Rom. 8:32) the angels when they sinned, but cast them into hell and committed them to chains of deepest darkness to be kept until the judgment ...'.

65 For the role of Samaritan claims regarding the setting of Genesis 22 in the formation of the Aqedah see Hayward, 'Present State' 133; I. Kalimi, *Early Jewish Exegesis and Theological Controversy: Studies in Scriptures in the Shadow of Internal and External Controversies* (Assen 2002).

66 *Beloved Son* 119–21. Levenson suggests a specific allusion to Jerusalem in Gen. 22:8: *yir'eh-lô haśśeh*, 'he will see to the sheep', (121). For other reasons to see a reference to Jerusalem in Genesis 22 see F. Stolz, *Strukturen und Figuren im Kult von Jerusalem* (BZAW 188, Berlin 1970), 207–8. Arguably, the wordplay is assumed in Isa. 2:1–4. It certainly lies behind Luke 19:41–4.

made known to all that you are faithful to me in everything which I say to you. *Go in peace*' (18:16b). Thus, for Jubilees, the site of Isaac's near sacrifice is both the mountain of vision and the place that provides peace. This will be the site of Jerusalem, the city of vision and of peace.

It cannot be a coincidence that vision and peace figure prominently in the Book of Watchers. As we have seen, the book is framed as a blessing (1:1, 8 and 36:4, cf. 12:3, 22:14; 25:7). In fact it is a blessing of the kind that Aaron is to bless over the people of Israel according to Num. 6:22–7 *at the sanctuary*. In the same introductory chapter that defines the book as a blessing emphasis is also placed on the fact that Enoch is a righteous man 'whose eyes were opened by God, who had a *vision* of the Holy One and of heaven' (1:1). In that vision 'the Great Holy One will come forth from his dwelling 'he will *appear* with his army, he will *appear* with his might host …' (1:4). God 'will make *peace* with the righteous … he will bless and help … light will shine upon them, and he will make *peace* with them' (1:8, cf. Num. 6:24–6). Clearly, in chapters 6–8, the irruption of violence and chaos caused by Asael, Shemihazah and their crew disturbs the peace of creation. But Enoch assures the readers that to those who disobey the order of creation God says 'There will be *no peace* for you!' (5:4). And when Enoch is sent to tell the watchers of their fate *four* times he tells them they will have no peace:

> In 12:5–6 the (righteous) angels send Enoch to tell the watchers that because 'they wrought great desolation on the earth — 'You will have *no peace* or forgiveness'. And concerning their sons — in whom they rejoice — the slaughter of their beloved ones they will see; and over the destruction of their sons they will lament and make petition forever, and they will have no mercy *or peace*.'
> Whereupon, immediately (13:1) Enoch proceeds and says 'to Asael (Gk: Azael), 'Go! You will have *no peace*'.'

Whilst the angels are no longer able to have a vision of heaven (13:5), Enoch has a visionary audience with God enthroned in splendour (14:8–16:4), at the end of which God himself reiterates the message Enoch is to deliver to the fallen watchers:

> 'Say to them, 'You will have *no peace*'.' (16:4)

God provided for, 'saw to' the needs of, Abraham on the mountain. So too Enoch assures the righteous that after the watchers and their children are punished humanity's needs will be taken care of: 'all the righteous will escape, and they will live until they beget thousands, and all the days of their youth and their old age *will be completed in peace*' (10:17). After the atonement achieved at this judgement creation will return to its paradisal bounty 'and then truth *and peace* will be united together for all the days of eternity and for all the generations of men' (11:2).

Clearly, vision and peace are prominent themes in the core chapters of the Book of Watchers. And given the allusions to Genesis 22 and all the other indications of the work's specific religious and political purpose, this must be a thinly veiled proclamation that it is *Jerusalem* where the *vision of peace* and the bounty of creation will be restored to the people of God; a point in fact then reiterated in chapters 25–7. No true vision and no true peace will be found at another sanctuary, whether it be that of the old Northern Kingdom at Dan or the new Samaritan sanctuary at Shechem.

The Book of Watchers and the Tradition History of the Aqedah

For the most part, our discussion of 1 Enoch's use of Genesis 22 and its literary and conceptual constellation has served to clarify the purpose and structure of the material in 1 Enoch, some of which is otherwise puzzling. We now have the opportunity to consider ways in which the use of Genesis 22 in 1 Enoch sheds light on the biblical text's interpretative history and the origins of the Aqedah.

Levenson has highlighted the ways in which the older Canaanite material and the role of Genesis 22 as a foundational cult legend for the Jerusalem temple anticipate themes that emerge much later in the Aqedah.[67] If our teasing out of the intertextual web of biblical allusions in 1 Enoch 6–14 is on the mark, then we are led to the following proposal: as a third or fourth century BCE text of considerable significance for emerging Judaism, the Book of Watchers bridges the gap between, on the one hand, *Genesis 22 in its Canaanite and Israelite religious context* that has been so freshly illuminated by Jon Levenson and, on the other, *the Aqedah of much later, chiefly targumic and rabbinic tradition*. And, *assuming the truth of the connections we have made between* 1 Enoch *and biblical and extra-biblical material*, some conclusions for the history of the Aqedah are fairly certain. It is also possible, with a little imaginative mirror reading of 1 Enoch, to hypothesise features of the Aqedah (the tradition of interpretation of Genesis 22) that were known to the author(/compiler) of 1 Enoch. The following points are more or less certain:

1. In the third or fourth century BCE Genesis 22 was widely known (not just to the author of 2 Chr. 3:1) as a story that legitimized the Jerusalem sanctuary. And, for

---

67 *Beloved Son* 173–99.

some, this interpretative judgement was particularly important for the polemic against the Samaritan temple at Shechem.

2. Several considerations mean Isaac's conscious offering of himself for the slaughter was assumed at this time.[68] First, we have seen that in the pagan context children are sometimes old enough to be conscious of their fate and steps are taken to limit their distress. In Genesis 22 Isaac is old enough to carry the wood for the fire. Although the text says nothing of his reaction as it becomes clear that he is to be the victim, any reader familiar with the realities of child sacrifice in the ancient world must wonder whether he protested. The text's silence on this point speaks eloquently for the fact that he did *not*. And, as we have seen, Genesis 22 was read in conjunction with Judges 11 where Jephthah accepts her fate willingly. In Judg. 11:36 Jephthah's daughter declares 'My father, if you have opened your mouth to the LORD, do to me according to what has gone out of your mouth …'. In Pseudo-Philo's Biblical Antiquities 40 Jephthah's daughter herself cites Isaac's example as a willing sacrifice as precedent for her own compliance (40:2). This reading of Genesis 22 through the lens of Judges 11 is perfectly natural and could have taken place any time after the two texts are included in Israel's canon. Indeed, we have found indications that the Book of Watchers is the first extant witness, several hundred years before Pseudo-Philo, to the combination of Judges 11 and Genesis 22. And, we have suggested that the willingness of Isaac's self-sacrifice is presumed by the Book of Watchers since it is implicitly contrasted with the efforts of the watchers and their children to have their condemnation dropped.[69]

3. In Judges 11 the beloved weeps over her fate and her companions weep with her. In Pseudo-Philo's version of Judges 11 this weeping is developed at length and Seila's companions include the trees of the field and the beasts (40:3, 5–7). As we have seen, the late first century BCE 4Q225 now anticipates the theme of weeping in Genesis Rabbah's witness to the Aqedah tradition. But already in the Book of Watchers, in the fourth–third centuries BCE, the watchers weep over the death of their beloved. That they do so should probably be explained not just because of the *literary* influence of Judges 11, but also because of the realities of child sacrifice in ancient Israel and its Canaanite context. On this evidence, ancient readers of Genesis 22 must,

---

68 This would mean the theme is not first read out of Genesis 22 in the context of Jewish martyrdom (as Vermes, Scripture 202–4, and Levenson, *Beloved Son* 188, suggest) since the Book of Watchers antedates the Maccabean crisis.

69 It should be noted that Jud. 8:26–7 and now perhaps also 4Q225 2 ii 8 attest the tradition that it was not just Abraham, but also Isaac whose obedience was tested.

early in the text's *Receptionsgeschichte,* have meditated on the lack, or implicit presence, of weeping in the biblical story.

4. It is likely that the author of 1 Enoch 1–36 thought what happened in Genesis 22 carried expiatory significance. The sacrificing of the beloved son had, in Israel's ancient Near Eastern context, expiatory, or, more especially, propitiatory power.[70] It is an act which assuages the wrath of the god(s) and it releases divine power against the worshipper's enemies (see esp. Judges 11 and 2 Kgs 3:26–7). Jewish readers of Genesis 22 throughout antiquity cannot have been unaware that this is how child sacrifice functioned. As Levenson has argued, Genesis 22 does not so much serve to negate the act of child sacrifice as transform it and, thereby, give a particular interpretation to Israel's God-ordained sacrifices, particularly the various forms of substitution for the firstborn. As an event that provides the conceptual foundations of Israel's cult where atonement takes place, the obedience of Abraham (and Isaac) probably carried with it the expiatory, or propitiatory, significance of literal child sacrifice.[71] This would certainly give added depth to the significance of God's punishment of the watchers in 1 Enoch. The watchers' children consume human blood only to satisfy their voracious lusts. These are the demons of the sacrificial cults of Israel's neighbours. Under the judgement of the one true God these demons have neither the forgiveness nor the peace that true atonement effects. By contrast, Enoch is installed as Israel's archetypal (high) priest, with access to the inner sanctum of the sanctuary that will later be built at Jerusalem (1 Enoch 25–6) where true peace, atonement and the vision of God will be available. The watchers write out prayers of memorial in their attempt to seek forgiveness through Enoch's intercession. These, again, are perhaps a foil to the prayers of memorial that *are* answered at Jerusalem, particularly in the New Year cycle of festivals.[72]

These four points I consider *probable,* if not certain. Three other corollaries to our mirror reading of Genesis 22 in the Book of Watchers are *possible* but far from certain.

---

70 For the texts see n. 45 above.

71 In the light of Levenson's work, a pseudepigraphic text which now warrants a fresh investigation as a witness to the Aqedah and its propitiatory logic is Apocalypse of Abraham 25 where the sacrificing of boys to a bronze statue is the picture Abraham is shown to give the inner meaning of Israel's priesthood and temple sacrifices.

72 For prayers of memorial for forgiveness during the festivals of *Tishri* see 4QFestival Prayers (1Q34 + 1Q34bis; 4Q507–9), esp. 4Q509 frag. 12 i, which has some interesting linguistic and conceptual points of correspondence to parts of 1 Enoch 13–14.

5. In the Book of Watchers Enoch is the archetypal (high) priest. The watchers, once they have left their heavenly domain, are no priests at all; they rely on Enoch to intercede for them. And, we should note, their seeing the death of their beloved renders them unclean through corpse impurity and, therefore, disqualifies them from cultic service (cf. Leviticus 21). There is perhaps here the assumption, found in Philo and later rabbinic texts (and, perhaps now 4Q225),[73] that Abraham was a priest when his offering of his beloved was spared.[74]

6. I have mentioned the likelihood that the fall of the watchers material is related to Yom Kippur. This may then mean that the binding of Isaac was tied liturgically to New Year festivals already in the third/fourth centuries BCE long before the formation of the synagogue liturgy. Since Jubilees shows, without obvious polemic against Autumn new year festivals, that Genesis 22 was read in association with Passover at roughly the same time, it may be wise now to refrain from playing off against one another Passover and New Year festival settings for the Aqedah's tradition history, as has sometimes been done.

7. Apocalyptic features of the Aqedah are present already in Jubilees. That is to say, in Jubilees the story in Genesis 22 is an occasion for the revelation of heavenly secrets: behind the empirical events of Abrahamic history there stands a battle between God, with the Angels of the Presence, and demonic forces, led by Prince Mastema who tries to undermine Abraham's election (17:15–16; 18:9–13). In Genesis 22 itself, of course, the LORD communicates through his angel (v. 11, 15). But in the Aqedah the angels multiply. A group of 'angels of holiness' are present in the Qumran version of the story attested in 4Q225 (frag. 2 col. ii 5). It is not clear in 4Q225 whether Abraham and Isaac see the angels. But where the biblical text says no more than that Abraham heard the angel's voice, Jubilees has the Angel of the Presence *appear* to him (18:14). Later the targums stress the visionary theme, and this too was perhaps a part of the traditional reading of Genesis 22 known to the Book of Watchers. There, as we have seen, Enoch, who is in various ways a type of Abraham, sees the heavenly world, including the angels and even God himself, whilst the watchers and their beloved are denied any visionary privilege. A visionary theme is already prominent in Genesis 22 and parallels in Phoenician inscriptions speak of the visions received by those making child sacrifices.

---

73 For a genealogy of priesthood in 4Q225 see n. 62 above.

74 Philo, De Abr, 198; Num. Rab. 4:6; PRE 8:2; 31:3; Cyrian, De bono Poenitentiae, 10; John Chrysostom, De Lazaro Concio, 5.

In theory, it may have been that the later Aqedah was influenced by an association between Genesis 22 and the material in 1 Enoch 10–14. But this is highly unlikely. For one thing, the interaction with Genesis 22 in the Book of Watchers is allusive. For another, more importantly, there is scant evidence that the rabbinic tradition and the targums were interested in the Book of Watchers. No explicit reference to the angel story occurs anywhere in the later retellings of Genesis 22. Whatever the exact form of interpretation of Genesis 22 known to the author (or compiler) of the Book of Watchers, there is, I submit, a cumulatively strong case that the earliest material of 1 Enoch provides a valuable witness to the long and highly complex history of engagement with one of scripture's most challenging and profound passages.

'and you know everything before it happens …':
A Complaint Against the Inaction of the Most High in 1 Enoch 9[*]

Siam Bhayro

Introduction

The Shemihazah and Asael Narrative, comprising chapters 6–11 of 1 Enoch, is located within the Book of Watchers (1 En. 1–36).[1] As it now stands, this narrative tells how a group of angels descend to the earth and fornicate with human women, causing a race of giants to be born and ravage the earth, the intercession of the four archangels and the intervention of the Most High. Whilst judgements are pronounced upon the sinful angels and their giant progeny, particularly the angel Asael, salvation from the impending deluge and the joys of a restored earth are promised to the righteous progeny of the 'son of Lamech'.

In this paper, I am particularly concerned with the intercession of the archangels in 1 En. 9:1–11. 1 Enoch 6–11 has long been considered a composite unit, made up of a number of strata.[2]

---

[*] This paper is an expanded form of the presentation I delivered at the annual conference of the British Association for Jewish Studies, Durham (UK), 2003, the subject of which was 'Jewish Prayer'. I would like to thank Professor Robert Hayward for the invitation to participate in this conference. At the end of this paper, I append the Ethiopic text of 1 Enoch 9:1–11, with a translation and textual notes.

[1] The Book of Watchers can be divided as follows: Introduction (1 Enoch 1–5); the Shemihazah and Asael Narrative (1 Enoch 6–11); the Petitions of the Giants (1 Enoch 12–16); Enoch's Journeys (1 Enoch 17–36). For the latest discussion of the structure of the Book of Watchers, see G.W.E. Nickelsburg, *1 Enoch 1: A Commentary on the Book of 1 Enoch, Chapters 1–36; 81–108* (Hermeneia, Minneapolis, MN 2001), 165–228.

[2] That 1 Enoch 6–11 contains at least two cycles within it was pointed out as far back as R.H. Charles, *The Apocrypha and Pseudepigrapha of the Old Testament* (2 vols, Oxford 1913), II, 191. See C.A. Newsom, 'The Development of 1 Enoch 6-19: Cosmology and Judgement' in *Catholic Biblical Quarterly* 42 (1980), 310–29, especially 313–14 where Newsom summarises the theories on the redaction of 1 Enoch 6–11. It is generally agreed that the core stratum of 1 Enoch 6–11 is the Shemihazah Narrative, to which were added either one or two other layers. This is discussed in more detail below. Different theories, concerning the literary development of 1 Enoch 6–11, have been advanced, notably by P.D. Hanson, 'Rebellion in Heaven, Azazel, and Euhemeristic Heroes in 1 Enoch 6-11' in *Journal of Biblical Literature* 96 (1977), 195–233; G.W.E. Nickelsburg, 'Apocalyptic and Myth in 1 Enoch 6-11' in *Journal of Biblical Literature* 96 (1977), 383–405 (and more recently in his

The Shemihazah Narrative

It is generally agreed that the core stratum of 1 Enoch 6–11 is the Shemihazah Narrative (SN), which, based upon Gen. 6:1–2,[3] tells of the descent of the 'sons of God' in order to choose human wives for themselves. This narrative defines the sons of God as being angels who descend to the earth with the intention of fornicating with human women. In doing this, the angels cut themselves off from their heavenly estate once and for all (1 En. 6:1–6). This core stratum subsequently uses Gen. 6:4 as a basis for its account of the giant progeny of the union between the sons of God and the daughters of men. This giant progeny causes destruction upon the earth and the annihilation of humanity (1 En. 7:1–5). This results in the cry of the earth and the spirits of the slain for the intervention of the Most High (1 En. 7:6 and 8:4). The Most High duly intervenes, pronouncing judgements upon both the angels who descended and their giant progeny (1 En. 10:9–14).[4] The primary emphasis of this core stratum is upon the sexual nature of the transgression, the resulting devastation and defilement of the earth, and the punishment meted upon the fallen angels and their giant progeny.

Nickelsburg and Hanson agree in identifying the following references as comprising the core SN:[5] 1 En. 6:1–7:1c; 7:2–6; 8:4–9:5; 9:7–8b; 9:9–11; 10:1–3; 10:11–11:2. Dimant differs in that she considers 1 En. 8:4 as belonging to one of the later strata.[6] I consider the following references to comprise the core SN: 1 En. 6:1–6; 7:1-6; 8:4; 10:9–14.[7]

---

commentary; see note 1); C. Molenberg, 'A Study of the Roles of Shemihaza and Asael in 1 Enoch 6-11' in *Journal of Jewish Studies* 35 (1984), 136–146; D. Dimant, '1 Enoch 6–11: A Methodological Perspective' in Paul J. Achtemeier (ed.), *Society of Biblical Literature 1978 Seminar Papers* (Missoula 1978), I, 323–39. The following is a summary of the detailed analysis contained in my PhD dissertation: S. Bhayro, *A Text-Critical and Literary Analysis of 1 Enoch 6–11*, unpublished PhD dissertation (University College London, 2000).

3   It has been argued that the SN actually predates Gen. 6:1–4, and that the latter is dependent upon the former, although this view is almost universally rejected – see Nickelsburg, *A Commentary on the Book of 1 Enoch*, 166.

4   Although chiefly based upon Gen. 6:1–2 and 4, the author of the SN appears to have drawn also upon the account of Absalom's rebellion against David as well as other literary devices. I hope to discuss this in more detail elsewhere in the future.

5   Hanson, 'Rebellion in Heaven', 197; Nickelsburg, 'Apocalyptic and Myth', 384–6 and *A Commentary on the Book of 1 Enoch*, 165.

6   Dimant, '1 Enoch 6-11', 323–6.

7   Thus I would dramatically shorten the core stratum of 1 Enoch 6–11. According to both Nickelsburg and Hanson, the main passage that deals with the punishment of the giants, 1 En. 10:9–10, is not part of the core SN. I think that these verses are part of the original SN because, coupled with the

The AN-second stratum hypothesis

There are two main hypotheses concerning the later strata of 1 Enoch 6–11. The first, advanced by Hanson and formerly by Nickelsburg, identifies the Asael Narrative (AN) as the second stratum of 1 Enoch 6–11.[8] The second, advanced by Dimant and of late by Nickelsburg,[9] identifies the Angelic Instruction (AI) revision as the second stratum. Hence according to Dimant, the AI revision precedes the AN revision (see below).

The AN relates how the angel Asael brought illicit and destructive teachings to the inhabitants of the earth. These teachings involved the use of natural substances for illicit purposes. Thus mankind was taught metalwork, which enabled the production of weaponry and the spread of violence upon the earth. Furthermore, womankind was taught the use of make-up and jewellery, which led to fornication (1 En. 8:1–2). In response to this illicit instruction, the Most High decrees that Asael is to be bound beneath the earth until the final judgement. At the final judgement, Asael, to whom all sin is imputed, is to be thrown into the fire (1 En. 10:4–6 and 8).

According to this hypothesis, the early development of 1 Enoch 6–11 is as follows: SN → SN + AN → [SN + AN] + AI. Thus the core SN was revised with the incorporation of the AN and to this new composite unit was added the next stratum — the Angelic Instruction (AI) revision. According to Nickelsburg's original hypothesis, following the insertion of the AN into the SN, a third stratum was added in which the motif of instruction found in the AN was put into the core SN.[10]

The AI-second stratum hypothesis

Dimant, however, provides an alternative analysis of the development of 1 Enoch 6–11, in which the first revision was the incorporation of the AI stratum: SN → SN + AI → [SN + AI] + AN. Thus, according to Dimant, the second stratum introduces the element of instruction distinct from the AN tradition, and then the AN was

---

judgement pronounced upon the fallen angels, they tell of the punishment of the two groups of villains in the core SN.

8   Hanson, 'Rebellion in Heaven', 226; Nickelsburg, 'Apocalyptic and Myth', 386.

9   Nickelsburg, *A Commentary on the Book of 1 Enoch*, 191 (esp. n. 2).

10   Nickelsburg, 'Apocalyptic and Myth', 384–6, 399–400. As stated above, Nickelsburg has since reversed his view of the development of these strata.

subsequently attracted into the SN + AI composite unit through their common instruction elements. Dimant notes that 1 Enoch 6–7 and 9 make up a cohesive narrative that is interrupted by the list of angels and teachings of chapter eight. Thus Dimant assumes that 1 Enoch 8 is a later insertion.[11] Dimant then analyses 1 Enoch 8 in detail, concluding that it too is of a composite nature. Whilst 1 En. 8:3–4[12] deal briefly with each angel, giving just his name and teaching, 1 En. 8:1–2 are completely devoted to Asael and his eight teachings. Furthermore, whilst the teachings of the angels in 1 En. 8:3 are related linguistically to their names, the teachings of Asael appear to bear no relationship with his name at all. Thus Dimant divides 1 Enoch 8 into two strata — the AI stratum of 1 En. 8:3–4, and the AN stratum of 1 En. 8:1–2.[13] Dimant then suggests that the AN was later attracted into the SN + AI unit by the instruction motif which characterised the first revision of the narrative.[14]

Whilst agreeing with the main thrust of Dimant's AI-second stratum hypothesis, I am inclined to regard 1 En. 8:4 as being part of the original SN. This hypothesis commends itself for two reasons. Firstly, the original narrative would then have described the complaint of the earth (1 En. 7:6), followed by the complaint of humanity (1 En. 8:4), which then brings the response of the Most High. Secondly, the content of 1 En. 8:4, with its description of humanity's anguished lament, is consistent with the role of humanity as victims in the SN. The later revisions are less sympathetic to humanity,[15] and, as such, would probably not present their cry as a

---

11 Dimant, '1 Enoch 6–11', 323. Thus far, this line of argument is consistent with the analyses of Hanson and Nickelsburg discussed above.

12 Although Dimant's arguments are concerned with 1 En. 8:3–4, I would prefer to limit her conclusions to 1 En. 8:3. The reasons for this are discussed below.

13 Dimant, '1 Enoch 6–11', 323–4. The distinction between the AI and the AN strata is also apparent in that the crafts taught by Shemihazah and his companions are occult crafts, whilst those taught by Asael are non-occult skills, such as metalwork, which are then misused by humanity. Furthermore, whilst the angels of the AI stratum are identified with those of the SN who sinned, Asael himself is not mentioned as sinning, rather he leads others into sin through his teachings. Dimant notes that this distinction, between the AI and the AN, is maintained throughout 1 Enoch (cf. 1 En. 13:1–2/13:3 and 86:1/86:3) — see Dimant *idem.*, 326–7, 335 (n. 35).

14 Dimant, ibid. 326–9. This is contrary to Nickelsburg's original hypothesis, discussed above, in which the instruction motif found within the AN prompted the insertion of the AI stratum into the SN + AN unit.

15 For example, the AN strongly suggests that humanity sinned by misusing metalwork, itself a morally neutral skill, leading to violence and fornication. This changes humanity's status from hapless victim of angelic sin (SN) to willing participant in, and possibly even cause of, angelic sin.

motivating force behind the Most High's response. I consider the following references to comprise the AI stratum: 1 En. 6:7-8; 8:3; 10:7.[16]

The Son of Lamech revision

As discussed above, the core SN is essentially based upon Gen. 6:1–2 and 4, which probably have nothing to do with the following flood story.[17] At some point, however, an exegetical breakthrough was made in which the flood story was associated with the preceding 'sons of God' unit. Thus the mingling of the sons of God with the daughters of men ceases to be a neutral act, as it appears in Gen. 6:1–4, and becomes a wicked act which is part of the rationale behind the deluge.[18] This association of Gen. 6:1–4 with the flood story underlies the Son of Lamech (SL) revision of 1 Enoch 6–11. This revision introduces aspects of the Biblical flood narrative into the Watcher story. The verses which comprise this revision are 1 En. 10:1–3 and 15–19.[19] The Noahic elements introduced in this revision include the deluge, the survival of one man and his seed to repopulate the earth and the motif of planting.

Molenberg argues for an organic development of these later strata, due to the changing circumstances, concerns and notions of sin of the people this work was

---

16 Regardless of the validity of Dimant's assertion that in 1 En. 8:3, 'we have another version of the list with Shemihazah as the first' (i.e. 1 En. 6:7), it is certainly conceivable that the AI-reviser selected some names from the list of Shemihazah's angelic comrades, and ascribed to each one the teaching of a specific craft related to its name. I consider the first list in 1 En. 6:7, however, also to be part of the AI revision. The insertion of the list of twenty angelic leaders allows the construction of the subsequent passage that describes the teachings of some of those angels.

17 It is generally accepted that Gen. 6:1–4 forms a literary unit distinct from the following flood story of Gen. 6:5–8:19. Van Ruiten notes how all the Biblical allusions and references to the flood story make no connection whatsoever with the preceding story of the mingling of the sons of God with the daughters of men; see J. Van Ruiten, 'The Flood Story in the Book of Jubilees' in F.G. Martínez and G.P. Luttikhuizen (eds), *Interpretations of the Flood* (Leiden 1998), 79–80.

18 This line of exegesis is found in Jubilees 5 and 7; CD 2; Testament of Naphtali 3, 3; Maccabees 2 etc.; see Van Ruiten ibid. 80–1.

19 Both Hanson and Nickelsburg consider the SL revision to be part of the core SN; cf. Hanson, 'Rebellion in Heaven', 197; Nickelsburg, 'Apocalyptic and Myth', 384 and *A Commentary on the Book of 1 Enoch*, 165. Molenberg follows suit; cf. Molenberg, 'A Study of the Roles of Shemihaza and Asael', 137. The problem with this view is that the Noahic elements are well defined and limited to two sections of the narrative — were they dispersed more evenly throughout 1 Enoch 6–11, there would be more credence to the view that they were originally part of the core narrative. Furthermore, there is no trace of the flood story in the preceding strata (SN, AI and AN), and the reference to the flood story in the SL revision is really only possible once humanity's role is changed from victim (SN) to participant (AI and AN) in the angelic rebellion.

disseminated amongst.[20] Thus the earlier SN was a condemnation of sexual sin and impurity, to which later writers added similar condemnations of the occult (AI) and weapons/cosmetics (AN).

The Angelic Prayer revision[21]

This brings us to the passage in question — the Angelic Prayer (AP) of 1 En. 9:1–11. Previous analyses of 1 En. 9:1–11 have distributed it amongst the various strata (SN, AI and AN).[22] But the narrative makes perfect sense without this section, with the cry of the spirits of the slain prompting the immediate response of the Most High in chapter ten. There are also two further indications that the AP was inserted into the narrative last of all.

Firstly, this prayer shows the concerns of the author(s) as they change through the successive strata:

- SN   sexual impurity (1 En. 9:8)
- AI   mantic arts (1 En. 9:7)
- AN   weaponry and cosmetics (1 En. 9:6)

But the really interesting thing is that the priorities of the author(s) of the AP are the reverse of the order of the strata as just outlined. Thus it appears that the author(s) of this prayer wrote it with the later concerns uppermost in mind, thus reducing the original concern of the narrative to the last mentioned. Secondly, the mention of all four archangels at the start of the chapter implies that it was composed after the rest of the narrative, as these archangels appear dispersed amongst the various strata through chapter ten.

Purpose of the AP

As stated above, the narrative would have read well enough without the insertion of the AP, as the intervention of the Most High (1 Enoch 10, originally verses 9–14)

---

20 Molenberg, 'A Study of the Roles of Shemihaza and Asael', 145–6.

21 Nickelsburg considers this chapter at length in his commentary; see Nickelsburg, *A Commentary on the Book of 1 Enoch*, 202–14. His discussion of angelic intercessors is particularly noteworthy, giving a thorough account of similar occurrences in the Hebrew Bible, Apocrypha and Pseudepigrapha, Qumran literature and the New Testament (208–10).

22 Hanson, 'Rebellion in Heaven', 195; Nickelsburg, 'Apocalyptic and Myth', 384 and *A Commentary on the Book of 1 Enoch*, 165; Molenberg, 'A Study of the Roles of Shemihaza and Asael', 137.

would have immediately followed the cry of the spirits of the slain (1 En. 8:4) as well as, prior to the insertion of the later strata, the cry of the ravaged earth (1 En. 7:6). It is this observation that helps us discern the reason for the AP's composition and insertion into this part of the narrative.

The original narrative, with its description of divine intervention in response to injustice, runs contrary to the course of human affairs. The point is that the Most High evidently does not intervene immediately following the appeal of the righteous for justice. Human history, and particularly the period in which this narrative was produced,[23] witnessed events of extreme trauma for those who considered themselves to be righteous, and yet their hopes for divine intervention in the affairs of humanity to put things right were not realised.

It is this understanding that enables us to explain the insertion of the AP into the narrative. The prayer of the four archangels very much expresses the distress of the final compiler of 1 Enoch 6–11 with the present state of affairs. The conflict between the experience of the author(s), distressed at the violence and devastation suffered by his people, and his doctrine, which espouses the sovereignty and justice of the Most High, expresses itself in the angels' statement:

> ... the whole earth has been filled with blood and iniquity ... and you know everything before it happens ... and yet there is nothing which you say to us ... (1 En. 9:9–11)

Thus it is the apparent inactivity of the Most High, his failure to act and put a stop to the suffering of the righteous, which is the most distressing aspect of this lament.[24]

Underlying this distress, however, is an implicit hope that the cries of the suffering righteous will indeed invoke the Most High's intervention. Thus 1 En. 9:2 mentions the cries of humanity reaching the gates of heaven and stirring the intercession of the four archangels. It is through these archangels that the Most High then intervenes on behalf of the righteous elect. This is probably the response to prayer that was desired by those who composed and read this text. Thus this prayer functioned as a blueprint for prayer — a template for intercession by which the righteous sought to provoke the kind of divine intervention that follows in 1 Enoch 10.

---

23 On this, see Nickelsburg, *A Commentary on the Book of 1 Enoch*, 169–70 and below.

24 Nickelsburg also comments upon the 'disjunction' between God's omniscience and inactivity — see Nickelsburg, *A Commentary on the Book of 1 Enoch*, 214. He also compares this prayer with other Jewish prayers from the Hellenistic period and, most significantly, observes that this prayer contains no element of petition and is rather an 'indictment' at God's inaction. In this respect, of all the Jewish Hellenistic prayers, Nickelsburg compares it to the prayer of Susanna; see Nickelsburg, *A Commentary on the Book of 1 Enoch*, 205–6.

The Sectarian Setting for the Prayer

A closer look at this prayer suggests that it was composed in a strongly sectarian setting. From the Qumran Aramaic fragments 4QEn[a] 1 iv g and h, we know that 1 En. 9:1 used the nouns דם 'blood' and חמסה 'violence' in reference to the scene of destruction witnessed by the four archangels.[25] It is this דם and חמסה, of which the earth and its slain inhabitants complain, that provokes the intercession of the archangels.

The use of these Aramaic nouns is most interesting as it recalls the following Hebrew phrase that occurs twice in the book of Habakkuk:[26]

... מדמי אדם וחמס־ארץ ...

... because of the blood of man and the violence of the earth ...

Taken out of context, this phrase from Habakkuk describes well the situation upon the earth as a result of the birth of the giants.

The exposition of this phrase in the Qumran commentary to Habakkuk reveals a strong exegetical tradition. In 1QpHab, Hab. 2:8 reads:[27]

(8) *Because you have plundered many nations, all the remnant of peoples will despoil you, because of the blood of man and the violence of the earth, the city and all its inhabitants.*[28]

---

25 J.T. Milik, *The Books of Enoch: Aramaic Fragments of Qumrân Cave 4* (Oxford 1976), 157–8, 342 and plate IV.

26 Hab. 2:8 and 17. In keeping with his identification of 1 En. 9:1–5, 7-8b and 9–11 with the core SN, and his favouring of an external circumstance for this narrative (see note 33 below), Nickelsburg does not establish a link between 1 En. 9:1 and 1QpHab. Rather, he simply identifies the Aramaic חמסה with the Hebrew חמס of Gen. 6:11, thus ignoring its coupling with דם, and prefers to see humanity still as victims ('[the author] makes the human race the victims rather than the perpetrators of the violence'); see Nickelsburg, *A Commentary on the Book of 1 Enoch*, 208. This is not so straightforward, however, as the AP does indeed refer to the role of humanity in devastating the earth. Thus Asael is blamed for teaching iniquity rather than committing it, with the assumption that humanity actually did it (1 En. 9:6). Similarly, Shemihazah teaches incantations, but it is assumed that humanity performed them (1 En. 9:7). Also, the devastation of the earth is caused through the offspring born to human women who, in the process of procreation, defiled the angels (1 En. 9:8–9). Compare also the retelling of this story in Jub. 4:15 and 5:1, in which the women actually seduce the angels. It appears that the male author(s) of the later strata of 1 Enoch 6–11 is eager to blame women for society's ills, hence the reference to cosmetics and jewellery, and the accusatory tone of 1 En. 9:9 — *And as for the women, they have borne giants, and through this the whole earth has been filled with blood and iniquity.*

27 The *editio princeps* of 1QpHab is M. Burrows, *The Dead Sea Scrolls of St. Mark's Monastery - Vol. 1 The Isaiah Manuscript and the Habakkuk Commentary* (New Haven 1950).

The commentary offered in the Qumran text relates this to the 'wicked priest', and the corrupt priesthood in Jerusalem, who opposed the 'teacher of righteousness'. The actions of this wicked priest are described in the commentary to the previous verses:

> 'Will not suddenly your creditors arise and your agitators awake? And you will be for a despoiling
> to them. Because you have plundered many nations, all the remnant of peoples [will despoil you'
> — the interpretation of the matter is ab]out **the priest who rebelled**...[29]

Thus the Qumran community's exposition of Hab. 2:7–8 is based upon the idea that the violence of the earth (חמס־ארץ) and blood of man (דמי אדם) resulted from rebellion. This idea is completely absent in Habakkuk 2, which deals with the Babylonians being used by God to execute judgement upon the nation of Judah. The Qumran commentary, however, identifies the Babylonians of Habakkuk 2 with the wicked priest and the corrupt Jerusalem priesthood. Thus the exposition of these verses in the Qumran commentary is a good example of eisegesis — reading the desired interpretation into a text. This eisegesis places the rebellion within an inner-Jewish sectarian conflict between the teacher of righteousness and the wicked priest and his followers.

This combination of 'the violence of the earth and the blood of man' with 'rebellion', a rather distinctive line of interpretation, also occurs in 1 Enoch 6–11, which uses דם and חמסה in the context of the rebellion of the Watchers. Thus we have, in 1QpHab and our own Enochic narrative, a common eisegetical approach to the construction of a polemic.[30] The manifestation of this common eisegetical approach in 1QpHab is certainly sectarian, so it is reasonable to assume that its occurrence in 1 Enoch 6–11 is also sectarian in context.[31]

---

28 Translations of 1QpHab are my own — for the text, see Burrows, *The Dead Sea Scrolls of St. Mark's Monastery*, plate LIX.

29 See Burrows ibid. plate LVIII. The restorations made in this section are virtually certain.

30 Furthermore, both texts concern the application of Babylonian images to a Jewish situation. In 1QpHab, the marauding Babylonians who spoil the earth are equated with the corrupt priesthood who spoil the Jews. In 1 Enoch 6–11, the practice of Babylonian divination is the object of the polemic. On this, see my dissertation, and also S. Bhayro, 'Daniel's "Watchers" in Enochic Exegesis of Genesis 6:14' in G.J. Brooke (ed.), *Jewish Ways of Reading the Bible* (JSS Supplement 11, Oxford 2000), 58–66.

31 Whilst a common eisegetical approach appears beyond doubt, the question of influence between 1 Enoch 6–11 and 1QpHab is more complex. The following chart illustrates the problem:

Thus it is reasonable to suggest that the prayer for divine intervention in the affairs of humanity contained in 1 En. 9:1–11 is not simply a plea for intervention against the enemies of the Jews in the Second-Temple Period, but also a plea for intervention against those Jewish groups that opposed the sect of the author.

Historical context

As we noted above, the author of 1QpHab relates the rebellion and the ensuing blood and violence to the wicked priest and his followers, i.e. those Jews who oppose his own sect. Similarly, 1 Enoch 6–11 discusses the rebellion of angels who deserted their heavenly station (cf. Jude 6). Thus it is clear that the crisis referred to by these texts is not an external threat to Judaism from gentile powers, but actually an internal Jewish sectarian conflict.[32] This may help us discern the historical context for the prayer.

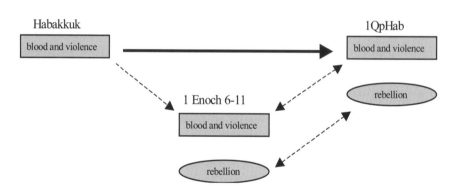

In this chart, a broken line indicates possible influence, whereas an unbroken line indicates certain influence. We can be sure that the blood and violence of 1QpHab comes from Habakkuk, so we are searching for the origin of the combination of blood and violence with rebellion. 1 Enoch 6–11 has the same combination of motifs. We are not able to deduce whether this combination of motifs is due to influence between 1 Enoch 6–11 and 1QpHab, or whether their occurrence is due to the use of a well-established literary device in both 1 Enoch 6–11 and 1QpHab.

32 Attempts to discern the historical setting of 1 Enoch 6–11 have not been well received. Nickelsburg, seeking a period in which Palestine experienced traumatic upheavals, favours the Diadochi Wars (323–302 BCE) in which the land of Israel changed hands at least seven times. Thus Nickelsburg tentatively suggests the end of the fourth century BCE for the period of composition; see Nickelsburg, 'Apocalyptic and Myth', 391 and *A Commentary on the Book of 1 Enoch*, 170. This external approach is rightly rejected by Collins, who argues for an internal conflict that is not linked to a specific historical event. He notes that the narrative does not refer explicitly to any historical event or person. For Collins, this demonstrates that it was not written for a specific period, as a polemic concerning current events, but for a general sectarian world-view, as a polemic warning of impending judgement against those not within the sect; see J.J. Collins, 'Methodological Issues in the Study of 1 Enoch:

If we are to seek a specific crisis that would have prompted the composition of the AP, rather than just a general sectarian world-view (see note 33), then there are three points that must be taken into account. Firstly, accepting the above hypothesis of a link between the AP section and 1QpHab, the issue of historical context probably revolves around the identification of the teacher of righteousness and his adversaries, the corrupt priesthood. It is probably this corrupt priesthood that brings violence and bloodshed upon the sect of the author.

Secondly, as the AP section suggests, we are looking for a period some time after this violence and bloodshed have begun, as the AP betrays a frustration at the lack of divine intervention following these events.

Thirdly, whilst 1 Enoch 6–11 may not refer explicitly to historical events, it may refer to them allegorically when it refers to the sins of the rebels. As we noted above, these change through three successive strata, and are then mentioned in reverse order in the AP. The first is sexual defilement, the second is religious defilement, and the third is violence, presumably against the sect of the author. This sequence may reveal much about the period in which the prayer was composed.

The identity of the teacher of righteousness is, of course, an unresolved problem and is certainly beyond the scope of this paper. But as an example of how the method outlined above works, let us consider the latest discussion of this problem.[33] Geller argues that the teacher of righteousness is Simon II,[34] the pro-Seleucid High Priest who flourished around the start of the second century BCE, only to die not long after the Seleucids gained control of the land of Israel. According to Geller, the Qumran community was organised no sooner than 160 BCE for the 'express purpose of waiting for the Messiah to come'.[35]

This period of roughly forty years, between the death of Simon II and the establishing of the Qumran Community, corresponds well to the statement in the Damascus Document that there was a forty year period between the death of the

---

Reflections on the Articles of P.D. Hanson and G.W. Nickelsburg', in Paul J. Achtemeier, (ed.), *Society of Biblical Literature 1978* Seminar Papers I, 315–22, especially 320–1. Similarly, Hanson, partly on the basis of the AP section, places the origins of the narrative within a sectarian apocalyptic movement comparable to the Essenes and the Hasidim; see Hanson, 'Rebellion in Heaven', 219–20. Whilst agreeing with Collins that this narrative should be placed in the context of a Jewish sectarian conflict, I disagree with the general approach, and below I argue that we can discern references to specific historical circumstances in 1 Enoch 6–11.

33 The latest discussion is that of M.J. Geller, 'Qumran's Teacher of Righteousness – a suggested identification' in *Scripta Judaica Cracoviensia* 1 (2002), 9–19.

34 Shimon Ha-Saddiq.

35 Geller 'Qumran's Teacher of Righteousness', 18.

Teacher and the end of those who opposed him (CD 20:11–12).[36] This forty-year period was extremely traumatic for the Jerusalem high-priestly office, due to the political struggles between the Oniads and Tobiads. The following is a summary of the salient points:[37]

- Circa 240 BCE

Following the victory of Ptolemy III in the Third Syrian War, the pro-Seleucid High Priest Onias II was severely weakened. Much of his power was transferred to the pro-Ptolemaic Joseph, son of Tobiah.[38] Crucially, Joseph was supported financially by the Samaritans.[39] According to a second-century account of the Samaritan Schism, the Samaritan priesthood arose due to a mixed marriage. Thus, according to Schäfer, there was an 'internal dispute among the Jerusalem priesthood over the mixed marriage question'.[40] The labelling of Samaritan support for the Tobaids as the support of sexually defiled priests would have proved an irresistible propaganda ploy for the Oniads.

- Circa 200 BCE

Following the victory of Antiochus III in the Fifth Syrian War, the pro-Seleucid High Priest Simon II[41] was politically ascendant. Simon II died at the height of his power, and was succeeded by Onias III who was quickly outmanoeuvred by the Tobiads.[42]

- Circa 175 BCE

Decades of Oniad/Tobiad struggles brought Jerusalem to the brink of civil war. With the accession of Antiochus IV, the Tobiads purchased the high-priestly office for Jason, brother of Onias III, but later purchased it for Menelaus, who was not from the Zadokite priestly line. Menelaus had Onias III assassinated. Under both Jason and

---

36 See Geller ibid. 11.

37 For a convenient summary of this period, see P. Schäfer, *The History of the Jews in Antiquity: The Jews of Palestine from Alexander the Great to the Arab Conquest* (translated by D. Chowcat; Luxembourg 1995), 13–63. See also E. Schürer, *The History of the Jewish People in the Age of Jesus Christ (175 B.C.–A.D. 135)*, I: (revised and edited by G. Vermes and F. Millar, Edinburgh 1973), 125–88.

38 This transfer of power was an innovation, thus showing the extent of Tobiad domination at this point; see Schürer, *The History of the Jewish People*, 140.

39 Schäfer, *The History of the Jews in Antiquity*, 20.

40 Schäfer ibid. 4.

41 Son of the High Priest Onias II.

42 Schäfer ibid. 32.

Menelaus, Hellenising policies popularised pagan practises associated with Hermes and Hercules even among the priesthood.[43]

- Circa 163 BCE
Following the death of Antiochus IV, Menelaus was executed and the Zadokite Alcimus was made High Priest, thus restoring the legitimate high-priestly line. Onias IV, son of Onias III, fled to Egypt and established a rival sanctuary. Alcimus murdered sixty Hasidim (thus turning against the pietists) and was subsequently forced to flee Jerusalem.[44]

- Circa 160 BCE
Having returned to Jerusalem following the defeat of Judas the Maccabee, Alcimus demolished the wall of the inner court of the temple in order to allow access for non-Jews. Following his death soon afterwards, there was no High Priest for seven years.[45]

- Circa 153 BCE
Jonathan the Maccabee, a non-Zadokite, became High Priest.[46]
In these events, it is possible to discern the elements present in the various strata of 1 Enoch 6–11, culminating in the AP. Firstly, there is the accusation of sexual defilement among parts of the priesthood (the Samaritan Schism). The support of a supposedly sexually defiled priestly line for the Tobiads under Joseph may have occasioned the composition of the core SN as anti-Tobiad propaganda.

We then see the religious corruption due to Tobiad influence, particularly in the policies accompanying the reigns of the Hellenising Jason and the illegitimate High Priest Menelaus, which were accompanied by the participation of the priests in illegitimate religious practices. This would have distressed the pietists further, and may have led to the incorporation of the AI stratum, with its emphasis on religious defilement, into 1 Enoch 6–11.

Following the accession of Alcimus as High Priest in the legitimate Zadokite line, the pietists would have had renewed hope, which would fit in with the statement in CD 20:11–12.[47] But this hope was soon dashed, however, with the persecutions

---

43 Schäfer ibid. 34–9.
44 Schäfer ibid. 49.
45 Schäfer ibid. 51.
46 Schäfer ibid. 51.
47 Of course, CD 20:11–12 could also refer to the relief of the pietists following the death of Alcimus around 160 BCE. It is worth noting that initially the pietists accepted Alcimus as legitimate; Schäfer, ibid. 49.

against the Hasidim. It is at this time that the AN stratum, with its emphasis on violence, may have been composed.

With the restoration of Alcimus, and the admission of pagans into the temple inner court, the pietists would have had their sectarianism reinforced. The failure of human attempts to resolve the situation, particularly with the defeat of Judas the Maccabee, would have stimulated the hope for divine intervention and justice, the like of which underlies the SL revision. The apparent delay in this intervention may have then stimulated such prayers as the AP.

If we accept this scenario, then the composition of the early strata of 1 Enoch 6–11 would coincide with the struggles between the Oniads and Tobiads in the first decades of the second century BCE, with the accompanying issues of Hellenisation and corruption in the priesthood. After a period of time, during which it became evident that an immediate divine intervention had not occurred, the withdrawal of a pietist sect to Qumran to wait for the Messiah probably provoked the composition of intercessory prayers such as the AP. This would fit in with Milik's assessment of 4QEn[a], the earliest of the Qumran Enoch manuscripts that contain 1 Enoch 6–11, which he dated palaeographically to the first half of the second century BCE.[48]

Conclusion

The AP section of 1 Enoch 6–11 was composed after the rest of the narrative, to express distress at the inactivity of the Most High. It was composed in a climate of sectarian strife, in which disputes over sexual and religious purity had spilled over into a bloody power-struggle and persecution of the pietist party. The probable time of composition coincided with the establishing of the Qumran community. This was around the time of the reign of Alcimus, during which hopes of a restoration of a righteous Zadokite High Priest were finally destroyed. This caused the pietist party to look back and grasp the memory of the last effective Zadokite High Priest — Simon II.

---

48 Milik, *The Books of Enoch*, 22 and 140.

Appendix

The Ethiopic text of 1 En. 9:1–11

The following section presents my readings of seven Ethiopic manuscripts.[49] My aim has not been to produce an eclectic or critical text of the Ethiopic version of 1 En. 9:1–11, but rather to add to the body of evidence by providing new readings from seven manuscripts.[50]

The base-text is EMML 6686, which is a seventeenth century manuscript from the monastery Debra Libanos in the Shewa region of Ethiopia. This is used for the base-text because it is a good example of a manuscript which some would suggest was produced by the scribal revisions of the late medieval/early modern period.[51] In this way, it resembles Rylands Ethiopic MS. 23, which was used as the base-text for

---

49 Print-outs of these manuscripts were kindly supplied by the Hill Monastic Manuscript Library which houses the Ethiopic Manuscript Microfilm Library. I would like to express gratitude to both the HMML and Dr. Getachew Haile for their assistance and permission to publish readings of these manuscripts.

50 In order to represent these seven manuscripts faithfully, most types of variants have been listed. In order that we are not over-burdened with trivial variants, however, most of the simply orthographic variations, which would be normalised in a critical edition, have been omitted. For a discussion of manuscript errors and normalisation, see T.O. Lambdin, *Introduction to Classical Ethiopic (Ge'ez)* (Atlanta 1978), 13–14. See also Knibb's comments on how the method in Charles' edition is questionable because it 'sometimes makes the use and interpretation of his evidence difficult'; M.A. Knibb, *The Ethiopic Book of Enoch* (Oxford 1978), II, 5–6. The following, however, should be noted:
- EMML 1786 is damaged in parts, so variants are only noted where the manuscript is legible. Absence of noted variants does not necessarily imply that EMML 1768 agrees with EMML 6686.
- The following sets of symbols are very often indistinguishable:

ሐ and ኀ   ጎ, ጐ and ኈ
ሰ and ሠ   ዐ and ዓ

In such instances, the notes assume that the manuscript in question agrees with EMML 6686.
- The vowels ዾ and ዺ are often indistinguishable, especially in the angelic names. Again, the notes assume that the manuscript in question agrees with EMML 6686.
- The punctuation of the text differs from manuscript to manuscript. To overcome this, I have punctuated the text as follows:
፥ between words
። at the end of each verse.

51 It has been suggested that the various parts of the Ethiopic version of the Bible were subject to a series of revisions beginning with those of Abba Salama during the fourteenth century. The circumstances and periods of these revisions remain uncertain, however, and various hypotheses have been advanced. For a detailed discussion of the different hypotheses, see E. Ullendorff, *Ethiopia and the Bible* (Oxford 1968), 36–62.

Knibb's edition.[52] As well as readings of EMML 6686, notes are given for the following manuscripts:[53]

EMML	36	late 18th – early 19th century	Church of St. Raguel, Entoto, Addis Ababa.
EMML	1768	late 15th century	Monastery of Hayq Estifanos, Ambassal, Wallo.
EMML	1950	17th – 18th century	Monastery of Hayq Estifanos, Ambassal, Wallo.
EMML	2080	12th – 13th century/15th century[54]	Private library of Mamher Hayla Maryam, Ambassal, Wallo.
EMML	2436	17th century	Church of Ankobarr Madhane Alam, Ankobarr, Shewa.
EMML	2440	dated 1663 CE	Church of Ankobarr Madhane Alam, Ankobarr, Shewa

1 Enoch 9:1-11

Ge'ez

[1] ወአሜሃ ፡ ሐወጹ ፡ ሚካኤል ፡ ወገብርኤል ፡ ሱርያን ፡ ወኡርያን ፡ እምሰማይ ፡ ወርእዩ ፡ ብዙኃ ፡ ደመ ፡ ዘይትከዓው ፡ በዲበ ፡ ምድር [(a)] ወኩሎ ፡ ዓመፃ ፡ ዘይትገበር ፡ በዲበ ፡ ምድር ።

[2] ወይቤሉ ፡ በበይናቲሆሙ ፡ ቃለ ፡ ጸራኃቲሆሙ ፡ ዕራቅ ፡ ጸርሐት ፡ ምድር ፡ እስከ ፡ እንቀጸ ፡ ሰማይ ።

[3] ወይእዜኒ ፡ ለክሙ ፡ አቅዱሳነ ፡ ሰማይ ፡ ይሰከዩ ፡ ነፍሳተ ፡ ሰብእ ፡ እንዘ ፡ ይብሉ ፡ አብኡ ፡ ለነ ፡ ፍትሐ ፡ ኀበ ፡ ልዑል ።

[4] ወይቤሉ ፡ ለእግዚአሙ ፡ ንጉሥ ፡ እስመ ፡ እግዚአሙ ፡ ለአጋእዝት ፡ ወአምላኮሙ ፡ ለአማልክት ፡ ወንጉሦሙ ፡ ለነገሥት ፡ ወመንበረ ፡ ስብሐቲሁ ፡ ውስተ ፡ ኩሉ ፡ ትውልደ ፡ ዓለም ፡ ወስምከ ፡ ቅዱስ ፡ ወስቡሕ ፡ ውስተ ፡ ኩሉ ፡ ትውልደ[(a)] ፡ ዓለም ፡ ወቡራክ ፡ ወስቡሕ [(b)] ።

[5] አንተ ፡ ገበርከ ፡ ኩሎ ፡ ወሥልጣነ ፡ ኩሉ ፡ ምስሌከ ፡ ወኩሉ ፡ ክሡት ፡ በቅድሜከ ፡ ወግሁድ ፡ ወአንተ ፡ ትሬኢ ፡ ኩሎ ፡ ወአልቦ ፡ ዘይትከሀለ ፡ ይትኃባእ ፡ እምኔከ ።

---

52 Knibb, *The Ethiopic Book of Enoch II*, 25 (note 9).

53 For full details of these manuscripts, see W.F. Macomber and G. Haile, *A Catalogue of Ethiopian Manuscripts Microfilmed for the Ethiopian Manuscript Microfilm Library, Addis Ababa and for the Hill Monastic Manuscript Library, Collegeville* (Collegeville, MN 1975–).

54 EMML 2080 is twelfth–thirteenth century according to Macomber, but Hable Selassie asserts that it is from the fifteenth century. Tiller states that it is a late fifteenth century manuscript, but unfortunately gives no reason for this assertion: see P.A. Tiller, *A Commentary on the Animal Apocalypse of 1 Enoch* (Atlanta 1993), 143.

⁶⁾ርኢኬ ፡ ዘገብረ ፡ አዛዝኤል ፡ ዘከመ ፡ መሀረ ፡ ኵሎ ፡ ዓመፃ ፡ በዲበ ፡ ምድር ፡ ወአግሃደ ፡ ኅቡአተ ፡ ዓለም ፡ እለ ፡ ይትገበራ ፡ በሰማያት ፡፡

⁷⁾ ወአመረ ፡ ስብዓታተ ፡ ስምያዛ ፡ ዘእንተ ፡ ወሀብኮ ፡ ሥልጣን ⁽ᵃ⁾ ፡ ይኩንን ፡ እለ ፡ ምስሌሁ ፡ ኅቡረ ፡፡

⁸⁾ ወሐሩ ፡ ኀበ ፡ አዋልደ ፡ ሰብእ ፡ ኀቡረ ፡ ወሰከቡ ፡ <u>ምስሌሆን</u> ፡ ምስለ ፡ እልኩ ፡ አንስት ፡ ወረኵሱ ፡ ወአግሀዱ ፡ ሎን ፡ እሎን ተ ፡ ኃጣውአ ፡፡

⁹⁾ ወእንስትኒ ፡ ወለዳ ፡ ረዓይተ ፡ ወበዝ ፡ መልእት ፡ ኵላ ፡ ምድር ፡ ደም ፡ ወዓመፃ ፡፡

¹⁰⁾ ይእዜኒ ፡ ናሁ ፡ ይጸርሑ ፡ ነፍሳት ፡ እለ ፡ ሞቱ ፡ ወይሰክዬ ፡ እስከ ፡ አንቀጸ ፡ ሰማይ ፡ ወዓርገ ፡ ገዓሮሙ ፡ ወኢይክሉ ፡ ወፂአ ፡ እምቅድመ ፡ ገጸ ፡ ዓመፃ ፡ ዘይትገበር ፡ በዲበ ፡ ምድር ፡፡

¹¹⁾ ወአንተ ፡ ተአምር ፡ ኵሎ ፡ ዘእንበለ ፡ ይኩን ⁽ᵃ⁾ ፡ ወአንተ ፡ ተአምር ፡ ዘንተ ፡ ወዘዚአሆሙ ፡ ወአልቦ ፡ ዘትነግረነ ፡ ወምንት ፡ መፍትው ፡ ንረስዮሙ ፡ በእንተ ፡ ዝንቱ ፡፡

(Underlined sections are omitted in the main body of the text, but the scribe notes them in the margins.)

Notes for Ethiopic mss:

Verse 1
EMML 36   አሜሃ instead of ወአሜሃ
                   ሱርያል ፡ ወኡራኤል instead of ሱርያን ፡ ወኡርያን
EMML 1768 ⁽ᵃ⁾ inserts ታሕተ
EMML 1950 ወሱርያን instead of ሱርያን
EMML 2080 ወሱርኤል ፡ ወኡርያል instead of ሱርያን ፡ ወኡርያን
                   ዘይትከ0ው instead of ዘይትከዓው
                   0መፃ instead of ዓመፃ
EMML 2436 ወሱራኤል ፡ ወገብርኤል instead of ወገብርኤል ፡ ሱርያን
                   ወኡርያል instead of ወኡርያን
EMML 2440 አሜሃ instead of ወአሜሃ
                   ወሱርያን instead of ሱርያን

Verse 2
EMML 36   ጸራሕቲሆሙ instead of ጸራኃቲሆሙ
EMML 1768 ጸራኀቲሆሙ instead of ጸራኃቲሆሙ
EMML 2080 ጸራኀቲሆሙ instead of ጸራኃቲሆሙ
EMML 2436 ጸራሆሙ instead of ጸራኃቲሆሙ

Verse 3
EMML 1768 በሎሙ ፡ ለቅዱሳን instead of ለክሙ ፡ አቅዱሳነ
                   ነፍሰ instead of ነፍሳተ
EMML 1950 ቅዱሳነ instead of አቅዱሳነ
EMML 2080 ቅዱሳነ instead of አቅዱሳነ

49

ገበ ፧ ልዑል precedes አብኡ ፧ ለነ ፧ ፍትሐ

EMML 2436 ገበ ፧ ልዑል precedes አብኡ ፧ ለነ ፧ ፍትሐ

Verse 4

EMML 36 ለእግዚአሙ instead of ለእግዚአሙ

እግዚአሙ instead of እግዚአሙ

omits ወስምክ ፧ ቅዱስ ፧ ወስቡሕ ፧ ውስተ ፧ ኩሉ ፧
ትውልደ ፧ ዓለም ፧ ወሮ

EMML 1950 ለንጉሥ instead of ንጉሥ

EMML 2080 ለእግዚአሙ instead of ለእግዚአሙ

እግዚአሙ instead of እግዚአሙ

መንበረ ፧ ስብሐቲክ instead of ወመንበረ ፧ ስብሐቲሁ

[a] omits ትውልደ

EMML 2436 አምላኮሙ instead of ወአምላኮሙ

[a] omits ትውልደ

[b] inserts አንተ

EMML 2440 ለንጉሥ instead of ንጉሥ

Verse 5

EMML 36 ቅድሜከ instead of በቅድሜከ

EMML 1950 ቅድሜከ instead of በቅድሜከ

ዘይትከህል instead of ዘይትከህል

EMML 2080 ቅድሜከ instead of በቅድሜከ

EMML 2436 ወአንተ instead of አንተ

EMML 2440 ቅድሜከ instead of በቅድሜከ

Verse 6

EMML 36 ወአግሀደ ፧ ገቡአተ instead of ወአግየደ ፧ ገቡአተ

EMML 1768 ወአግሁዱ instead of ወአግየደ

EMML 1950 ዘመሐረ instead of ዘከመ ፧ መሀረ

ወአግሁደ instead of ወአግየደ

EMML 2080 አዘዚኤል instead of አዛዝኤል

0መ9 instead of 9መ9

ወአግሁደ ፧ ገቡአተ instead of ወአግየደ ፧ ገቡአተ

EMML 2436 አመ9 instead of 9መ9

ወአግሁደ instead of ወአግየደ

EMML 2440 ወአግሁደ instead of ወአግየደ

Verse 7

EMML 36 ስብአታተ instead of ስብዓታተ

omits ገቡረ

EMML 1768 አመረ instead of ወአመረ

ስብእ instead of ስብዓታተ

EMML 2080 ስብአታተ ፧ ስምያዘ instead of ስብዓታተ ፧ ስምያዘ

ወሀብከ instead of ወሀብከ

EMML 2436 ወስምያዘ ፧ አመረ ፧ ስብአታተ

instead of ወአመረ ፧ ስብዓታተ ፧ ስምያዘ

ገቡረ occurs following ይኩኑን

EMML 2440 [a] inserts ከመ

Verse 8
EMML 36   ወሐሩ instead of ወሐሩ
              ጎቡረ instead of ጎቡረ
              ወአግሃዱ instead of ወአግሀዱ
EMML 1768 omits ጎቡረ
              ሎቱ ፤ ኩሎ ፤ ኃጢአተ
              instead of ሎን ፤ እሉንተ ፤ ኃጣውአ
EMML 1950 ወሐሩ instead of ወሐሩ
EMML 2080 ወሐሩ instead of ወሐሩ
              ኩሎ ፤ ጎጢአተ instead of እሉንተ ፤ ኃጣውአ
EMML 2436 omits ጎቡረ
              ወአግሃዱ instead of ወአግሀዱ
              ኩሎ ፤ ኃጢአተ instead of እሉንተ ፤ ኃጣውአ
EMML 2440 ወሐሩ instead of ወሐሩ
              ለእልኩቱ instead of ምስለ ፤ እልኩ

Verse 9
EMML 1768 ወአንስትሰ instead of ወአንስትኒ
              በዝ instead of ወበዝ
              ኩሉ instead of ኩላ
EMML 1950 ወአንስትሰ instead of ወአንስትኒ
EMML 2080 ወአንስትሰ instead of ወአንስትኒ
              ወ0መq instead of ወጎመq
EMML 2436 ወልዶ instead of ወለዳ
              በዝመልዓት instead of ወበዝ ፤ መልአት
EMML 2440 ረአይተ instead of ረዓይተ

Verse 10
EMML 36   ወይእዜኒ instead of ይእዜኒ
              ገ0ርመ instead of ገጎርመ
EMML 1768 ነፍስ instead of ነፍሳት
              እሉ instead of እለ
              ወኢይክል instead of ወኢይክሉ
EMML 1950 ወይእዜኒ instead of ይእዜኒ
              ገ0ርመ instead of ገጎርመ
EMML 2080 ወይእዜኒ instead of ይእዜኒ
              ነፍሳተ instead of ነፍሳት
              ወ0ርገ instead of ወጎርገ
              0መq instead of ጎመq
EMML 2436 ወይእዜኒ instead of ይእዜኒ
              ወአርገ instead of ወጎርገ
              አመq instead of ጎመq
EMML 2440 ወይእዜኒ instead of ይእዜኒ
              ወ0ርገ instead of ወጎርገ

Verse 11
EMML 36   omits but notes following at top of page:
              አንተ ፤ ተአምር ፤ ዘእንበለ ፤ ይኩን ፤ ወ
              ንሬስዮሙ instead of ንረስዮሙ

51

EMML 1768 ታአምር instead of ተአምር (both times)
(a) inserts ወአንተ ፡ ታአምር ፡ ኩሎ ፡ ዘእንበ ፡ ይኩን
EMML 2080 ዝትነግረነ instead of ዘትነግረነ
EMML 2440 ወምንተ instead of ወምንት

Translation

1) And at that time[55] Michael and Gabriel,[56] Suriel and Uriel[57] watched from heaven and they saw the abundance of blood that was being spilled upon the earth[58] and all the iniquity that was being done upon the earth.

2) And they said among themselves, 'The earth laid bare sends the sound of their cries[59] up to the gate of heaven'.

3) 'And now to you, O holy ones[60] of heaven, the souls of men complain[61] while they say, "Present for us a suit unto the Most High"'.[62]

4) And they said to their Lord the King,[63] 'Lord of lords and[64] God of gods and King of kings, and the throne of whose glory *is* in all the generations of the world, and Thy name *is* holy and praised in all the generations of[65] the world, and[66] blessed and praised'.[67]

5) 'Thou[68] hast made everything, and dominion over all[69] *is* with Thee,[70] and everything *is* uncovered and open in front of Thee, and Thou seest everything, and nothing can be concealed from Thee[71].'

---

55 EMML 36, 2440 omit the initial *and*.

56 EMML 1950, 2080, 2436, 2440 insert *and*. Note also that EMML 2436 inverts the names Gabriel and Suriel.

57 The translation of the angelic names given above is according to EMML 36, 2080 and 2436 which terminate the last two with ል - -*l*. This is better than the ን - -*n* used in the other manuscripts.

58 EMML 1768 inserts *beneath*.

59 Lit. *cries the sound of their cries*; see A. Dillmann, *Ethiopic Grammar*² (2ⁿᵈ enlarged edition by C. Bezold; translated by J.A.. Crichton; London 1907), 432–3, where Dillmann discusses such examples of verbs which govern an accusative derived from themselves for the sake of emphasis.

60 EMML 1950, 2080 omit the vocative *O*.

61 EMML 1768 reads *And now the souls of men complain concerning them to the Holy Ones of heaven*.

62 EMML 2080, 2436 read *Unto the Most High present for us a suit*.

63 EMML 1950, 2440 insert an accusative marker - *to the King*.

64 EMML 2436 omits *and*.

65 EMML 2080, 2436 omit *the generations of*.

66 EMML 36 omits *and Thy name is holy and praised in all the generations of the world and* by homoioteleuton.

67 EMML 2436 adds 2.m.s. pronoun - *and blessed and praised art Thou*.

68 EMML 2436 reads *And Thou*.

69 For the translation of ሥልጣን ፡ ኩሉ as *dominion over all*, see Dillmann, *Ethiopic Grammar*², 463.

70 Dillmann comments on this particular use of the preposition ምስለ as having the sense of the Latin *penes* - i.e. ምስሌከ = *is (to be found) within Thee* - see Dillmann, *Ethiopic Grammar*², 400.

71 For this rendering of the final clause, see Dillmann, *Ethiopic Grammar*², 494.

[6] 'See then[72] what 'Azāz'ēl has done, how[73] he taught all iniquity upon the earth and he revealed[74] the secrets of eternity which were made in heaven.'

[7] 'And[75] Samyāzā, *to* whom Thou gave authority[76] to rule over those who are together[77] with him, has shown incantations.'

[8] 'And they went into the presence of the daughters of men together[78] and they laid down with them, with[79] those women, and they were defiled and they revealed to them[80] these sins.'[81]

[9] 'And as for the women,[82] they have borne giants, and[83] through this the whole earth has been filled[84] *with* blood and iniquity.'

[10] 'Now behold![85] The souls that have died cry out and complain up to the gate of heaven. And their wailing has gone up, and they are not able to go out by reason of[86] the face of the iniquity which is being done upon the earth.'

---

72 Or *Now see* ... .

73 For the rendering of ዘከመ as *how*, see Dillmann, *Ethiopic Grammar*[2], 537–8.

74 EMML 1768 reads *and they revealed*. Knibb cites a further five manuscripts with this reading; see Knibb, *The Ethiopic Book of Enoch* I, 26. This reading is not original, however, as both the Greek versions (CP and Syncellus) present their equivalent of this verb in the 3rd person singular. This is one of the characteristic readings of the Eth. I family of manuscripts, and probably represents an attempt on the part of the Ethiopic tradition to harmonise an apparent discrepancy in the narrative. According to this verse, Azazel is responsible for all of the evils perpetrated upon the earth, whilst in the following verses, Samyaza and the angels who accompanied him are also mentioned. Furthermore, Samyaza and his angels have already been listed as having taught forbidden arts to humankind (e.g. 1 En. 8:3). Thus the reading *and they revealed* as opposed to *and he revealed* solves this problem. This solution was not maintained, however, as the Eth. II manuscripts confirm.

75 EMML 1768 omits *And*.

76 EMML 2440 inserts ከመ - *that he should rule* ... . This has been added to smooth out the syntax of this clause.

77 EMML 36 omits *together*. Note also that EMML 2436 places it awkwardly following ይኴንን - *to rule over*. The *together* element should not be omitted, however, as is confirmed by both the Greek versions - CP and Syncellus: τῶν σὺν αὐτῷ ἅμα ὄντων.

78 EMML 1768 & 2436 omit *together*.

79 EMML 2440 omits *with*.

80 EMML 1768 reads ሎቱ - *to him*, rather than the expected ሎን - *to them* (f. pl.), which is an obvious error. Dillmann highlights the form ሎንቱ as an alternative to ሎን; see Dillmann, *Ethiopic Grammar*[2], 406. Thus the scribe probably meant to write ሎንቱ for ሎን, and erroneously wrote ሎቱ instead.

81 EMML 1768, 2080 & 2436 read *every sin*.

82 EMML 1768, 1950 & 2080 use a different suffix - i.e. ወአንስቲሰ rather than ወአንስቲኒ. Although very similar in meaning, the reading ወአንስቲሰ can also mean *And the women on the other hand ...*

83 EMML 1768 & 2436 omit *and*.

84 EMML 1768 has the adverb ኵሎ rather than the adjective ኵላ - i.e. *and the earth is completely filled* ... .

85 EMML 36, 1950, 2080, 2436 and 2440 read *And now behold!* This *And* ... is also attested in both CP and Syncellus, so it is probably the better reading.

87 For the rendering of እምቅድመ as *by reason of*, see Dillmann, *Ethiopic Grammar*[2],400

[11] 'And Thou knowest everything before[87] it happens, and Thou knowest this and that which pertains to each of them[88], and *yet* there is nothing which Thou sayest to us. And what is fitting for us to do with them concerning this?'

---

87 For the use of ዘእንበለ + subjunctive = *before*, see Dillmann, *Ethiopic Grammar*², 545.

88 Lit. *and that which is of each of them.*

Pleas for Deliverance from the Demonic in Early Jewish Texts

L. T. Stuckenbruck

In Jewish literature from the Second Temple period, prayers to God for deliverance from malevolent beings — whether they be Satan, Belial, Lilith, or any other assortment of single or multiple evil spirits — mark an innovation from the biblical tradition.[1] Though prayers of deliverance are frequently addressed to God in the Hebrew Bible, these would be petitions seeking rescue from one's own shortcomings,[2] from dangers and distresses associated with opponents or enemies,[3] or from a premature or unwanted afterlife.[4] However, scholars frequently take for granted, and therefore have neglected to notice, that by the turn of the Common Era petitionary prayers became concerned with rescue or protection from afflictions attributed to spiritual forces.[5] In tandem with this development, a further emphasis began to manifest itself: the recitation of songs or certain words within songs can provide effective protection from demonic disturbance. Songs used for such a purpose have been characterised as 'magical incantions' by Bilhah Nitzan,[6] whose study of these has focused mostly on the Maskil songs preserved among the Dead Sea fragments of both 4Q510–511 and 11QPsAp^a (=11Q11).

With respect to prayer, broadly understood, this growing concern to deal with the problem of spiritual powers could take a number of forms in the non-biblical Second Temple literature. First, prayers — or, rather, 'adjurations' — could be addressed

---

1   Even 1 Sam. 16:14–23, in which David uses music (v. 23) to make Saul feel better when he is troubled by an evil spirit, nothing is said about a song with words effecting the cure. See, by contrast, Pseudo-Philo 60:1–3; 11Q5 col. xxvii, lines 9–10 (David composed four psalms to be recited over 'the stricken ones'); and 11Q11 (=11QPsAp^a, four psalms of which the third, attributed to David, is an incantation addressed to Belial). These later texts, however, are not prayers specifically addressedto God.

2   See e.g. Ps. 27:12; 39:8; 51:14; 79:9.

3   See e.g. Gen. 32:11; Jos. 2:13; Judg. 10:15; 1 Sam. 12:10; 2 Kgs 21:14; 1 Chr. 6:36; 16:35; Ps. 6:4; 17:13; 22:20; 25:20; 31:1–2; 31:15; 40:13; 43:1; 59:1–2; 69:14, 18; 70:1; 71:2, 4; 82:4; 116:4; 119:134, 170; 120:2; 140:1; 142:6; 143:9; 144:7; 144:11; Isa. 44:17.

4   So, in particular, Job 33:24, 28.

5   Indeed, there is no single instance in the Hebrew Bible in which God is specifically invoked for deliverance against another deity.

6   *Qumran Prayer and Religious Poetry* (Studies on the Texts of the Desert of Judah, 12, Leiden 1994), esp. 227–72.

directly to the evil being or beings to compel them to certain activity (e.g. 11QPsAp[a] col. iv, lines 4–6; col. v, lines 6–11; and 4Q560 frg. 1 col. ii, line 6). This form becomes more widespread amongst, for example, Jewish adjurations circulated through the much later Hekhalot literature, texts from the Cairo Geniza, incantion bowls, and Greek Magical Papyri.[7] Second, there is evidence from the Second Temple period that songs, chants, or hymnic prayers could be recited in order to neutralise the harm associated with demonic beings. Such songs could take several forms; (a) they could be declarations that focus on the nature and activity of God (as, for example, in the adaptation of Psalm 91 in 11QPsAp[a] col. v);[8] (b) they could be addressed to a righteous one or righteous ones reminding them to rely on God who will act on their behalf (4Q511 frg. 10, lines 7–12; cf. 11QPsAp[a] cols. ii–iv); or (c) they could be declarations about God that are preceded or followed by a writer's first person claim that he occupies a special position in countering being able to counter malevolent activity of spiritual powers (4Q510 frg. 1, lines 2–8; 4Q511 frg. 8, line 4–10; frg. 35, line 1–8; frgs 48–51, lines 1–6; 4Q444 frg. 2 col. i//4Q511 frg. 121). Third, along the lines of more conventional Jewish prayers of petition, some texts contain songs or prayers that praise God directly and then implore God to remove, disempower, or drive away an evil being or beings (so 11Q5 col. xix, lines 15–16; 4Q213a frg. 1 col. i, line 17; Jub. 1:19–20; Jub. 10:1–6; 12:19–20; Tob. 8:4–8).[9]

In the discussion that follows, I would like to explore the nature and specific function of the deliverance prayers identified in the last mentioned category, that is, those which address God by praising God and/or describe God's character and then petition God for protection against (a) malevolent being(s). While such petitions reflect an adaptation of a form that is widespread in biblical tradition, it is surprising

---

7   See e.g. D.L. Penney and M.O. Wise, 'By the Power of Beelzebub: An Aramaic Incantation Formula from Qumran (4Q560)', *Journal of Biblical Literature* 113 (1994), 627–50 and J. Naveh, 'Fragments of an Aramaic Magic Book from Qumran', *Israel Exploration Quarterly* 48 (1998), 252–61, who draw comparisons between the Dead Sea and some of these later texts.

8   Psalm 91, in its adapted form in 11QPsAp[a], is integrated into the previous three exorcistic psalms; see Hermann Lichtenberger, 'Ps 91 und die Exorzismen in 11QPsAp[a]', in Armin Lange, Hermann Lichtenberger, and K.F. Diethard Römheld (eds), *Die Dämonen. Demons* (Tübingen 2003), 416–21. Unlike the foregoing psalms, the text sustains the address to God throughout and thus although it is not formally an incantation, its recitation was intended to function in the same way.

9   For reasons that will become clear below, it does not seem necessary here to include two similar, though essentially different, prayers: the prayer attributed to Abraham in 1QapGen col. xx, lines 12–16 (see below) and the prayer of the four angels on behalf of humanity in 1 En. 9:4–11 which is primarily a form of complaint; see George W.E. Nickelsburg, *1 Enoch 1: A Commentary on the Book of 1 Enoch, Chapters 1–36; 81–108* (Hermeneia, Minneapolis 2001), 205–6 (cf. Susanna vv. 42–3).

that there is not more evidence for them. Is one therefore to infer that such prayers were relatively rare or that their occurrences in texts are literary developments, rather than reflections of praxis? The following considerations will thus ask about the degree to which the anti-demonic petitionary prayers reflect a religious practice with which the hearers and readers of the texts might have been familiar. In other words, to what extent did the authors of these passages, especially given the literary contexts in which they appear, regard all or any part of the petitions as exemplary models for prayer?

11Q5 Column XIX ('Plea for Deliverance')

Here we have to do with the most classic of a prayer against the demonic. In 11Q5 column xix, which is also preserved in two of the six fragments belonging to 11Q6, such a prayer is preserved as part of a larger manuscript that also consists of biblical psalms and other hymnic compositions, as well as a piece that lists compositions attributed to David.[10] Since both 11Q5 and 11Q6 are copied in Herodian hands, they provide evidence for the prayer at the turn of the Common Era, though the compilation itself is surely earlier.[11] Significantly, unlike the other petitionary prayers to be considered below, we have here to do with a piece composed as a prayer *per se*, that is, it is not a text embedded by an author within a larger narrative or story.

The prayer, originally 24 or 25 verses, is not completely extant; some lines at the beginning are missing, as well as one at the end.[12] However, a large portion of the prayer (18 lines from 20 verses) is preserved. The structure of what is extant is as

---

10   For a description of the contents of the six fragments of 11Q5, see J.A. Sanders, *The Psalms Scroll of Qumrân Cave 11 (11QPsᵃ)* (Discoveries in the Judaean Desert of Jordan IV, Oxford 1996), 5. See further Peter W. Flint, *The Dead Sea Psalms Scrolls and the Book of Psalms* (Studies on the Texts from the Desert of Judah 17, Leiden 1997), 190. According to J. van der Ploeg, 11Q6 is an exact copy of 11Q5; cf. idem, 'Fragments d'un manuscrit de Psaumes de Qumrân (11QPsᵇ)', *Revue Biblique* 74 (1967), 408–13. It is possible, in addition, that 4Q87 (= 4QPsᵉ) is a copy of the same collection; see Flint, *The Dead Sea Psalms Scrolls*, 160–4.

11   Armin Lange argues for a date as early as the first half of the second century BCE in 'Die Endgestalt des protomasoretischen Psalters und die Toraweisheit: Zur Bedeutung der nichtessenischen Weisheitstexte aus Qumran für die Auslegung des protomasoretischen Psalters', in E. Zenger (ed.), *Der Psalter in Judentum und Christentum* (Herders Biblische Studien 18, Freiburg 1998), 108.

12   Sanders, *The Psalms Scroll*, 76 argues that the psalm probably began on the previous column xviii; regarding the end of the prayer, see James A. Sanders with J.H. Charlesworth and H.W.L. Rietz, 'Non-Masoretic Psalms', Princeton Theological Seminary Dead Sea Scrolls Project, vol. 4a: *Pseudepigraphic and Non-Masoretic Psalms and Prayers* (Tübingen 1997), 193 (hereafter PTSDSS).

follows: In lines 1–5 the psalmist reflects the view that only living creatures can praise God and therefore implies that God should spare him from death (cf. Isa. 38:18–19; Ps. 6:4–5).[13] There follows in lines 5–12 the author's declaration of YHWH's character and faithfulness which he recalls through his own experience and for which he offers YHWH praise. On the basis of this thanksgiving for YHWH's deeds, the petition ensues in lines 13–16. In the petition, the author begins with a plea for forgiveness and purification from 'my iniquity' (ll. 13–14), requesting instead that he be granted a 'spirit of faith and of knowledge' and not be dishonoured in ruin/iniquity (l. 14).[14] The remainder of the petition on lines 15–16 is formulated as follows:

אל תשלט בי שטן ורוח טמאה מכאוב ויצר רע אל ירשו עצמי

Do not allow to rule over me a satan or unclean spirit;

do not let pain and an evil inclination take possession of my bones.

The first thing to notice is the functional equivalence here between 'satan' and 'unclean spirit'. Though the latter expression seems to draw on language from Zech. 13:2,[15] here it designates a demonic being which, if an Enochic aetiology is assumed, may be traced to disembodied spirits that originally belonged to the pre-diluvian giants.[16] As for the former, it is not, at first sight, clear whether the author is seeking protection from a specific being called 'Satan' (as is translated by Sanders and in PTSDSS) or is calling attention to a kind of being who, more functionally, takes an adversarial role. The juxtaposition with 'unclean spirit' may suggest that 'satan' is not a proper name (see below on the Aramaic Levi prayer).[17] At the same time, however, the use of the term goes beyond its application in the Hebrew Bible to an angelic

---

13 See e.g. PTSDSS, 193 n. 6.

14 On the difficulty of interpreting בעווה as either 'in ruin' (Ezek. 21:32) or 'in iniquity' (Dan. 4:24), see PTSDSS, 194 (n. 13) and 195 (n. 13).

15 See Armin Lange, 'Considerations Concerning the "Spirit of Impurity" in Zech 13:2', in *Die Dämonen*, 254–68 (here 254–55; bibliography in n. 8).

16 See e.g. Philip S. Alexander, 'The Demonology of the Dead Sea Scrolls', in Peter Flint and James C. VanderKam (eds), *The Dead Sea Scrolls after Fifty Years. A Comprehensive Assessment* (2 vols.; Leiden 1999), 331–53 and Loren T. Stuckenbruck, 'The Origins of Evil in Jewish Apocalyptic Tradition: The Interpretation of Genesis 6:1–4 in the Second and Third Centuries B.C.E.', in Christoph Auffarth and Loren Stuckenbruck (eds), *The Fall of the Angels* (Themes in Biblical Narrative 6; Leiden 2004), 87–118 (esp. 99–110) for discussions of wider network of related references in 1 Enoch (esp. chs 10, 15–16) and the Dead Sea materials (*inter alia* of Book of Giants, 4Q444; 4Q510–511; and 11Q11).

17 This would, then, be in contrast with Jub. 10:11, in which 'Satan' is the named equivalent for Mastema as the ruler of demons on the earth; cf. also Test. Dan 5:6.

being subservient to God (cf. Num. 22:22, 32; Ps. 109:6; even Job 1–2 and Zech. 3:1–2) or as a general designation for one's enemies (1 Kgs 11:23, 25; Ps. 71:13; 109:20, 29). Beyond any usage in biblical tradition, 'satan' here functions as a general designation for a demonic being whose activity is not subservient to YHWH.

Though further observations about the petition will be made below when we consider the parallel prayer text in *Aramaic Levi*, a more general point about the compilation of psalms in which this petition is found should be made. Whereas James Sanders argued in his edition of the scroll that the compilation in 11QPs[a] was produced by the Qumran community,[18] Peter Flint has emphasized that the absence of peculiarly Qumranic expressions and calendrical affinities with those groups within which the early Enochic works and Jubilees were composed suggest that this collection probably predates the formation of the Qumran community and thus enjoyed a wider circulation.[19] If Flint is correct and if the 'Plea for Deliverance' was in the psalmic compilation, then it is likely that its petition that YHWH act on behalf of the pious speaker of the prayer to disempower 'a satan' and 'an impure spirit' cannot be assigned to a single, and relatively isolated, group. This view is strengthened by our consideration of the following text.

Aramaic Levi Document: Prayer of Levi (4Q213a=4QTLevi[a] frg. 1 col. i, line 10) and Jubilees 1:19-20

This text, published by Michael E. Stone and Jonas C. Greenfield,[20] has been dated by J.T. Milik to the late second–early first century BCE,[21] though the document which it

---

18 James A. Sanders, *The Dead Sea Psalms Scroll* (Ithaca, New York 1967), 158, designated it the 'Qumran Psalter'.

19 See the discussion by Flint in *Dead Sea Psalms Scrolls*, 198–200. While continuing to underscore the consistency between the ideas in the scroll and those of the Qumran community, Sanders has more recently adopted a less narrow view about its origins, arguing that the compilation was acquired by the community; see Sanders, 'Psalm 154 Revisited', in G. Braulik, W. Gross, and S. McEvenue (eds), *Biblische Theologie und gesellschaftlicher Wandel. [Festschrift] für Norbert Lohfink S.J.* (Freiburg 1993), 296–306 (here 301–2).

20 Initially in 'The Prayer of Levi', *Journal of Biblical Literature* 112 (1993), 247–66 (with photograph) and then in G. Brooke et al. (eds), *Qumran Cave 4. XVII: Parabiblical Texts, Part 3* (Discoveries in the Judaean Desert, XXII; Oxford 1996), 25–36 and Plate II.

21 So J.T. Milik, 'Le Testament de Lévi en araméen', *Revue Biblique* 62 (1955), 398–408.

preserves was likely composed during the third century BCE.[22] Since the wording of the Aramaic text corresponds closely to that of the more complete Greek manuscript from Mt. Athos (Athos Koutloumous no. 39, at *Testament of Levi* 2:3), the latter was used by Stone and Greenfield to reconstruct many of the lacunae in 4Q213a.[23]

The prayer, within the later Testament of Levi attributed to Levi just prior to his vision of heaven (cf. 4Q213a col. ii, 14–18) and commission to become a priest (2:5–4:6), reflects its larger, now fragmentary, literary context.[24] After Levi makes preparations through cleansing and gestures (col. i, lines 6–10), a text of his prayer is given (col. i, line 10–col. ii, line 10). The prayer, according to Robert Kugler, may be loosely structured as follows: (a) col. i, lines 10–16 — pleas that God cleanse him from evil and wickedness, show him the holy spirit, and endow him with counsel, wisdom, knowledge, and strength, in order that Levi may find favour before and to give praise to God; (b) col. i, line 17 — a petition that God protect him from evil; and (c) col. i, line 18-col. ii, line 10) — a series of requests arising from what precedes, namely, that Levi be cleansed and sheltered from evil (Grk. vv. 12 and 14), that wickedness be obliterated from the earth (Grk. v. 13), and that Levi and his offspring be placed in God's service for all generations (Grk. v. 18; col. ii, lines 8–9). The petition for protection in column i, line 17 (Grk. v. 10) is remarkably close to that of 11Q5 column xix, lines 15–16 (see above); it reads as follows, with reconstruction based on the Greek:

וא[ל תשלט בי כל שטן [לאטעני מן ארחך

καὶ μὴ κατισχυσήτω με πᾶς σατανᾶς πλανῆσαί με ἀπὸ τῆς ὁδοῦ σου

And do n]ot let rule over me any satan [to lead me astray from your path.

The context suggests that the petition here is concerned with demonic threat. In the text Levi asks to be kept far from 'the unrighteous spirit (Grk. v. 7-τὸ πνεῦμα τὸ

---

22 For a full discussion on both date and provenience of the document, see Robert Kugler, *From Patriarch to Priest. The Levi-Priestly Tradition from* Aramaic Levi *to* Testament of Levi (SBL Early Judaism and Its Literature 9, Atlanta 1996), 131–8.

23 So e.g. Stone and Greenfield, 'The Prayer of Levi', 257–58 (Aramaic and Greek texts, respectively, from which the citations here are taken).

24 My present comments follow, unless otherwise indicted, the line numeration from 4Q213a, rather than the versification derived from the Greek text. However, the content is partially reconstructed by referring to the Greek, as in the eclectic translation of Stone and Greenfield, 'The Prayer of Levi', 259–60. See now the text and reconstruction by Henryk Drawnel, *An Aramaic Wisdom Text from Qumran* (JSJS 86, Leiden 2004), 174–9 and the comment on this text by E. Eshel, Jonas C. Greenfield and Michael E. Stone, *The Aramaic Levi Document* (SVTP 9, Leiden 2004), 129–30, in which the plea by the patriach is traced back to Ps. 119:133b.

ἄδικον) and evil thoughts and fornication and hubris'; by contrast, he asks to be shown 'the holy spirit (Grk. v. 8-τὸ πνεῦμα τὸ ἅγιον) and counsel and wisdom and knowledge and strength'. On the other side of line 17, in a text not extant in the Aramaic, Levi asks for protection (Grk. v. 12): 'and let your shelter of power shelter me from every evil (ἀπὸ παντὸς κακοῦ)'. In using the term 'any satan', then, the writer summatively personifies what Levi wishes to be delivered from: 'any satan'.

This only difference between the Aramaic formula in 4Q213a and the Hebrew formula in 11Q5 is the addition of 'any' (כל) in the former. This addition makes it even more clear than in the 'Plea for Deliverance' that 'satan' is not being used as a proper name.[25] Given the similarity between the petitions in 4Q213a and 11Q5, is there any genetic link? The parallel is striking in its similarity to Psalm 119:33b: ואל תשלט בי כל און ('and do not let any iniquity rule over me'). Therefore, several have argued that both texts reflect a 'common interpretation' of Psalm 119.[26] This view, if correct, would (a) show how writers were personifying concepts associated with evil, in this case in the same way when inspired by the same text and (b) suggest that the inclination to do so was more generally widespread than the evidence preserved in the texts. Armin Lange, however, maintains that a dependence on Psalm 119 is not in view and that, instead, a literary dependence between the two documents is more likely. For this perspective Lange offers two reasons: (1) it is unlikely that both 4Q213a and 11Q5 column xix would have independently substituted 'iniquity' with 'Satan' and (2) both texts exhibit 'extensive parallels in demonic thought'.[27] Lange goes on, plausibly, to posit a literary dependence between the texts, in which the Aramaic petition depends on its formulation in the 'Plea for Deliverance'.[28] More significantly, Lange notes a parallel between the petition in 11Q5 column xix and Jub. 1:19–20,[29] in which Moses pleads that God not deliver Israel 'into the hand of their enemy, the gentiles, lest they rule over them' and that God 'not let the spirit of Beliar rule over them to accuse them before you and ensnare them from every path of

---

25 See Stone and Greenfield, 'The Prayer of Levi', 262, who draw attention to the use of the same expression ('every satan') in 1QH isolated frg.'s 4 and 45.

26 So David Flusser, 'Qumrân and Jewish "Apotropaic" Prayers', *Israel Exploration Journal* 16 (1966), 194–205 (here196–7); Kugler, *From Patriarch to Priest*, 73; Stone and Greenfield, 'The Prayer of Levi', 263.

27 Lange, 'Spirit of Impurity' (see n. 14 above), 262.

28 Ibid. However, Lange's argument for the secondary nature of the petition in 4Q23a on linguistic grounds that in Aramaic one would have expected the verb מלך instead of שלט is in itself less persuasive; cf. Klaus Beyer, *Die aramäischen Texte vom Toten Meer* (Göttingen 1984), 709–10 and idem, *Die aramäischen Texte vom Toten Meer. Ergänzungsband* (Göttingen 1994), 422.

29 Ibid., 262 n. 38.

righteousness so that might be destroyed from your face'.[30] The wording of the passage, as in the 'Plea for Deliverance', does not contain an equivalent for כל and the mention of 'satan' has been replaced by the more proper name in the designation 'the spirit of Beliar' and reformulated as a verb that describes the activity of the demonic Beliar as an accuser of God's people.

These considerations suggest that both Levi's prayer and Moses' intercession in Jub. 1:20 reflect the influence of a tradition that is extant through the 'Plea of Deliverance'. If this is correct, then we may offer to observations: First, the writers of both texts have adapted the generally formulated prayer text to suit the purposes of their narrative, doing so in different ways. Whereas the author of Jubilees has transformed the ambiguous 'satan' of 11Q5 into a proper name Beliar while retaining an the adversarial function, the author of the prayer of Levi has regarded 'satan' as a type of demonic being. Second, the existence of the deliverance prayer in 11Q5 demonstrates that the attestation of the petitions for deliverance within larger narratives that have shaped them (i.e. in 4Q213a and Jubilees 1), does not mean they bear no relation to religious practice. This last point will be important to keep in mind as we consider the other passages on deliverance below.

EXCURSUS: Is a Prayer of Deliverance Implied in *Genesis Apocryphon* Column xx, lines 12–16?

Lange has claimed that a text in *Genesis Apocryphon*, composed some time during the second century BCE, contains a prayer that belongs to a genre of 'hymnic exorcism'.[31] Though I am not so sure that the passage provides further evidence of a prayer for rescue from a demon, a brief discussion of Lange's claim may assist in delineating more specifically just what constitutes such a petition.

The document, which paraphrases the accounts of patriarchs' lives based on Genesis, is preserved in a number of columns (xix–xxii) that focus on the story of Abraham. In response to Pharaoh's abduction of his wife Sarah, an account inspired

---

30 The translation is that of O.S. Wintermute, in James H. Charlesworth (ed.), *The Old Testament Pseudepigrapha* (2 vols.; Garden City, New York 1983–1985), II, 53 (hereafter Wintermute, *OTP*).

31 'The Essene Position on Magic and Divination', 382. See further A. Lange, '1QGenAp XIX$_{10}$ – XX$_{32}$ as Paradigm of the Wisdom Didactive Narrative', in H.J. Fabry, A. Lange, and H. Lichtenberger (eds), *Qumranstudien. Vorträge und Beiträge der Teilnehmer des Qumranseminars auf dem internationalen Treffen der Society of Biblical Literature, Münster, 25–26. Juli 1993* (SIJD, 4, Göttingen 1996) 191–204, esp. 197–8.

by Gen. 12:10–20 and 20:1–18, Abraham utters a prayer not contained in the biblical text. The text of the prayer is given in English translation as follows:

Blessed are you, O God Most High, my Lord, for all ages,

for you are Lord and the Mighty One over everything

and over all the kinds of the earth you are mighty

to execute judgement over them all.

And now I raise a complaint, my Lord, against Pharaoh Zoan, king of Egypt,

because my wife has been taken from me by force.

Carry out for me judgement against him,

and show your great hand over him and over all his house.

Do not let him be able tonight to defile my wife away from me,

so that they might know you, my Lord,

that you are Lord of all the kings of the earth.

Without doubt this is a prayer of protection. If the text of the prayer is anything to go by, the readers are led to think that the protection is being sought from God in relation to Pharaoh who, by having taken Sarah into his household, threatens to violate her sexual purity. The reader does not yet know, however, precisely what the nature of that protection is going to be like. Ironically, the protection occurs when God, in answer to Abraham's prayer, sends an evil spirit (רוח באישא, lines 16–17) to afflict Pharaoh; this is ironic, because in the end Pharaoh requests Abraham to pray for the evil spirit to be removed (a prayer, the text of which is not given; cf. line 29).

On the nature of the prayer, Lange comments that 'Because the spirit was sent by God in response to Abraham's prayer this prayer should be understood as an incantation.'[32] This description of what is going on is, however, not clear. In making this claim, Lange has inferred that the prayer uttered by Abraham to get rid of the evil spirit mentioned in lines 28–29 'alludes to a prayer similar to' the one for which the text is given in the preceding lines. However, it is inappropriate to regard Abraham's prayer in lines 12–16 as a 'hymnic exorcism' for the following reasons: (a) The prayer is itself completely unrelated in the narrative to the expulsion or driving away of the evil spirit from Pharaoh. Instead, its answer is seen in the very opposite: God sends the evil spirit to 'protect' Sarah! (b) It is Abraham's second prayer, for which no wording is provided, that restores Pharaoh from the afflictions brought on by the spirit. The prayers, the texts of which are, respectively, given and not given, serve two

---

32 'The Essene Position on Magic and Divination', 382.

different functions that are to be understood as distinct parts in a narrative sequence. While Abraham may be said to have uttered a prayer of deliverance from a demonic being, the wording for this prayer is not provided.

Jubilees 10:3-6

Jubilees 10:3–6 contains a prayer attributed to Noah. At the request of his sons, Noah utters a petition in order to curb the activities of evil spirits who have been deceiving and afflicting them in the aftermath of the great flood (vv. 1–2). The text of the prayer is as follows:

> (v. 3) … God of the spirits which are in all flesh,
>> who has acted mercifully with me and saved me and my sons
>>> from the water of the Flood
>> and did not let me perish as you did the children of perdition,
>>> because great was your grace upon me,
>>> and great was your mercy upon my soul.
> Let your grace be lifted up upon my sons,
>> and *do not let the evil spirits rule* over them,
>>> lest they destroy them from the earth.
>> (v. 4) But bless me and my sons.
>> And let us grow and increase and fill the earth.
>> (v. 5) And you know that which your Watchers, the fathers of these spirits, did in my days
>> and also these spirits who are alive.
> Shut them up and take them to the place of judgment.
>> And do not let them cause corruption among the sons of your servant, O my God,
>>> because they are cruel and were created to destroy.
>> (v. 6) And *let them not rule over* the spirits of the living
>>> because you alone know their judgement.
>>> And *do not let them have power over the children of the righteous now and forever.*[33]

Formally, the prayer has a two-fold structure. First, it opens with a declaration of God's activity on behalf of Noah and his sons in saving them from the destruction of the Flood, summed up in the phrase 'great was your mercy upon my soul' (v. 3). Thus the prayer initially assumes a posture of thanksgiving and praise. The second, more

---

33   The translation of Wintermute, *OTP*, II, 75–6 (italics my own).

extensive, part of the prayer consists of a two-fold petition: (1) God is asked for a blessing to 'grow and increase and fill the earth', which is reminiscent of Gen. 9:1, 7.[34] (2) As almost a precondition to such a blessing, Noah petitions God to punish 'the spirits', the offspring of the fallen angels, because of their destructive activities by consigning them to a place of judgement. The petition, indeed the prayer as a whole, closes with the plea that 'the children of the righteous' (also called 'the spirits of the living') not be subject to the destructive spirits' rule.

With respect to its content, the prayer the prayer has been made to reflect the preceding and following narrative in Jubilees. The evil spirits referred to are those of the giant offspring of the Watchers and the women they deceived (v. 5; 5:1–11; 7:21–4). Though they began as creatures with a human flesh (v. 3; cf. 5:8), they became spirits when they killed one another. And so, after the deluge,[35] Noah's descendants (i.e. his grandchildren) are being threatened by the activities of the impure demons. It is in response to this that Noah's prayer is formulated. The narrative following the prayer describes the divine response to Noah's petition: God has the angels bind the demons (10:7). Noah's petition that his grandchildren not come under demonic power is, however, not addressed with finality. Mastema, the chief of these punished spirits, begs to be allowed to exercise his (rightful) authority, given that the greatness of human sin is inevitable (v. 8). God responds by having nine-tenths of the spirits consigned to the place of judgement below (v. 9) while a limited number (one tenth) may carry out Mastema's orders (cf. v. 9). In the end, Noah is taught various herbal remedies through which the afflictions brought about by the evil spirits on his offspring could be curbed (v. 12). In its position between the ante-diluvian catastrophes and the deluge, on the one hand, and the containment and punishment of malevolent forces, on the other hand, the prayer occupies a pivotal position in the narrative. Because of Noah's great piety, his prayer functions to set on course the temporary position of evil spirits until the eschatological judgement. God's response to his petition ensures that from now on, the evil that is manifest on earth represents

---

34 Cf. MT: 'God blessed Noah and his sons, and said to them, "Be fruitful and multiply, and fill the earth". In terms of inter-textuality, Noah's prayer in Jubilees makes God's act of blessing Noah the object of the petition. Significantly, no command in Jubilees is given to the first humans (see Gen. 1:28a). Thus the demons pose an obstacle to the carrying out of God's command after the flood; cf. James C. VanderKam, 'The Demons in the Book of Jubilees', in *Die Dämonen* (cf. bibliography in n. 8), 339–64 (here 343).

35 In contrast to the *Book of Watchers* (1 Enoch 1–36; esp. chs 6–16), Jubilees says nothing explicitly about the great flood being the manifestation of God's punishment against the Watchers and giants for their activities; cf. Stuckenbruck, 'The Origins of Evil', 111–12.

an essentially defeated power whose activity has already been contained. This strong link to the literary context means that the prayer is here really conceived as *Noah*'s prayer, and in its present form does not draw on a prayer that would have been uttered by anyone. Thus the wording of the petition that God punish the demonic spirits is 'historicised', that is, it takes into account what the author believed were the specific circumstances faced by the patriarch after the great flood.

Despite the strong connection between the content of the prayer and the surrounding narrative, two elements in its wording suggest that the horizon of the implied readers of the author's time is in view. First, at the end of the prayer, the plea to curtail the spirits' power no longer simply refers specifically to Noah's grandchildren. Although the designation 'the sons of your servant' could refer to his immediate family, the inclusion of 'the spirits of the living' and, especially, 'the children of the righteous henceforth and forever' is concerned with righteous humanity who live from Noah's day until the end. There is a sense, then, in which Noah's prayer is also a plea for protection on behalf of all righteous ones who come after him, and readers would have understood themselves to be included in this protection.[36] Second, the conclusion of the petition, which is both brief and conventional in form, implies a familiarity with this sort of prayer among the readers, who perhaps may have been accustomed to reciting it to ward off evil spirits. To this extent, the attribution of such a petition to Noah not only anchors this prayer within a pivotal point of salvation history, but also allows it to function within a framework of understanding that gives pious confidence when they pray that their petitions for deliverance from demons are concerned with destructive powers whose judgement has been decisively executed in the past and therefore will become fully manifest in the future. In short, what to the readers was perhaps a conventional prayer for deliverance from afflictions associated with malevolent powers has in Jubilees 10 been placed within an eschatological context that inspires trust in God's justice, both past and future.

Jubilees 12:19–20

Another prayer of deliverance is attributed to Abram in 12:19–20:

> (v. 19) ... My God, O Most High God,

---

36   The same may be implied by Moses' intercessory prayer in Jub. 1:19–20.

you alone are God to me.

And you created everything

and everything which is the work of your hands.

And you and your kingdom I have chosen.

(v. 20) *Save me from the hands of evil spirits*

which rule over the thought of the heart of man,

and do not let them lead me astray from following you, O my God,

but establish me and my seed forever,

and let us not go astray now and forever.[37]

As with 10:3–6, the prayer is given a two-fold structure. The first part the one praying addresses God, declaring him as the only God, the one who is creator of all things (v. 19). The plea in the second part asks for deliverance from the rule of evil spirits who would lead astray from offering exclusive devotion to God.[38]

As in the case of Noah's petition in chapter 10, the content of this prayer is bound up with and reflects its literary context. It is uttered just before Abram receives God's promise of a land for him and his progeny. Earlier in the narrative, the story about Abraham is prepared for in chapter 11, where Noah's progeny is said to have engaged in activities of violence and social oppression (v. 2). In addition, they began to fashion idols, and thus come under the influence of malevolent 'spirits' who, under Mastema's rule, led people astray and to commit sin and impurity (vv. 4–5). Abram's piety, introduced from 11:14, begins to reverse the post-diluvian decay; at an early age, his prayers 'to the Creator of all' are described as tantamount to the rejection of his father Terah's worship of idols (11:16; 12:2–8, 12–14). At one point, Abram exhorts his father not to worship idols fashioned by human hands, but rather 'the God of heaven' who has 'created everything by his word' (12:3–4). We may note, therefore, that although it does not specifically refer to idols, Abram's confession in 12:19 incorporates themes already provided in Abram's story.

The mention of 'evil spirits' in the plea for deliverance is less easily related to Abraham's story. Lange rightly argues that, since the prayer occurs while Abram is making observations about the stars at night (12:16), these spirits must be the stars linked with 'astrology'.[39] Abram, after all, recognises that it is wrong for him to

---

37 The text given follows the translation of Wintermute, *OTP*, II, 81 (italics my own).

38 As 4Q213a, the prayer in Jub. 1:20 and 12:20 refers to demonic activity as 'leading astray', a motif that occurs in the narrative before Noah's prayer in 10:3. The 'Plea for Deliverance' in 11Q5, however, makes no mention of this.

39 Lange, 'The Essene Position on Magic and Divination', 383.

prognosticate even the weather — for example, whether or not it will rain — since such activity detracts from the conviction that such a matter is God's to decide. In sitting alone at night, Abram thus finds himself resisting the temptation to adopt the instruction about 'the omens of the sun and moon and stars within all the signs of heaven' attributed to the Watchers and discovered after the deluge by Cainan, Noah's great-grandson, who 'sinned' because of it (8:1–4). However, why does the nomenclature of 'evil spirits' occur in the prayer and not a more direct reference to the heavenly bodies Abram has just seen? Though the 'spirits' coming from the giants are featured in the periods associated with Enoch and Noah, they are nowhere explicitly mentioned in the early part of Abram's story; moreover, though the connection between demonic spirits and idols is mentioned in 11:4–5, the link is not explicitly made here.

Nonetheless, in the later part of the Abraham story of Jubilees, several passages are illuminative: the angel's explanation of the significance of the law of circumcision (15:30–2), the account about the sacrifice of Isaac (17:15–18:19); and the blessings pronounced by Abraham over Jacob (esp. 19:27–9). In 15:30–2, the angel's instruction to Abraham, circumcision is explained as a means by which God rules over his people Israel, over whom 'he made no angel or spirit rule' (v. 32). The rest of the nations, by contrast, are ruled by spirits who lead them astray (v. 31). The link already made in 11:4–5 between evil spirits and the worship of idols (cf. 22:16) suggests that Abram's prayer in chapter 12 regarding his 'seed' is one that is ultimately answered when God separates Israel from the nations of the earth to become the people he will protect (15:32). In 17:15–18:19, 'Mastema' is identified as the one who sought to distract Abraham from obedience to God in the sacrifice of Isaac (17:16; 18:12). In 19:28, Abraham pronounces a blessing over Jacob: 'may the spirit of Mastema not rule over you or over your seed in order to remove you from following the Lord who is your God henceforth and forever …'. Abraham's story thus exemplifies how his prayer for deliverance from the rule of 'evil spirits' is answered: His obedience to God thwarts Mastema's plan to test his character; and God's separation of Israel as his elect people is God's response to Abram's prayer of deliverance (and perhaps also the prayers of Moses and Noah).

For all the connections between Abram's prayer in chapter 12 and the narrative, the subject matter of the petition itself remains conventional, that is, it is formulated in a way that is not fully bound into the literary context. The petition for deliverance from the rule of 'evil spirits' (rather than, simply, from the rule of Mastema, as the story bears out) is formulated generically. As such, it is a petition by the pious that expresses the desire to stay away from idolatry. Moveover, similar to Noah's petition at 10:6, Abram's plea is concerned with all his progeny 'forever', which includes the implied readers of the story. With perhaps the exception of the Abram-specific phrase 'me and my seed forever', the prayer itself could be uttered by any of Abram's seed, that is, those whom the author regards as pious.

Tobit 8:4-8

This passage contains a prayer uttered by Tobiah and Sarah on their wedding night. It follows immediately after Asmodeus has been banished to Egypt by the archangel Raphael.[40] The angel's action ensues when Tobiah has followed his instructions by smoking a fish's heart and liver according to the recipe. In the storyline, of course, this protection is made necessary by the fact that Asmodeus had killed Sarah's previous seven bridegrooms on their respective wedding nights before the marriage could be consummated. With Asmodeus 'out of the way', Tobiah and Sarah pray as follows (according to the so-called long, short and 'third' Greek[41] recensions):[42]

Although Tobiah and Sarah have already been rescued from Asmodeus who is already banished to Egypt (v. 3), Codex Sinaiticus goes on nonetheless to regard their prayer as one of σωτηρία, which may mean 'salvation' or, better here, 'deliverance'. The shorter version, represented by Codices Vaticanus, Alexandrinus, and by the majority of the textual witnesses, does not present the prayer in this way, while the 'third' recension retains this understanding of the prayer as concerned with σωτηρία 'in this night' and adds the detail that describes the threat as coming from 'an unclean

---

40 Cf. 1 En. 10:4 — God instructs Raphael to 'bind Asael/Azazel and to throw him into the darkness...'. It is not clear whether the prayer in Tobit 8 is reminiscent of the Enochic tradition (and, therefore, links Asmodeus to the fallen angel tradition). It may be significant, however, that the link is made in the much later Christian Testament of Solomon 5:3 where Asmodeus is identified as one of the offspring of the fallen angels ('born from a human mother and an angel').

41 Unfortunately, none of the Dead Sea scroll fragments of Tobit preserve this part of the book.

42 The English translation of the first two columns follows J.A. Fitzmyer, *Tobit* (CEJL, Berlin/New York 2003), 238, while the third column is my translation. In each case, the italics are my own. The manuscript texts (under the sigla G2, G1, and G3, respectively) are now conveniently presented synoptically, with introductions, by Stuart Weeks, Simon Gathercole, and Loren Stuckenbruck, *The Book of Tobit: Texts from the Principal Ancient and Medieval Traditions. With synopsis, concordances, and annotated texts in Aramaic, Hebrew, Greek, Latin, and Syriac* (Fontes et Subsidia ad Bibliam pertinentes, 3, Berlin 2004).

Studies in Jewish Prayer

Cod. Sinaiticus	Cod. Vaticanus	Ferrara 1871
(4) After the others had gone out and closed the door of the bedroom, Tobiah got up from bed and said to Sarah, 'My sister, get up and let us pray and *beg our Lord to grant us mercy and deliverance.*	(4) When the two of them were closed in, Tobiah got up from bed and said, 'My sister, get up and let us pray that the Lord may take pity on us.'	(4) And Tobiah said to Sarah, 'Sister, get up and let us pray and *beg before the Lord that he may take pity on us and* (do) *grant deliverance in this night*
(5) She got up, and they began to pray, *begging that deliverance might be accorded them.* Tobiah prayed, 'Praise be to you, O God of our ancestors, and praised be your name for all generations and all your creation praise you for ever and ever!	(5) Tobiah began to pray, 'Praise be to you, O God of our ancestors, and praised be your holy and honourable name for all generations! May the heavens and all your creatures praise you!	(5) And Tobiah said, 'Praised be the Lord God of our ancestors, and praised be your name for generations forever! May the heavens and all your creation praise you!
(6) You made Adam, and made his wife Eve to be a helper and support. From the two of them has come the whole human race. You even said, 'It is not good for the man to be alone; let us make for him a helper like himself.'	(6) You made Adam and gave him his wife Eve as his helper and support. From them has come the whole human race. You even said, 'It is not good for the man to be alone; let us make him a helper like himself.'	(6) You made Adam and gave him his wife Eve as a helper like himself. From them both has come the human race. You even said, 'It is not good for the man to be alone; let us make for him a helper like himself.'
(7) Now I am taking this kinswoman of mine as wife not out of lust, but with sincerity. Grant that she and I many find mercy and grow old together	(7) Now I am taking this kinswoman of mine as wife not out of lust, but with sincerity. Grant that I may find mercy and grow old together with her'	(7) Now, Lord, you know that I am taking this woman of mine not out of lust, but according to the righteous decree of your law, so that we may be shown mercy, Lord, she and I, and *that you put a curse on the unclean demon,* even giving us children, Lord, and blessing.'
(8) They both said, 'Amen, amen!'	(8) She said with him, 'Amen!'	(8) And they said together, 'Amen!'

70

demon' whom God is being petitioned to curse.[43] Especially important here is the longer version attested in Codex Sinaiticus,[44] in which the notion of 'protection' is not entirely irrelevant to the purpose of the prayer. It may be noted, however, that it is at first sight not a straightforward matter to regard the couple's prayer as a plea for protection. Indeed, two problems with such a reading should be addressed: First, why pray for protection when the demon has already been driven away or banished? Second, the prayer seems more like a petition that implores God to bless their marital union (so that σωτήρ might be interpreted as a desire for children), in that it appeals to the way God had set up marriage at the beginning in creating Adam and providing him a helpmeet in Eve.

However, the mention of Adam and Eve is more than simply an appeal to 'the beginnings'. One could argue, after all, that in the biblical tradition, God's creation of the man and his helpmeet is, of course, followed by Eve's encounter with the serpent. Further, one could surmise that, although nothing is said about this incident in the prayer itself, the immediate context suggests an analogy between the first couple's confrontation and what Tobiah and Sarah have just done. Finally, one might infer that the story in Tobit represents a 'reversal' of the biblical tradition, so that Tobiah and Sarah, who have overcome the dangerous power of Asmodeus, are portrayed as the couple who wish to exemplify what God must have originally set up marriage to be like. Whereas death follows the incident in Eden, Tobias has been delivered from death. As attractive as this intertextual reading might be, the prayer itself invites a reading that takes its literary context in Tobit, both immediate and remote, into closer account.

The prayer, as it stands, functions in a two-fold manner: First, it celebrates the fact that this marriage between Tobiah and Sarah, against all odds, has actually come

---

43 Moreover, see the Lat. Vulgate (Cod. Amiatinus) to 8:4 — Tobiah and Sarah pray *ut eis sanitas donaretur*, though here the underlying Γρεεκ for *sanitas* may simply refer to the couple's wish to have children. In what may ultimately be a secondary insertion of this early tradition may be found in the late 13th century Hebrew version of Tobit in the North French Miscellany (Add. 11639) in the British Library. In this version Tobiah petitions God, after praising God extensively for God's omnipotence, omniscience and justness, to 'deliver me' (ynlychv) and to 'drive away Satan' (וחצילני) so that he will 'not afflict or do evil to us'. On this manuscript and its textual character, see Weeks, Gathercole, and Stuckenbruck, *The Book of Tobit*, 37–9.

44 The affinity between the longer recension (imperfectly preserved in Cod. Sinaiticus and the Old Latin manuscript tradition) and the Dead Sea scroll fragments of Tobit has added considerable weight to scholarly arguments which have favoured its priority over the so-called shorter recension; see the discussions by Carey A. Moore, 'Scholarly Issues in the Book of Tobit Before Qumran and After: An Assessment', *Journal for the Study of the Pseudepigrapha* 5 (1989), 65–81 and Fitzmyer, *Tobit*, 3–28.

about. The marriage itself is only consummated because Asmodeus has been banished.[45] This banishment, carried out by Raphael, signifies and gives expression to the defeat of evil. In the narrative, this event comes about as an answer to the prayer of Sarah who, in 3:11-15, has complained to God for unjustly having allowed her to acquire the false reputation of being a 'husband killer' (Cod. Sin. v. 8 - ἡ ἀποκτέννουσα τοὺς ἄνδρας σου; Lat. Vulgate and the short Greek recension speak of her 'strangling' her husbands). God acts immediately, according to 3:16–17, by sending Raphael to give Sarah in marriage to Tobiah and (then) to free her from the wicked demon Asmodeus. Here the marriage is here understood as God's response to Sarah's complaint as if it were a petition. In chapter 8, God's activity through Raphael reaches its proper conclusion, and God is — at the beginning of the prayer — blessed and praised.

Second, and less prominently, the prayer asks for deliverance. In the present context, this petition relates to protection from any return of the demon. This does not mean that the couple are seriously worried that, though Asmodeus has been driven away, he could be expected to come back time and again to plague and afflict them; there is no hint of such in any of the versions or recension of the book. Instead, this is a prayer for deliverance *post eventum*: Tobiah is made to articulate in prayer what he has already done by applying the magical recipe that Raphael revealed to him. According to 6:8, the instructions by Raphael to Tobiah on what to do with the fish's heart and liver emphasize the completeness of the result:

As for the fish's heart and liver, you can smoke them in the presence
    of a man or woman afflicted by a demon or an evil spirit,
and the affliction will flee from him (sic!);
and they will never stay with him any longer. (Cod.Sin.)
4Q197 frg. 4 col. i, 13 - and thei[r] encounters will [neve]r occur again
(לעלם [וֹ]יסחרון סחרתהו[ן][לֹא])

Thus, the angel's role aside, the marriage is the result of two acts on the part of Tobiah: the application of a magical recipe and the utterance of a plea for deliverance which, like the recipe, is said to ensure that the defeat of Asmodeus stays that way.

---

45 On the later notion of Asmodeus as an offspring of the fallen angels, see n. 39 above. Two medieval Hebrew and Aramaic versions of Tobit introduce Asmodeus as 'the king of demons' (cf. the so-called 'Münster' text of Constantinople 1516 to 3:8, 17; North French Miscellany to 6:14; the Neubauer Aramaic version to 3:8, 17; and so-called 'Hebrew Gaster' to 3:17).

As a petition directed at God who is blessed and praised, the prayer further expresses what the book articulates elsewhere: the deliverance has ultimately occurred because of God's activity, and not that of Raphael. This anticipates Raphael's own clarification to Tobit and Tobiah about his part in the story in 12:15–18; Tobit, upon gaining back his sight, may have blessed the angels alongside God (cf. 11:14–15), but Raphael explains that he is a carrier of prayers before God and that what he has done for them 'was not owing to any favour of mine... but to the will of God' (12:18). In the end, as in the petition in chapter 8, the praise goes to God: 'praise him and sing to him all your days' (12:18).

Unlike the petitionary prayers in Jub. 1:19–20, 10:3–6, and 12:19–20 considered above, the prayer in Tobit 8 is thoroughly made to reflect the storyline. Thus, while the praise of God followed by the petition that the marriage be long-lasting plausibly represents a prayer that readers could have owned for themselves, I find no suggestion that the implied reader would have been familiar with the utterance of a prayer about marriage that seeks deliverance from demonic power.

Conclusion

Not all the prayer-texts concerned with demonic spirits are apotropaic, 'magical', incantations, or even exorcistic (if we take the etymology of that term seriously). Rather, alongside and perhaps even prior to, the development of adjurations and recitations that invoked spirits directly or expected words to wield power in and of themselves, a world view — one which maintained that human and spiritual beings share social space — came, quite naturally, to include malevolent forces within the framework of traditional prayers for deliverance provided through biblical tradition. From the Second Temple period, we do not have very much evidence for such petitions; with the exception of the 'Plea for Deliverance' in 11Q5 column xix, what we do have is petitions that are conveyed in forms that have been narrativised by their respective literary contexts. Nonetheless, there is enough evidence to demonstrate that these petitions were part of Jewish religiosity from at least the third century BCE. As such, these prayers may provide the most formative background for early Christian-Jewish practice known through the final, and climactic, petition in the 'Lord's Prayer' attributed to Jesus in the Matthew's gospel: 'Do not lead us into temptation, but deliver us from the evil one'.[46]

---

46 Mt. 6:13: ῥῦσαι ἡμᾶς ἀπὸ τοῦ πονηροῦ, which is not included in the Lukan version of the prayer (11:4). The possibility that the prayer in Matthew's text refers to demonic evil is strengthened if, similarly, the making of oaths is ascribed to 'the evil one' in 5:37.

Prayer and Incantation in the Dead Sea Scrolls

Archie T. Wright

Introduction

A large corpus of material amongst the Scrolls has been identified as containing some form of prayer or hymn. Esther Chazon notes that the Scrolls offer in excess of two hundred previously unknown hymns and prayers along with portions of approximately one hundred and twenty-five biblical psalms. Each of these texts lends insight into the religious practice and spiritual life of early Judaism, in particular, the key element of prayer.[1] This facet of Judaism was apparently no less important during the time that the documents found at Qumran were being collected or written by the community. Included amongst this group of documents are several prayers that fall into the genre of incantation.[2] Although these prayers do not necessarily enhance our understanding of the developing anthropology, they do reveal how humans interacted with evil spirits in Judaism during the Second Temple Period. I will attempt to show, from the language of some of the incantations, that the Watcher tradition found in 1 Enoch 1–36 and its description of the origin of evil spirits perhaps influenced the authors of some of the incantation texts of the Scrolls.

---

1   See Esther Chazon, 'Hymns and Prayers in the Dead Sea Scrolls', in Peter W. Flint and James C. VanderKam (eds), *The Dead Sea Scrolls After Fifty Years A Comprehensive Assessment*, (2 vols, Leiden 1998), I, 244–70. It is possible that some of the prayers and hymns encountered in the Qumran material will reflect similar prayer traditions found in the later rabbinic period. In both cases, lack of the Temple edifice, due to the community's voluntary separation and the Temple's destruction in 70 CE, may have spurred similar responses to the need for a substitute for sacrificial worship. This may be what is alluded to in 11Q5 col. xviii, lines 9–11. The author states 'the person who gives glory to the Most High is accepted like one who brings an offering, like one who offers rams and calves, like one who makes the altar greasy with many holocausts'.

2   The term 'incantation', if it is to be given a technical definition, must carry with it some key concepts. First, the person must be operating under some kind of authority, whether it is by divine name or a word of power. Second, it requires a repetition of what can be defined as a certain formula of words given to the person by a figure who is connected with the authority, i.e. a prophet, diviner, etc. These words must then be spoken directly to the spirit in question or the divinity in question.

Incantation prayers are one of the two main formulae for magical texts found in the Scrolls.[3] The first group includes those which are concerned with divination, omens, and foretelling (e.g. 4Q186; 4Q561; and 4Q318). The second group includes those concerned with prayers that request or enforce a defence against evil spirits (e.g. 4Q510; 4Q511; 4Q444; 4Q560; 11Q5; and 11Q11). The second category can be subdivided into possibly three forms. In the first, the person addresses the spirit directly by invoking the Divine Name. In the second (although this prayer may be categorized as a hymn of thanksgiving), the person makes a direct plea to God for his protection from the evil spirit. And in the third, the person invokes the praise and glorification of God in order to stop the activity of the evil spirits in his or her life. We will examine briefly an example of each of these types of prayers.

11Q11 (11QPsAp^a): Invoking the Divine Name

The first form of incantation is found in 11Q11.[4] This document dates from early first century CE and contains six columns of text in a very fragmentary condition. J.P.M. van der Ploeg has identified within 11Q11 columns i–v three incantations against evil spirits followed by a version of Psalm 91 in column vi.[5] Van der Ploeg, followed by Émile Puech, has suggested that the prayers from 11Q11 are the four prayers mentioned in 11Q5 col. xxvii which describe four prayers that David prayed over the possessed.[6] Puech concludes the four prayers are from an ancient Israelite

---

3   See Alexander, 'Wrestling Against Wickedness in High Places: Magic in the Worldview of the Qumran Community', in Stanley E. Porter and Craig A. Evans (eds), *The Scrolls and Scriptures Qumran Fifty Years After* (Sheffield 1997), 318–37.

4   Cf. also 4Q560 frag 1 ii, in which the person praying directly addresses the evil spirit. It is difficult to discuss this text in any detail due to its very fragmentary nature: it lacks the presence of the Divine Name. For a thorough discussion, see Douglas L. Penney and Michael O. Wise, 'By the Power of Beelzebub: An Aramaic Incantation From Qumran (4Q560)', *Journal of Biblical Literature* 113 (1994), 627–50. Penney and Wise argue the presence of these incantation prayers in the DSS is due to the intense spiritual battle going on within Judaism with spiritual forces outside of the community.

5   See J.P.M. Van der Ploeg, 'Le psaume XCI dans une recension de Qumran', *Revue Biblique* 72 (1965) 210–17.

6   The idea that these are prayers said over the possessed is based on the word הפגוע[ים] in col. v line 2. See Émile Puech, '11QPsAp^a: Un rituel d'exorcismes. Essai de reconstruction', *Revue de Qumrân* 14 (1990), 377–408.

ritual and were adopted by the Qumran community for prophylactic and incantation purposes.[7]

According to Van der Ploeg, the prayer begins in column ii lines 2–4 with the mentioning of David's son Solomon.[8] These lines may allude to a tradition in which Solomon has the ability, through the wisdom of song, to exorcise demonic spirits (see Josephus, Antiquities, 8:45; Wisdom of Solomon 7 [second century BC]; Testament of Solomon [first century CE?]). Although the fragmentary nature of the text resists a precise interpretation, it seems to suggest that one is told to invoke the name of the Lord (יהוה) against evil spirits. However, we must assume the presence of the Divine Name in this particular column. This is followed in lines 10–12 by words that glorify God for his works, although much of this text is reconstructed.[9]

Column 3 (again fragmentary) continues with a reminder of the creative works of God (lines 1–4); this is followed by a call to all creation to witness against those who sin against God (lines 4–7).[10] It is from these lines that one may question if these

---

7   Van der Ploeg suggests 11Q11 columns 2, 3, and 4 contain a series of prayers against evil spirits that invoke the Divine name. The term 'invoke' is a key to understanding these psalms as incantations. Puech and later García Martínez/Tigchelaar reconstruct col. ii line 2 (col. i for Puech) with ויקרא.

8

1. [ ]	שׁמֹ[]
2. [ ]	[ה שלומה] [ ] ויקרֹ[א
3. [ ]	הרו[חות] [והשדים]
4. [ ]	[אלה [הש]דים וש]ר המשט[מה

1.   ?
2.   [   ] Solomon, [ ] and he shall invo[ke
3.   [the spi]rits, [ ]and the demons, [
4.   [   ] These are [the de]mons. And the p[rince of enmi]ty.

9

10.	]ביחוה אלוהי אלים אשר עשה] את השמים
11.	[ואת הארץ ואת כול אשר בם א[שר הבדילו [בין]
12.	[האור ובין החושך...] עד[...]

10.   [on YHWH, God of gods, he who made] the heavens
11.   [and the earth and all that is in them, w]ho separated
12.   [light from darkness ...] ...[...

The reconstruction is based on the use of the verb הבדיל in Genesis 1. Other possible uses are the separation of Israel from the nations in Lev. 20:24, in Qumran literature, the separation of the community from Israel (1QS v 1; CD vi 14); separation between pure and impure in CD vi: 17. García Martínez suggests it could be related to demons in the sense of impurity: see Florentino García Martínez, Eibert J.C. Tigchelaar and Adam S. Van der Woude (DJD XXIII; Oxford 1998), 192.

10

4.	עשה את ה[אלה בגבור]תו משביע לכול מ[לאכיו]
5.	[א]ת כול ז[ר]ע הקודש [אשר הת[י]צבו לפני[ו ויעיד א[ת
6.	[כול הש]מים ו[את כול] הארץ] בהם [אשר יעש]ו [על

77

columns are a series of three prayers, as suggested by Van der Ploeg, or a pair of incantations (found in cols. iv and v) that are introduced in columns ii and iii with a reminder to the reader, or hearer, of the effect these prayers had in the life of Solomon.

The fragmentary nature of the document makes it extremely difficult to determine what may have been original. Some of the difficulties are revealed by observing the attempts at reconstruction and translation of col. iii, lines 4–5, by Puech and García Martínez/Tigchelaar.[11] Martínez and Tigchelaar read, '(the Lord—YHWH) who summons all [his] a[ngels] and all [the holy] se[ed] to st[a]nd before [him …]'. Puech reads, 'He adjures every ang[el to help] all of the ho[ly seed] who are st[a]n[d]ing before [Him …]'.[12] These two translations represent two very different understandings of one event. García Martínez and Tigchelaar reconstruct with language that is characteristic of a scene of judgment (i.e. a summons to stand before the Lord) going as far as to suggest a possible reading of '(God) adjures the bastards and the seed of evil to appear before him'.[13] Puech, meanwhile, uses language that is representative of the commissioning of a task based on the idea that angels are often told to assist the righteous.

It is possible that 11Q11 col. iii is alluding to the tradition of the judgment of the Watchers in 1 En. 10:13–14 for their rebellion against God, which we may also find in Ps. 82:6–7. The author of 11Q11 has set this story before the incantation that follows in column iv as a reminder to the reader or hearer of the fate that awaits the spirits that afflict him or her. This may support the idea that the incantation will not bring about the immediate destruction of the evil spirit; that destruction must wait for the eschaton. In the meantime, however, the incantation will provide immediate protection against these afflicting spirits.

7.]כול אי[ש חטא ועל כול א[דם רשע ו[הם יודעים

4. (*YHWH*) made t[hese through] his [streng]th, who summons all [his] a[ngels]

5. and all [the holy] se[ed] to st[a]nd before [him, and calls as witness]

6. [all the he]avens and [all] the earth [against them] who committed against

7. [all me]n sin, and against every m[an evil. But] they know.

11   See Puech, '11QPsApᵃ' and García Martínez/Tigchelaar, *Dead Sea Scrolls*, II, 1203.

12   Puech's reconstruction and translation is based on the idea in 1QS iii, 24 — 'the God of Israel and the angel of his truth assist all the sons of light'; and 1QM xiii, 10 — 'from of old you appointed the Prince of Light to assist us'.

13   משביע לכול מ[מזרים [וא]ת כול זר[ע הרשע [אשר הת]י[צבו לפני] DJD XXIII, p. 194, note on line 4–5.

The text that follows in column iv describes the incantation that is spoken by the individual or group who invokes the Divine Name against the spirits.[14] This prayer is a direct speech used to terrify the spirit with a description of its fate.[15] The punishment is described in lines 7–9 ('who will [bring] you [down] to the great abyss, [and to] the deepest [Sheol.] And …[…] … And it will be very dark [in the gr]eat [abyss'). This is similar to the description of the punishment of the angels described in 1 En. 10:4–5 — 'Bind Azazel by his hands and his feet, throw him into the darkness. And split open the desert which is in Dudael, and throw him there. And throw on him jagged and sharp stones, and cover him with darkness; and let him stay there forever, and over his face that he may not see light'[16] (cf. also col. v, lines 8–10).[17] It is difficult to determine direct influence of the Book of Watchers (hereafter, BW) on this prayer, but the similarity in language suggests the possibility.

A second incantation prayer in this document is found in column v. This prayer is a direct address to an evil spirit in which the person invokes the Divine name, יהוה (see line 4). This is the only prayer of the three suggested by van der Ploeg and Puech that can be clearly attributed to David. There are several allusions to the Book of Watchers in this particular prayer. The threat levelled against the evil spirits in line 6 resonates with the interaction between God and the evil spirits in the Book of Watchers. Although there is some argument over the reconstruction of 11Q11 col. v line 6,[18] it is possible the author was alluding to the spirits of the giants in the Book of Watchers — 'who are you [oh offspring of] man and of the seed of the ho[ly one]s'? מי אתה [הילוד מ[אדם ומזרע הקד[ושי]ם.[19] It is possible this line is describing the hybrid offspring of the angels and humans in 1 Enoch 7:2 and 15:8–9. In 11Q11 col. v lines

---

14 It can be argued that the end of the incantation in column V line 3, 'Amen, Amen, Selah', (usual in Jewish magical incantations) indicates the prayer was recited in a public setting.

15 Cf. perhaps *Book of Giants* — 4Q530 ii, 20–4. The giants and nephilim become frightened when they hear of their fate.

16 Translation of Knibb, *Ethiopic Enoch*, II, 87–8.

17 'YHWH [will bring] you [down] [to the] deepest [Sheo]l, [he will shut] the two bronze [ga]tes through [which n]o light [penetrates.] [On you shall] not [shine the] sun …'.

18 There have been two other proposed reconstructions of the lacunae [oh offspring of]. J.P.M. van der Ploeg reconstructs it with מי אתה [ותירא מ[אדם following an example in Isa. 51:12 ('Who are you that you fear men'?). García Martínez suggests this is too long for the space and does not make sense syntactically. The second suggestion, from Puech, is מי אתה [ארור מ[אדם ('Who are you cursed of man'?), which he contends corresponds to the curses of Belial and the spirits in other DSS; see 1QS ii, 4–7; 1QM xiii, 4–5; CD xx, 8; 4Q175 23. García Martínez argues that translating ארור as a jussive is unwarranted. See DJD XXIII, 198–201.

19 'Holy ones' (קדשים) identifies the angels in the biblical psalms (Ps. 89:6, 8; cf. Zech. 14:5 — 'God comes with his holy ones'). Daniel 8:24 identifies the destruction of 'holy people', קדשים.

6–10, the evil spirit is told of the punishment that awaits it at the hand of the chief of the army of the Lord[20] in the darkness of Sheol, similar to what is found in col. v, lines 7–8. Again, the description of the fate of the evil spirits in this text seems to be informed by the Watcher tradition in 1 Enoch. Bilha Nitzan suggests the use of the Divine Name in this prayer is a clear distinction from other Jewish magical texts,[21] but the reason may be that the scribe is following the example of some of the biblical psalms, perhaps indicating the text did not originate at Qumran.

Psalm 6 is perhaps an example of an incantation that invokes the Divine Name in verses 8–10 (MT).[22] The psalm stresses the physical affliction that David is facing because of his adversaries (v.8 — 'my eye has wasted away with grief; it has become old because of all my adversaries'.), perhaps indicating the presence of an unclean spirit. In verses 9–10, David addresses his enemies, the workers of iniquity [a term attributed to evil spirits in 1 Enoch 9:1, 9)], by invoking the name of the Lord (יהוה) against them ('depart from me all you who do iniquity, for the Lord has heard the voice of my weeping'—cf. 1 En. 9:10). Verse 11 declares that by calling upon the name of the Lord, David finds deliverance from his enemies, 'All my enemies shall be ashamed and greatly terrified (בהל); they shall turn back, they shall be suddenly ashamed', language that is similar to what we find in 4Q510 frag 1 line 4. As Nitzan notes, 11Q11 is different from other magical texts, but the reason for this may be that it is simply following a typical 'biblical' psalm format (which may or may not be an incantation), rather than a specific magical incantation format.[23] This may account for what follows in column vi, a version of Psalm 91.

This column is in fragmentary condition making it difficult to determine the original make-up of the lines. However, van der Ploeg has reconstructed the text alongside the MT biblical text by which he noted at least twenty-five variants between the Qumran fragments and the MT text.[24] It appears likely that this biblical psalm was adopted by the Qumran community as an apotropaic prayer of protection against evil

---

20 Cf. Josh. 5:14–15; Dan. 8:11.

21 See Bilhah Nitzan, *Qumran Prayer and Religious Poetry* (trans. Jonathan Chipman, Studies on the Texts of the Desert of Judah 12, Leiden 1994), 235. Nitzan compares 4Q510–11 and other non-canonical writings found at Qumran. Puech argues the psalms are pre-Qumran and possibly prior to the canonization of scripture, see Puech, '11QPsAp^a', 401f.

22 The Hebrew קרא is here translated 'invoke', while the LXX uses ἐπικαλέω or a form of it.

23 See Robert J. Burrelli, 'A Study of Psalm 91 with Special Reference to the Theory that it was Intended as a Protection Against Demons and Magic', unpublished Ph.D. thesis (University of Cambridge, 1993).

24 For discussion on the variants see Burrelli, 'Psalm 91', 22ff.

spirits; however, it is difficult to determine the function of Psalm 91 during biblical times. There is evidence of a tradition of prayers or incantations against demons in the time of David and Solomon.[25] Hans J. Krause argues the Psalm was part of a liturgy to heal the sick that were being afflicted by evil spirits.[26] W.O.E. Oesterley suggests the Psalm is a polemic against the means employed to counteract the attacks of demons, i.e. magic. He argues that the Psalmist did not adopt the magic practices of contemporaries such as amulets or enchantments, but merely claimed the protection of Yahweh by invoking the name יהוה.[27] Later Jewish writings indicate the Psalm was used for protection against demons, but not as an incantation. The B. Shebuoth 15b states it is a song for evil encounters. The Midrash on Psalms identifies the 'arrow that flies by day' as the demon 'Lilith' found in Isaiah 34:14 and 'the plague (קטב) that rages at noon' as the demon from Deuteronomy 32:24 and Isaiah 28:2. This identification is also affirmed in b. Pesahim 111b, the LXX, and Aquila's translation of these passages.

The Qumran community apparently adopted the Psalm as an apotropaic prayer against evil spirits as a part of the need to relieve the problem of human suffering. This Psalm, along with the many others found amongst the Scrolls, could indicate this tradition predated the Qumran community perhaps as early as the biblical period.[28] If so, this may then push the date of the Watcher tradition earlier than the fourth or third century BCE currently assigned to BW. If we can demonstrate a need for relief from the attack of evil spirits in the biblical period or Persian period, then we can perhaps presume a similar earlier dating for the Watcher tradition. A thorough study of Old Testament demonology is beyond the scope of this paper; however, it is generally thought that hostile spiritual creatures existed in the biblical period.[29] Some of these

---

25 See Nitzan, *Prayer*, 251; Alexander, 'Wrestling Against Wickedness', 336; and Burrelli, 'Psalm 91', 21–9. The close of the text (line 14), although a reconstruction (סלה [וייע]נו אמן אמן), indicates that it is likely a liturgical prayer pronounced by the community in a public setting. See also I. Ta-Shma, 'Notes to "Hymns from Qumran"', *Tarbiz* 55 (1986), 440–2 [Hebrew] and J.M. Baumgarten 'The Qumran Songs Against Demons', *Tarbiz* 55 (1986), 442–5 [Hebrew] for use of Psalm 91 as an anti-demonic song.

26 See Hans-Joachim Krause, *Psalm 60–150 A Commentary*, trans. Hilton C. Oswald (Minneapolis 1989), 223.

27 See W.O.E. Oesterley, *The Psalms* (2 vols, London 1939), II, 407ff.

28 Eileen Schuller suggests, 'It is theoretically possible that in manuscripts from Qumran, there could be preserved previously unknown ancient psalms which had been composed in the Pre-exilic period, i.e., works which are, in fact, many centuries older than our earliest extant copies'. See Eileen Schuller, *Non-Canonical Psalms from Qumran: A Pseudepigraphic Collection* (HSS 28, Atlanta 1986).

29 For discussion of pertinent texts, see Burelli, 'Psalm 91', 62–97.

O.T. 'demons'[30] are identified in the list of evil spirits provided in 4Q510 lines 5–6, which are similar to those found in BW.[31] These creatures appeared to pose a threat to the people of Israel who then invoked the name יהוה in hymns or prayers of protection. Nitzan argues that when the hymns or prayers were recited, the 'demons' (i.e., the spirits of 1 En. 16:1) were forced to return to the depths of Sheol, which was their dwelling place.[32] However, the dwelling place of the evil spirits of the Watcher tradition is not in Sheol, but rather in the midst of humanity. Nevertheless, Psalm 91 does contain characteristics of other prayers of protection or deliverance similar to what we find in the second type of 'incantation', 11Q5 col. xix.

11Q5 (11QPsᵃ) Column XIX: Plea for Deliverance

This type of prayer is found in column 19 of the large 11Q5 (Psalm Scroll) and is titled 'Plea for Deliverance'.[33] J.A. Sanders proposed the psalm originally contained about twenty-four verses beginning in column 18.[34] The psalm is incomplete with possibly the first five lines missing from the text. The 'incantation' section of the prayer is found in column xix, lines 13–16, in which the person is making a direct plea to God (using the Divine Name, יהוה) for his forgiveness, strengthening, and protection from Satan and evil spirits.[35]

---

30 See for example Isa. 34:14 and 13:21–2.

31 See Nitzan, *Prayer*, 251.

32 Ibid. Although the demons of the O.T. appear to parallel the evil spirits of BW, there is no mention of their presence in Sheol in BW. This place is reserved for the spirits and souls of dead humanity.

33 (8) 'My soul cried out to praise your name, to give thanks with shouts (9) for your compassionate deeds, to proclaim your faithfulness, to the praise of you there is no end. I was near death (10) for my sins and my iniquities sold me to Sheol, but you (11) YHWH, did save me, according to your abundant compassion and abundant righteous acts. Also I (12) have loved your name and I have found refuge in your shadow. When I remember your strength my heart is strengthened (13) and upon your mercies I lean. Forgive my sin YHWH (14) and cleanse me from my iniquity. Grant me a spirit of faith and knowledge. Let me not stumble (15) in transgression. Let not Satan rule over me, nor an evil spirit; let neither pain nor evil inclination take possession of my bones'. A second copy of the prayer is suggested in 11Q6 frags 4–5. This very fragmentary text contains only small sections of thirteen of the sixteen lines that are thought to correspond closely with 11Q5 xix, see DJD xxiii, 43–4.

34 See J.A. Sanders, *The Psalms Scroll of Qumran Cave 11 (11QPsᵃ)* (DJD IV, Oxford 1965).

35 David Flusser identified a close affinity of 11Q5 xix to the Aramaic Testament of Levi found at Qumran (4Q213ᵃ frag 1 I), see David Flusser, 'Qumran and Jewish "Apotropaic" Prayers', *Israel Exploration Journal* 16 (1966), 194–205. 11Q5 xix line 15 (אל תשלט בי שטן) contains a similar phrase to that which is found in Aramaic Levi line 17 (אל תשלט בי כל שטן). See also the use of 'satan' in 1QH frag. 4 6; frag. 45 3 and 1QSᵇ 1.8. This of course does not necessitate a literary dependence in either direction (although both may be drawing on Ps. 119:133), but perhaps supports the idea of a

The psalm follows a biblical model in the way of form, content, and the vocabulary (García Martínez/Tigchelaar suggest it follows Ps. 105).[36] Sanders argues certain vocabulary used in 11Q5 col. xix differs from other Qumran documents relating to the spiritual battle of the community, i.e. the use of Satan and the evil inclination rather than Belial and the spirit of wickedness.[37] Sanders opts for a closer connection to rabbinic literature because of the presence of 'Satan' and 'evil inclination', but these terms are to be found in the O.T. (Job 1:6; 2:1 and Gen. 6:5). A connection to rabbinic literature, while insightful, should not suggest that the document is dependent on rabbinic ideas, but rather the language of the document may represent a developing tradition that is identified in rabbinic Judaism.

The prayer begins with the author acknowledging the greatness of God in lines 1–12. Within this praise, we find the author's recognition of God's sovereignty, mercy, loving kindness, and great deeds. This is followed by the acknowledgement by the author of his sin and the need for forgiveness and purification, perhaps recognizing a reason for the affliction of evil spirits. This is followed in lines 15–16 with a request for God's protection against Satan and unclean spirits. It may be assumed from these two lines that unclean spirits are responsible for physical affliction and the emergence of the 'evil inclination' in humanity. The term 'unclean spirit' may characterize further the developing anthropology of early Judaism. The term can only find definition if it is set against the human spirit, which then must be defined as a clean spirit, or an undefiled spirit.

The 'Plea for Deliverance' closes with a further praise of God and recognition of his grace. The author acknowledges his near death experience due to his sins and iniquity. He also recognizes his inclination to sin and the ability of evil spirits to lead

---

developing tradition within Judaism of personal incantations against evil spirits in the late second century BCE. There are also three later prayers in b. Berakhoth 60b, which have parallels to the Scroll material. Flusser argues it is possible that the 'Apotropaic' prayers of the Scrolls and later rabbinic literature can be traced back to Ps. 51. However, one major difference between the biblical psalms and the Scroll material is the 'demonization' of sin in the Scroll texts. The biblical psalms offer no counterpart to the Holy Spirit or willing spirit. Flusser suggests this is evidence for a late development of a belief in demonic powers as a parallel to positive spiritual powers inside and outside of humans and the dualistic movement at Qumran. See Ibid., 204.

36 García Martínez and Tigchelaar, in their reconstruction of 11Q5 frag E iii, contend the document contained Ps. 147:14–17 in the missing lines 1–4 and verses 18–20 make up lines 5–7. They also suggest the rest of the psalm is directly related to Psalm 105.

37 These characteristics would suggest a non-Qumran authorship. There are, however, at least three documents from Qumran that include the phrase 'evil inclination' — 4Q435, 4Q370, and 4Q422. Sanders suggests the psalm has possible parallels to 1QS col. iii–iv (cf. also 1 Enoch 84 for a similar type of prayer).

him in that direction, a characteristic of Qumran demonology. He therefore asks for a spirit of faith and knowledge to be strong against their attacks. There are several reasons in which one may question whether this psalm should be classified as an 'incantation.' First, there is no direct address to an evil or unclean spirit, however, there is evidence in the psalm of affliction by an evil spirit in the person's plea to God for deliverance (see lines 9, 13–14). Second, the person does not invoke the divine name in the sense of using it as a measure of authority against the spirit, but rather YHWH is simply the divinity addressed by the individual. This prayer should perhaps be categorized a prayer of thanksgiving for deliverance rather than an incantation.

4Q510 and 4Q511: Songs of the Maskil

The third form of incantation prayer is found in 4Q510 and 4Q511, the 'Songs of the Maskil'.[38] These two documents are quite fragmentary and contain some uncertainties in their reconstruction.[39] 4Q510 is made up of two fragments of which there are fourteen lines, nine on fragment one, and five on fragment two. 4Q511 is a much larger document that is made up of twenty-three fragments of (approx.) 130 lines. Similar language found in the two texts has prompted Nitzan and Alexander to suggest that 4Q510 and 511 are two copies of the same text by different scribes.[40]

The surviving text of 4Q510 frag 1 begins with four lines of praise directed towards the glory of God without using the Divine Name, יהוה (instead, אלהים is used).[41] Alexander suggests these apotropaic lines of thanksgiving are sectarian in

---

38 Armin Lange and Esther Chazon suggest a parallel to these two documents in 4Q444 (Incantation). I disagree with Lange's proposal that the beginning of 4Q444 should parallel 4Q510 frag. 1, lines 4–5. 4Q510 frag. 1, 4–5 is clearly set out as words of praise to terrify the demons. There is not the sense in 4Q444 that this is an incantation in the sense that 4Q510–11 are, but rather it seems to be closer to the wisdom text of 4Q417–18, which describes a spirit which is granted to the person in order to rebuke spirits which are trying to lead him or her away from God's Law. See 4Q444 frag 1 line 2, 'and they became spirits of dispute in my understanding of the statute', ויהיו לרוחי ריב במבנתי הוק. Cf. CD xvi, 4–5; iv, 12–15; v, 8; and 1QHᵃxi, 19–20.

39 See M. Baillet, 'Qumran Cave 4 III', DJD 7 (1982).

40 See Alexander, 'Wrestling Against Wickedness', 319 and Nitzan, *Prayer*. Arguably, this is a possibility, but it is also possible that 4Q510 is a single incantation out of a collection of prayers, a recipe book, of which 4Q511 may have served as the main body.

41 Cf. 4Q290 for use of אל for the name of God in asking for protection. The opening lines of 4Q510 and fragments of 4Q511 may have been an allusion to 1 En. 9:4–5, 11, which contain the prayer of the archangels concerning the evil which was being done by the Watchers and their offspring. The idea that the angels were worshipping alongside the covenanters may have influenced the author in adopting this method of prayer.

origin based upon the 'siege mentality' and the 'distinctive language of the Qumran group' contained in the hymn (i.e. 'sons of light' — 4Q510 frag 1, line 7; and 'men of Covenant' — 4Q511 frags 63–4, ii line 5).[42] The apparent failure to use the Divine Name (יהוה), which is found in other incantation texts, may be due in part to the author's recognition of the sanctity of the name and his fear to use it as a magical charm. However, it is possible, as Nitzan suggests, the text contained adjurations with the Divine Name that were subsequently lost.[43] The use of a divine name would follow the normal pattern of incantation prayers in which the name of the deity (in this case יהוה) is used as the word of power, rather than the words of glorification and praise of God, which we find in 4Q510–11.[44]

Nitzan suggests each of the 'Songs of the Maskil' can be divided into three primary components: a word of power, banishment of the demons, and the time in which the prayer will be effective.[45] These components can be identified in 4Q510. The 'word of power', which Nitzan identifies as the *praise and glorification of God* rather than the Divine Name, is found in lines 4–6.[46] In this instance, they are used to terrify and scatter the evil spirits — 'and I, a Sage, declare the splendour of his glory in order to frighten and terrify all the spirits'. The second component is the identification of all the spirits by the Sage which are turned away by the incantation (lines 5–6): the spirits of the corrupting angels, bastard spirits, demons, Lilith, owls, jackals, and those which strike suddenly. A description of several of these demons is found in the Book of Watchers, again offering a possible influence upon this document by the Watcher tradition (see 1 En. 19:1; 10:9).[47] The third component of Nitzan's formula (the time of effective prayer) is found in lines 6–8. Nitzan suggests

---

42   See also Esther Chazon, 'Hymns and Prayers'.

43   This theory, however, may perhaps be questioned due to the presence of the Hebrew אלהים.

44   See Ibid., 248–50.

45   Ibid., 244.

46

4. ואני משכיל משמיע הוד תפארתו לפחד ולב[הל]

5. כול רוחי מלאכי חבל ורוחות ממזרים שדאים לילית אחים ו[ציים...]

6. והפגעים פתע פתאום לתעות רוח בינה ולהשם לבבם ונתתם בקץ ממשל[ת]

7. רשעה ותעודות תעניות בני או[ר]

4. And I, a sage, declare the splendour of his glory in order to frighten and terr[ify]

5. all the spirits of the corrupting angels and the bastards spirits, demons, Lilith, owls and [jackals]

6. and those who strike suddenly to lead astray the spirit of knowledge, to make their hearts devastated. And you have been placed in the era of the rul[e of]

7. wickedness and in the periods of humiliation of the sons of lig[ht].

47   See also Isa. 13:21 and 34:14.

85

this is a warning to the spirits that their time is limited, but that their activity is permitted through Divine decree until the Day of Judgment (see Jubilees 10).[48] It is through this prayer of glorification of God that the people will find an immediate end to the demonic activity and a promise of an eschatological punishment of the spirits.

4Q511 is more complex than 510. The fragmentary nature of the document does not seem to allow the psalm to fit into Nitzan's formula of components listed previously. However, the document is clearly an incantation against evil spirits. Fragment 35 line 6f. identifies the task of the Maskil to exalt the name of God (?) and to (terrify) the spirits of the bastards (see 1 Enoch 10:9; and 4Q511 frags 48, 49, 51, lines 2–3).[49] The document also contains scattered words of praise and glorification of God (frag. 2 col. i, frags 28, 29, 30, 52, 54, 55, 57–9, 63–4). Fragment 10 appears to be the end of the list of demons that is given in 4Q510 frag. 1, lines 5–6. A point of significant difference in 511 is the numerous promises of protection by God in what appears to be eschatological language. Fragment 1 describes a region in which there are no evil spirits. Fragment 2, col. i states that God has removed the chief of dominions (cf. frag. 3). Fragment 8 describes the protection of the person in the secret (place) of El Shaddai amongst the holy ones (cf. Ps. 91:1). These promises of protection perhaps enforce the idea of an immediate deliverance from the affliction of the spirits while at the same time reminding the people of the final destruction of the spirits in the eschaton described in the Book of Watchers.[50]

Conclusion

The incantation psalms of the DSS reveal an apocalyptic world-view in Second Temple Period Judaism that recognized the presence of evil spirits at work in the world within the divine order. Some of the Scroll texts disclose vulnerability in the

---

48 Cf. 4Q511 frag. 35, 8–9. A second possible interpretation of these lines is that the Maskil is addressing the people. It is not clear who the 'you' is in the word *natatem* (you have been placed in the era of the rule of wickedness). If it is the people then it could be understood as a word of encouragement that the rule of the wicked is coming to an end. They are told that their lives will not come to an everlasting destruction during the period of humiliation.

49 'And through my mouth he startles [all the spirits of] the bastards, so to subjugate [all] impure [sinners]'.

50 Alexander contends the emphasis in the Qumran documents (e.g. 1QS iii, 20–4; 4Q174 1–3 I, 7–9; 4Q510 i 6; 11Q11 v, 5–8; 11QPs^a xix, 15) is on the psychological effects of the evil spirits upon the individual and community rather than the physical harm. Therefore, the primary weapon against the spirits is prayer that glorifies God; see Alexander, 'Demonology in DSS', 345–6.

human spirit that left a person open to attack by the subordinates of Beliar due to the inclination of the heart.[51] These evil spirits afflicted humanity with physical aliments, spiritual oppression, and possession (cf. 4Q560). In order to counteract the activity of these spirits, Judaism incorporated the magic practice of protection through prayer and the use of incantations. These prayers were used as weapons of spiritual warfare in order to protect the children of light from being persuaded by a host of evil spirits to follow the evil inclination.

The growing prominence of the belief in demons played a key role in the struggle of good versus evil in the Second Temple Period. As a result, anthropology developed in certain documents that empowered evil spirits to influence a person in an effort to draw him or her away from God and at the same time, permitted evil spirits to afflict or perhaps take possession of a human body (cf. 11Q5 xix, 15–16). Within this anthropology and demonology, three primary motifs are at work in the Scrolls that helped to formulate how the problem human suffering was being addressed in Second Temple Judaism. It was understood that humanity had a good and evil inclination. The evil side of this innate characteristic allowed the evil spirits who emerged from the Watcher tradition to cause people to digress from following God. It is because of these attacks that we see the prominence of the prayers that were used as a defence against the spirits. Within these prayers, we find allusions to the Watcher tradition, which was advanced in the second and first centuries BCE by the Scrolls and other Jewish literature to the depiction of the interaction of demons and humans we find in the Gospels.

What is unclear from the documents, which include incantations, is why there were multiple styles of the prayers. It is perhaps a result of the origin of each of the documents; was a document written in Qumran or was it adopted from outside the community? We can only offer informed speculation to these questions. Whether the documents are original to Qumran or not, the people used them in the fight between

---

51 There are several protective prayers or recitations in the Qumran literature, which are used against Belial, or those in his camp. See e.g. 1QS ii, 4–10 — 'against human followers of Belial'; 1QM xiii — 'against Belial and his lot of spirits who plot against the lot of God'; 4Q280 — 'against Melki-resha', the one who plots against the covenant of God'; and 4Q286 frag. 7 — 'against Belial and the spirits that plot with him'. 4Q560 suggests a physical possession or affliction of an individual by an evil spirit (during sleep?) that causes an undefined illness (cf. 4Q266 6. i, 5–6). 4Q560 frag 1, line 2 offers an amulet that presumably will protect the individual from these attacks. These types of prayers may be reflected in the instruction given to Noah by the archangel in Jubilees 10:12–14 which would protect his children from the attacks of *Mastema* and the evil spirits of the giants. Similar practices can be found in Tobit 6.8.

the forces of light and the forces of darkness within their dualistic worldview. The prayers we find in the Scrolls represent a developing tradition within Judaism of spiritual warfare that we find flourishing in Jewish mysticism[52] and in early Christian texts (cf. Ephesians 6).

We have established that these prayers contain terminology that implies the influence of BW upon the worldview of early Judaism and its use of various styles of prayer in the ongoing war in the spirit realm. The origin of evil spirits that the authors of 1 Enoch formulated is seen clearly in some of the documents discussed above. Some of the most significant are found in what is likely the best case for Qumran authored documents 4Q510–11. Other Scroll documents that closely resemble the biblical psalms and contain possible allusions to the Watcher tradition perhaps help support the idea that some form of the tradition of the Watchers was present in Judaism prior to the composition of 1 Enoch 1–36.

---

52 See, e.g., in the Qabbalah and the Hasidei Ashkanaz.

Prayer in Psalms of Solomon or The Temple, Covenantal Fidelity, and Hope

Bradley J. Embry

In an ancient and modern sense, prayer suggests communication with God. In this short paper on the concept of prayer in the Second Temple period document Psalms of Solomon, I will be arguing for a relatively specific understanding of this communicative aspect of the Jewish faith on the part of the authors.[1] This is to say, these authors understood prayer as communication with God, but defined such communication as an event that takes place in the Temple or Temple precincts. The concept of prayer in the document is, therefore, tempered by the authors' understanding of the relationship between God and his children Israel. As such, the

---

1 Implied in the term 'authors' should be the understanding that the document may reflect the work of several hands, i.e., author, editor, compiler. I do not press this point simply because the document does not *necessarily* reflect multiple hands. The structure and form of the document argues for a particular end in a complimentary and uniform fashion. As a result, I see no reason suggesting that the document is a collection of individual psalms from either a wide chronological period or from diverse life-settings. A contrary position is taken by Johannes Tromp 'The Sinners and the Lawless in Psalms of Solomon 17', *Novum Testamentum* 35 (1993) 345–61 who suggests a very wide period during which the psalms could have been composed. Note also Kenneth Atkinson, 'Towards a Redating of the Psalms of Solomon: Implications for Understanding the *Sitz im Leben* of an Unknown Jewish Sect', *Journal for the Study of the Pseudepigrapha* 17 (1998), 95–112 who tempers Tromp's wide sweep and suggests a period from 62–30 BCE based in large part on the grammatical observations of Tromp in addition to the historical activities of Herod the Great in killing off the Hasmonean line; cf. also Otto Eissfeldt, *The Old Testament: An Introduction* (Peter R. Ackroyd, trans.; Oxford 1965), 612; Emil Schürer, *The History of the Jewish People in the Age of Jesus Christ* v.I (Geza Vermes, Fergus Millar, and Matthew Black [eds], Edinburgh 1979), 301. The problem with this theory is that Herod was initially married to a Hasmonean, Mariamme, and the suggestion that his culling was not necessarily due to their being 'Hasmonean'. Against this grammatical note cf. M. de Jonge, 'The Psalms of Solomon' in *Outside the Old Testament*, Cambridge Commentaries on the Writings of the Jewish and Christian 4 (M. de Jonge [ed.], Cambridge 1985), 159–77 who explains the future to aorist shift as an indication of the shift towards the eschaton; and Joseph L. Trafton, *The Syriac Version of the Psalms of Solomon: A Critical Evaluation* (Septuagint and Cognate Studies 11, Atlanta 1985), 163–4. With respect to Psalms of Solomon specifically, there is little mention of any other uprisings, revolts or persecutions, such as Herod's sacking of Jerusalem in 37 BCE: cf. Josephus, *Antiquities* xiv, 448–64; also note E. Mary Smallwood, *The Jews Under Roman Rule* (Leiden 1976), 56–8.

concept of prayer in the document must be understood as a function of worship, with all the implications that accompanied worship in Second Temple Judaism.

To examine this connection between prayer and the more general topic of Jewish religious practice and establish an understanding of prayer in Psalms of Solomon I will examine the matter primarily from a linguistic standpoint. The strong connection between the Temple and the concept of prayer will be highlighted, and will serve to illustrate the authors' intent and expectation. By way of our conversation with the document on the point of prayer, we may then be able to gauge the authors' disposition towards the historical conflagration of Pompey's invasion and conquest of Jerusalem. First and foremost however, I will ask and try to answer this question: where did the authors envisage prayer to have taken place? Several words from the document are suggestive of a particular locale.

On 6 occasions in Psalms of Solomon, the Greek term ἐπικαλέω, meaning to 'call upon' is used.[2] This term is significant in LXX where it is used in a number of instances to render the Hebrew term שכן.[3] Note, for example, Exod. 29:45:

45) MT: I will *dwell* (ושכנתי) among the children of Israel and be their God.

But LXX has:

LXX: I will be called upon (ἐπικλήθησομαι) among the children of Israel and be their God.[4]

The use of the term ἐπικαλέω for שכן suggests something of the disposition of the translators to the purpose of the Temple as a centre for worship.[5] In the light of this, it may be posited that, for the translators of LXX, 'calling upon the Name of the Lord' carries a connotation of being in God's presence, a description best embodied in the Jerusalem Temple.

Of the 6 instances in which the term ἐπικαλέω is used in Psalms of Solomon, two may serve as typical examples. First, 6:1 reads:

Blessed is the man whose heart is prepared to call upon (ἐπικαλέσασθαι) the Name of the Lord, when he remembers the Name of the Lord, he shall be saved.

---

2   2:36; 5:5; 6:1; 7:7; 9:6; 15:1.

3   Cf. Exod. 29:45–6; Deut. 12:5, 11; 14:23; 16:2, 6, 11; 26:2.

4   Also note Deut. 12:15; 17:8, 10.

5   Certainly 'calling upon the Name of God' is not an uncommon occurrence in HB Pentateuch; cf. e.g., Gen. 4:26; 12:8; 13:4; 21:33; 26:25; and Deut. 4:7. Some of these refer to Israel's prehistory, e.g., Gen. 4:26 when men simply 'called upon the name of God'. Others are a response to God's revealing himself, e.g., Gen. 12:8; 13:4; 21:33; 26:25. Deut. 4:7 indicates an activity of the whole nation of Israel.

Pss.Sol. 15:1 is very similar:

> In my affliction I called upon (ἐπεκαλεσάμην) the Name of the Lord for help
>
> I hoped in the God of Jacob and was saved
>
> For you, O God, are the hope and shelter of the poor.

Bearing in mind the use of the term ἐπικαλέω in reference to the Temple by LXX, one might initially posit that the authors of Psalms of Solomon were themselves making a thinly veiled reference to the Temple. This opinion is strengthened when one examines the primary importance placed on the sanctity of the Temple and its sacrifices by the authors. The profanation of the Temple results in the punishments recounted in chapters 1, 2, and 8. In each of those chapters, the primary sin committed by the 'sons of Jerusalem' is their neglect of the Temple's sanctity and outright transgression of the purity laws.[6] Moreover, the constant reiteration of the 'Name of the Lord' in these examples strengthens the suggestion that they are of a priestly nature and that the Temple is of primary concern.[7]

Of those instances in which ἐπικαλέω is used in Psalms of Solomon, the coordinating Syriac term is ܩܪܐ. The Hebrew cognate, קרא, was often understood in later Jewish contexts as a synonym for 'prayer'.[8] Israel Drazin has pointed out that the Hebrew term קרא, with God as the object, came to be understood by the *Meturgemanim* as the activity of prayer. This is to say that 'calling upon' God was seen as tantamount to 'praying to' God.

With respect, then, to the issue of calling upon God or his Name in Psalms of Solomon, two points may be made. First, much as the translators of LXX envisaged

---

6   Note and compare 1:2 with 1:7–8; 2:1–2 with 2:3–5; and 8:11–13 with 8:14ff.

7   In the priestly material, however, the act of *invoking* the Divine Name is nowhere to be seen. This may be viewed in one of two ways. Either the P material does not see need for invocation of the Divine Name; or the legists are concerned, at a very early stage, with protection of the Divine Name from misuse. The former opinion should be discarded given the evidence of the Yom Kippur ceremony during which the High Priest invokes the Divine Name, cf. e.g., Sifre Numbers 39:12, m. Sotah 7.6. The latter opinion is commendable considering P's constant punctiliousness on proper religious practice, under which misuse of the Divine Name most surely falls; it results in careful delineation of vows and the use of God's Name therein, cf. e.g., Lev. 19:12.

8   On this point note Israel Drazin, *Targum Onkelos to Deuteronomy* (Baltimore 1982), 270, in which he points out that Hebrew 'call', when in reference to God, came to be understood as 'pray' by the Targumim. Michael Maher, 'The Meturgemanim and Prayer', *Journal of Jewish Studies* 41 (1990), 226, 239–42 discusses precisely this point and concludes that the Hebrew term קרא, when God is the object, is understood by the Meturgemanim as meaning prayer. The use of the term by the Syriac translator of Psalms of Solomon suggests that the authors understood the underlying Hebrew term, and its implications, in the same manner.

the Temple as the place wherein God was to be called upon, so too did the authors of Psalms of Solomon 1. Unlike some literature from Qumran, nothing in the document suggests that the authors held the Jerusalem Temple to be irrevocably defunct. The importance placed on Temple purity leads directly to the assertion that the authors of Psalms of Solomon were closely associated with the Temple and its sacrifices. As such, there is every reason to view the Temple and its associated ministrations as a dominant theme for the authors. The act of calling upon the Name of God, therefore, should be viewed within this context. Secondly, the rabbinic material clearly understood many of the instances in which the Hebrew term קרא was used as references to prayer. With respect to the Targumim, Michael Maher's point that '…the Targums had their origins in the synagogue and in the context of worship…' bears significance for Psalms of Solomon as the compilation seems intended, at least in part, as a liturgical text.[9] Psalms of Solomon agrees with LXX by suggesting that 'calling upon the Name of the Lord' is to take place within the Temple confines, and also with the rabbinic material in intimating that 'calling upon the Lord' is a synonym for prayer.[10] Further evidence may be adduced in support of this point.

A second term of some significance in the document is the Greek verb δέομαι. In his informative article, Maher suggests that one feature of the Targumim on the issue of prayer is an equivalency of various Hebrew terms. This is to say, verbs such as חלה, עתר, and נפל are oftentimes rendered by the *Meturgemanim* with the stock phrase צלי קדם — 'pray before'.[11] It is interesting to note that LXX, in rendering these terms, also tends to standardize them in much the same manner. For instance, the pertinent part of Deut. 9:18, where Moses is reiterating Israel's sins and appealing to God to spare them, reads:

(MT 9:18) And I fell (נפל) down before the Lord…

Neofiti renders this portion:

---

9   The chapter headings and insertion of διαψαλμα at Pss.Sol. 17:29 and 18:9 along with the occasional use of εἰς τὸ τέλος are indicative of a liturgical tone. On the liturgical nature of Psalms of Solomon, note P.N. Franklyn, 'The Cultic and Pious Climax of Eschatology in the Psalms of Solomon' *Journal for the Study of Judaism* 18 (1987) 5; H.St.J. Thackeray's comments in *The Septuagint and Jewish Worship* (London 1921); Eissfeldt, *The Old Testament: An Introduction*, 611.

10 The priestly benediction of Num. 6:19ff is an important element in this process and is highlighted in Pss.Sol. 9:9.

11 Maher 'Meturgemanim', 231–4, 236; cf. also S. Brock, 'Jewish Traditions in Syriac Sources' in *Journal of Jewish Studies* 30 (1979), 214–18 who gives evidence of the inclination of Syriac compositions to replicate Jewish interpretive trends such as those found in Targum and, later, Midrash.

(N) and I fell down in prayer (צלא), and I implored (בעא) before (קדם) the Lord…[12]

LXX, interestingly, gives this translation:

(LXX 9:18) And I prayed (δέομαι) before the Lord…

While certainly not as elaborate as some of the Targumim on this point, LXX seems to offer a very early example of a trend in which certain Hebrew terms are understood as specific references to prayer; a characteristic, so it would seem, of much post-biblical literature.

In Psalms of Solomon, δέομαι is used on two occasions, first in 2.22 and then again in 6.5. The passages are similar:

2:22) And I saw and prayed (ἐδεήθην) before the Lord (τοῦ προσώπου κυρίου)…

6:5) And he prayed (ἐδεήθη) before the Lord (τοῦ προσώπου κυρίου)…

In these two passages, note in particular the phrase 'before the Lord'. When taken in conjunction with the Greek term δέομαι, this phrase is certainly idiomatic and suggests a particular locale and proximity. Indeed, the phrase is significant in identifying the entry of the High Priest to the Holy of Holies on Yom Kippur (cf. Lev. 16:2, 14–15).[13] There, the location of the High Priest is established by the phrase אל-פני הכפרת — 'before the mercy seat'. Elsewhere in HB, the concept of 'praying before God' is suggestive of an appeal made before the presence of God in the Temple. Note the appearance of the idiom in 1 Kgs 13:6.[14]

MT 1 Kgs 13:6) …entreat the Lord (חל־נא את־פני יהוה) your God and pray (והתפלל)…

The LXX renders this verse:

---

12 Also N glosses and PsJ.

13 The phrase found in Leviticus 16 refers to the actual place of supplication, that is 'facing the place of mercy'— πρόσωπον τοῦ ἱλαστηρίου. Also of Moses and Aaron encamping 'before the Sanctuary' in Num. 3:38. M. Haran *Temples and Temple Service in Ancient Israel* (Oxford 1978), 26–7 has suggested that the phrase 'before the Lord' is idiomatic and is used almost univocally within the context of the Temple structure. He notes the evidence from Numbers (32:20–2) and Joshua (4:13) wherein some of the Israelite tribes are marching to battle 'before the Lord' — a clear reference to the presence of the ark within the camp. Based on this, Haran suggests that the phrase more generally refers to being before the *presence* of the Lord and is not necessarily tantamount to being in the Temple proper. But this in no way undermines Haran's emphasis on the phrase as technical language used in the context of the Temple and Temple worship, a position supported by some 230 occurrences of the phrase. The phrase's association with Temple worship stems, Haran argues, from the plain fact that the Temple was considered the 'dwelling-place' of God.

14 The phrase is used twice in the verse.

(LXX 1 Kgs 13:6) ...pray before the Lord (δεήθητι τοῦ προσώπου κυρίου) your God...(leaving off 'and pray'). (Syr.: ܐܠܗܐ ܟܡܪ ܐܠܠ ܟ — also no element for פלל).

Two things are important to notice. First, פלל is not represented by LXX. One explanation may be that whereas MT likely differentiated between חלה and פלל ('entreat' and 'pray'), LXX did not. This may be an act of economy on the part of LXX, rendering two Hebrew terms with one in Greek. Secondly, and most importantly, the phrase τοῦ προσώπου κυρίου is shown to be a representative of אל־פני יהוה and bears significance in light of the phrase in Psalms of Solomon. The context of 1 Kings 13 is Jeroboam's displeasure with the enigmatic 'man of God' and is set within the Temple at the altar of Bethel. Thus the phrase τοῦ προσώπου κυρίου, at least in 1 Kings 13, is set firmly within the parameters of the place wherein God's Name dwelled or was to be called upon. As Menachem Haran states:

> In general, any cultic activity to which the biblical text applies the formula 'before the Lord' can be considered an indication of the existence of a temple at the site, since this expression stems from the basic conception of the temple as a divine dwelling-place and actually belongs to the temple's technical terminology.[15]

With respect to Psalms of Solomon, insofar as the Temple is a key concept in the theological outlay of the document, the use of the phrase τοῦ προσώπου κυρίου is indicative of a specific locale, namely the Temple.[16]

With this understanding of τοῦ προσώπου κυρίου in mind, let us return to the Greek verb δέομαι and discuss the understanding espoused by the authors. In both instances from Psalms of Solomon cited above, the Syriac version uses the verb ܒܥܐ. The Aramaic cognate of this Syriac term is used in Targumim, Maher notes, to render or qualify not only expected Hebrew equivalents such as דרש, חלה, and בקש, but also

---

15 *Haran, Temples and Temple Service*, 26.

16 From a conceptual standpoint it is perfectly understandable to envisage τοῦ προσώπου κυρίου as indicative of being before the Lord in the Temple. This is particularly the case if one recalls Exod. 33:23 in which God passes before Moses but does not allow him to see His 'face' — πρόσωπον. That God dwells in the Temple leads to the obvious conclusion that when one approaches the Holy of Holies, one is presenting oneself before God's face. An idiom, while colloquial by definition, is still forceful because of the image it creates. Thus the close proximity engendered by the phrase τὸ πρόσωπον to indicate 'nearness' is only achieved by literally envisioning being in someone's face. Furthermore, presentation 'before the Lord' is an essential aspect of priestly legislation regarding sin and impurity. Note e.g., Lev. 4:4, 5:5 *passim*. It is interesting that appearance before the Lord is equally important to both the process of forgiveness and re-purification. See Milgrom, 'Priestly Doctrine of Repentance' in which he notes the confessional aspect to repentance in the legists' system; 'Leviticus' v. I, 302–4.

unexpected terms such as נפל (note Deut. 9:18) and נשא (Isa. 53:4).[17] Regardless of what the original Hebrew of Psalms of Solomon might have been, in light of the use of בעא by Targumim the appearance of ܒܥܐ in the Syriac version of Psalms of Solomon suggests a particular action to be undertaken before the Lord. When combined with the authors' passionate dedication to the Temple, Psalms of Solomon Syr. 2:24, ܘܗ݂ܒܝܠ ܠܩܒܠ ܐܦܘܗܝ ܕܡܪܐ, seems to be located within the Temple structure.[18] With the Syriac version in view, it seems likely that the Greek phrase is rendering the Hebrew phrase אל־פני יהוה. This adds strength to the suggestion that the authors' scope with respect to prayer is dictated by the Temple and its significance as God's dwelling place.[19]

So far, I have examined the 'where' of prayer within the document and now I will very briefly discuss the 'how' of prayer in the document. By 'how' I mean to suggest that there is a particular status that one must have in order to be fit to offer prayers to the Lord. This feature of Psalms of Solomon is, I think, a vestige of the priestly system of ritual preparation, readapted for the layman who wishes to offer a 'sacrifice of prayer'. A brief examination suggests as much.

An important theological tenet for the authors is that Israel is God's own inheritance.[20] This is indicated by references made to the covenant initiated with Abraham and finalized with Moses.[21] This theology of election is key to the authors' understanding of intent in reference to prayer.

A term of some significance in this respect is ἐπακούω. In the Pentateuch, LXX generally use this term to render the Hebrew verb שמע; but they also use it to render ענה (2x) and עתר (1x). Thus, on several occasions where HB may be distinguishing between 'hearing' and 'answering', LXX is not. What is most important for this present study is to understand that ἐπακούω, in light of the various LXX usages, can mean that God hears *and* answers.

---

17 Maher 'The Meturgemanim', 227–34.

18 It will be remembered that Amos makes a similar plea in Amos 7:5 and that Amos prophesied at Bethel, one of the two Temples of the Northern Kingdom, cf. 7:13.

19 Since the original Hebrew (or Aramaic) text of Psalms of Solomon is no longer extant, it is not always easy to deduce from the Greek what exactly may be behind the translated material. The Syriac version is valuable precisely because it represents a form of Psalms of Solomon in a Semitic language which may offer an indication of what the original may have read.

20 The inheritance issue is mentioned at 7:2, 9:1, 14:5, 17:23.

21 References to Abraham are made at 9:9 and 18:3; references to the Law are made at 4:8, 10:4, and 14:2.

In Psalms of Solomon, the term ἐπακούω appears on four occasions (1:2, 5:12, 7:7, and 18:2). Again, for the sake of space, I will deal with only two examples, 1:2 and 7:7. Note 1:2:

> 1.2) Suddenly I heard before me the sound of war
>
> I said, He will hear/answer me for I am full of righteousness

The expectation on the part of the author is that God will hear him. The reason given for God's attentiveness is that he (or 'it' as Jerusalem personified) is righteous. Within Psalms of Solomon, however, this righteousness is not considered to be a static characteristic; rather, it is predicated on the adherence of our authors to the covenantal obligations embodied within the Law of Moses. This characteristic, not shared by the sinners, fuels the authors' anthropological duality.[22] So in chapter 4, the unrighteous one is so called because he is said to 'deceitfully quote the Law' (4:8, cf. also 4:1). The central and key issue for the authors, stated at the outset of the document, is that righteousness is a prerequisite in order for God to hear one's prayer or appeal.

On this point, Pss. Sol. 7:7 offers a great deal of insight. Verse 6 is important in the light of my argument so I have included it here:

> 7.6) While your Name dwells (κατασκηνοῦν) in our midst, we shall receive mercy
>
> and the Gentile will not prevail over us.

> 7.7) For you are our protector and we will call to you (ἐπικαλεσόμεθα) and you
>
> shall hear/answer us (ἐπακούσῃ).

The first verse sets the location. The verb κατασκηνόω literally means to 'encamp' and certainly recalls the image of the Tabernacle in the wilderness. Earlier in the chapter (7:2), the authors implore God not to let the Gentiles 'trample on your holy inheritance'. The idea of the chapter when it reaches the v. 7 is clear: as long as the Temple remains as a place wherein one may call on God, the Gentiles will never rule over God's people, his inheritance. Moreover, the thrust of chapter 7 is that God will hear and answer those among whom he dwells. V. 7 must be set within this theology of election, and the image of God hearing his people when they call is predicated on that understanding. It is only to those who live according to God's precepts that he will listen.

---

22 Note 1:8; 2:3; 2:8; 9:2; 15:8, 10; compare 3:5–8 with 3:9–12; compare 4:23–5 with 4:1–22; compare 12:1-6a with 12:6b; 13:11; compare 14:1–5 with 14:6–9.

Central to prayer in the document is the understanding that righteousness by way of covenantal fidelity and cultic purity are prerequisites to offering prayer before the Lord. This preparedness is explicitly stated in 3:7; 6:1; 9:6; and 10:1f. In HB, the priestly code is saturated, indeed characterized by, a ritual preparedness. Always, when coming before the Lord, one must be clean and ritually pure, have on the proper clothes and be of the required type or class of people. So, whereas P focuses its punctiliousness on the ritual associated with a proper class or type of person, proper dress, and proper action at the proper time, Psalms of Solomon is more concerned with the individual's acceptance of the covenant and the avoidance of impurities. The two views do not differ in kind, but in degree. While P speaks specifically to a priestly audience, which prompted Menachem Haran to characterize it as an 'esoteric document', Psalms of Solomon both assaults the priesthood for the catastrophic misbehaviour, and seeks to encourage orthodox behaviour from the common man as well. This concern with the 'covenantal state' of an individual as elementary to coming before the Lord accords with the earlier observation that the Temple is in the purview of the authors. Just as the priestly writer from HB stresses the importance of ritual preparedness before entry into the presence of the Lord, so too does Psalms of Solomon with respect to prayer. For them, prayer is an institution of worship and sacrifice.

Finally, I want to discuss the expectation, or 'what', of prayer in the document. Throughout this paper I have been stressing the need for understanding general thematic principles in order to assess the particular concepts within the document. The question of 'what' prayer was for the authors is really a question of themes, one dependent on the groundwork already established in the first two questions of 'where' and 'how'. In short, passion for the Temple, its sanctity, one's own purity, and the Law of Moses govern the expectation of the authors.

First and foremost, it is important to stress that the document is one of assurance. In full view of the present conflagration, the authors are keen to point out that none of it is happenstance. A section from Psalms of Solomon 2 illustrates this point clearly. Note verses 6–15, which I will summarize and quote alternately:[23]

6–9) (summary): Israel is made captive and despised by all — this is a direct result of their sinfulness in vv. 3–5.

2:10) (quote): And the earth shall know all your righteous judgments, O God.

---

23 This is closely linked with the concept of discipline in the document, which is God's righteous action, note 5:4; 7:3; 8:7, 26; 9:2; 10:1–4; 14:1.

11–14) (summary): The Gentile conquerors humiliate and abuse the Jews in Jerusalem, about which the authors is deeply disturbed (14).

2:15) (quote): I shall justify you, O God, in uprightness of heart; for your judgments are right, O God.

Very briefly, the authors display nothing in the form of a 'crisis theology'. Rather, they are interested in pointing out that, in spite of appearances, all that has taken place has done so according to God's own judgment. Elsewhere I argue that this type of 'historical apologetic' is a symptom of the prophetic paradigm of HB.[24] Such a construction of crisis of judgment + assurance in purpose forms an 'historical apologetic'. This type of theological writing is prevalent in the HB prophets as well, and is characterized by a perception of history as viewed through a specific theological approach to God's relationship with Israel, i.e., God's divine plan. The progression of sin/punishment/repentance/forgiveness/redemption is played out in relation to historical events. When given enough time to develop in HB this progression culminates in the redemption of Israel.[25]

In Psalms of Solomon, this paradigm finds its conclusion in 17:21, which reads:

17:21) See Lord, and raise up for them their king, a son of David in the time which you know, O God, to rule over your child Israel.

Here the authors has reached the stage of messianic appeal, and, as the final instalment of God's divine plan, we could very well expect some type of redemption associated with the messianic advent. This is confirmed in 17:22ff. Just as the authors remained confident that the Lord was justified in punishing Israel elsewhere in the compilation, they are here confident that the Lord will complete the task of 're-purifying' and redeeming Israel. Pss Sol. 17:26ff tells of how the Messiah will perform this task. But the Messiah is simply a servant of God and a tool of His divine plan, initiated in the judgment upon the sins of Israel in chapter 1.[26] Thus this final appeal in 17 is a reflection of the expectation of the authors all along: God will

---

24 Note my forthcoming dissertation.

25 So in Isaiah 40–55; Jeremiah 46–51; Hos. 2:14–23, 14:1–9; Amos 9:11–15; Mic. 4:1–5:15, 7:1–20; Zeph. 3:9–20; and Mal. 2:17–4.6. Cf. John Eaton, *Vision in Worship* (London 1981), 1–39 wherein he discusses the close relationship between psalmody and prophecy.

26 The notion that the kingly Messiah will also purify or undertake the actions of a priest is to be found in HB. Kings such as Josiah and Hezekiah were both known and lauded for their religious reforms wherein they attempted to expunge all traces of religious syncretism.

institute His judgments as He has promised in the Law given to Moses. The 'what' of prayer in the document is to see this 'divine plan' enacted and fulfilled.

To conclude, I have examined three aspects of prayer within the document. First, it seems likely that the Temple was considered the most significant place wherein prayers were to be offered.[27] Secondly, it was noted that the intention of prayer within the document functioned as a call to righteousness. The authors are keen to remind the readers that God only hears and answers the prayers of the righteous. Thus the common man and priest alike must be prepared in their own way to go before the Lord. Generally speaking, Psalms of Solomon is a call to covenant fidelity and a return to legitimate Temple practices. Thirdly, it was suggested that the authors of the document expected their prayer, said in the Temple and conducted in righteousness, to be efficacious. God would hear and answer their prayers. Their assurance is predicated on the Law of Moses wherein God promises to dwell amongst his people. This is to say, prayer follows this paradigm: righteousness + location = the ear or attention of God. As such, their perception of God's covenant fidelity governed their expectation in prayer. In Psalms of Solomon, this 'expectation' was for the redemption of Israel and the establishment of God's kingdom on earth.

For Psalms of Solomon, prayer asserted God's hegemony over human history. As such, the authors held in unyielding terms that God would hear their pleas and, more importantly, answer them favourably. In short, the document itself could be viewed as a type of prayer. From the opening line of 'I cried unto the Lord' to the closing appeal referring to the created order, the authors are making one continuous reference to God's divine plan in history. Within that appeal are all the ingredients for prayer to be successful: it must be done in the Temple by those who obey the Law and with the purpose of establishing God's judgments and kingdom in the world.

---

27 The synagogue was very likely developing during this time, with roots extending back to the third century BCE in Egypt to the προσευχή, 'house of prayer'. Lee I. Levine, *The Ancient Synagogue* (New Haven, CT 2000), 1–40 has demonstrated the antiquity of this institution, but suggests that the synagogue as a replication of the Temple and the centre for Jewish worship is a much later development. Cf. also Joseph Gutmann, 'Synagogue Origins: Theories and Facts in *Ancient Synagogues: The State of Research* (Brown Judaic Studies 22, Chico, CA 1981), 1–7; *The Jewish Sanctuary* (*IR* 23:1, Leiden 1983); Donald D. Binder, *Into the Temple Courts: The Place of the Synagogues in the Second Temple Period* (SBL Dissertation Series 169, Atlanta 1999), 92–3. All agree that the term συναγωγή was, during much of the Second Temple Period, a designation for a type of gathering rather than a place. Interestingly, the term is found on four occasions in Pss.Sol., 10:7; 17:16, 43, 44.

The Prayer of Choni in Josephus Jewish Antiquities XIV 24

Niclas Förster

In antiquity petitionary prayer was a matter of controversy and critical debate especially among Hellenistic and Roman philosophers who expressed conflicting views on it. Thus it is worthwhile to examine aspects of this debate contained in the historical work of Flavius Josephus. The centre of attention will be the story of the death of the pious Choni, the so-called circle drawer, in the Jewish Antiquities (14:22–4). Amongst the Jews, Choni was famous for his petitionary prayers. Shortly before Rome interfered for the first time in Judean politics — during the period of the civil war between the two sons of Alexander Jannaeus, Aristobulus II and Hyrcanus II — Choni was killed because he allegedly refused to pray for the victory of one party involved in the war. Instead, he asked God in his prayer to remain neutral and to grant support to neither side. Josephus recorded this story, which appears at first glance like an anecdote of a legendary character and seemingly like a footnote to important historical events. It appears in truth as a carefully and intentionally selected incident that exemplifies the correct and true form of petitionary prayer; in this light, the murder of Choni, who was stoned to death because of the content of his prayer, seems even more despicable. In this part of his work Josephus draws for his non-Jewish readers the attractive image of an exemplary pious man and his prayer. The divine revenge on Choni's murderers that almost instantaneously ensued after his gruesome death was expected both by educated Jews and by pagans who read Josephus's book.

Before interpreting Choni's prayer in Antiquites 14:24, we must first take a quick look at the criticism of petitionary prayer in antiquity and its guiding principles. With the help of these principles, it becomes clear how Josephus modified the content of Choni's prayer in accordance with philosophical considerations. Thus the rejection of petitionary prayer in antiquity was a subject discussed among many contemporary philosophers and fused into their respective schools of thought. Nevertheless, many of the philosophical treatises on this topic remain lost to us today. A good example for the criticism of petitionary prayer which grasped the attention of educated circles in Hellenistic and Roman times is the orator Maximus of Tyre, who lived in the middle of the second century. He taught rhetoric in Athens for some time, visited Rome and was highly regarded by contemporaries. Forty-one speeches of his διαλέξεις on mostly philosophical subjects are preserved today. In his speeches Maximus assimilated the influence of different philosophical traditions, above all of Platonism, but he never got beyond a superficial knowledge of the treated topics. His fifth speech is a unique example of the philosophical criticism on petitionary prayer. In many manuscripts it is entitled Εἰ δεῖ εὔχεσθαι. In the first line Maximus concentrated his critical remarks about prayer on the egoism of the praying person. Above all he criticized most sharply those people, who selfishly prayed for themselves and who ignored the concerns, needs or interests of their fellow men. According to Maximus, one can even go so far as to say that many prayers completely contradicted each other and that their requests mutually excluded each other. If God chose to grant these wishes, he was always forced to give preference to one side or the other. Maximus illustrates prayers that in his view are foolish and selfish, by the example of the Phrygian king Midas,[1] who asked Dionysus for the ability to transform everything he touched into gold. When his wish was granted, he quickly realized how pointless it was, because his kingdom turned into gold and a famine broke out.[2] Maximus summarized the basic problem of these prayers as follows:[3] 'For what is it but an allegory of the misguided prayers of foolish men, who repent the very moment they gain what they have been praying for?'

The pagan rejection of egoistic prayer also influenced the Greek-speaking Jewish Diaspora. Its leading theologians tried to prove that Jewish piety met the requirements of philosophical thinking and that Jewish prayer was not selfish in its content. Traces of this opinion can be found in the literature of Hellenistic Judaism such as in the works of Philo from Alexandria. The same observation can be made in the writings of Flavius Josephus. Philo's remarks on the prayer of the Jewish high priest make clear the apologetic aim of Philo's thinking. Josephus' writings mirror the same goal. Thus Philo underlines in several passages of his works instances of the Jewish high priest praying during the service not only for the well-being of his own people but

---

1 G. Soury, *Aperçus de philosophie religieuse chez Maxime de Tyr, Platonicien éclectique. La prière - la divination - le problème du mal* (Collection d'études anciennes, Paris 1942), 16.

2 On the king Midas cf. M.C. Miller, 'Midas', *Lexicon Iconographicum Mythologiae Classicae* VIII 1, 846–51, 846–7.

3 Max.Tyr. 5, 1: τί γὰρ δὴ ἄλλο αἰνίττεται ἢ ἀνοήτου ἀνδρὸς εὐχὴν ἐπ' οὐδενὶ χρηστῷ, εὐχομένου μὲν ἵνα τύχῃ, μεταγιγνώσκοντος δὲ ἐπειδὰν τύχῃ. The text is taken from *Maximus Tyrius, Dissertationes*, M.B. Trapp (ed.), Bibliotheca Scriptorum Graecorum et Romanorum Teubneriana, (Stuttgart 1994), 38, 16–19. The translation is taken from *Maximus of Tyre, The Philosophical Orations* trans. with Introduction and Notes by M.B. Trapp, (Oxford 1997), 42–3.

altruistically for the entirety of mankind including all pagans and even the barbarians. Philo points out that this high-minded piety distinguishes the Jewish priest from his pagan contemporaries:

> Among the other nations the priests are accustomed to offer prayers and sacrifices for their kinsmen and friends and fellow-countrymen only, but the high priest of the Jews makes prayers and gives thanks not only on behalf of the whole human race but also for the parts of nature, earth, water, air, fire. For he holds the world to be, as in very truth it is, his country, and in its behalf he is wont to propitiate the Ruler with supplication and intercession, beseeching Him to make His creature a partaker of His own kindly and merciful nature.[4]

In the quoted passage Philo does not conceal that he wanted to contrast Jewish and pagan piety for apologetic reasons. He obviously wanted to defend his compatriots against the accusation spread amongst pagans that Jews are hostile towards all who do not share their belief and therefore direct their prayers against all pagans. According to Philo this insinuation could be disproved by the Jewish temple-cult and its priestly prayers:

> And therefore it astonishes me to see that some people venture to accuse of inhumanity the nation which has shown so profound a sense of using its prayers and festivals and first-fruit offerings as a means of supplication for the human race in general and of making its homage to the truly existent God in the name of those who have evaded the service which it was their duty to give, as well as of itself.[5]

In Philo's view the service in the temple was the centre of Jewish piety and mirrors the true essence of Jewish religion. Thus the Jewish philosopher wants to

---

4   Spec. Leg. I.17 (97) (Philo volume VII with an English translation by F.H. Colson, The Loeb Classical Library 320, (Cambridge MA 1998) 154: τῶν μὲν γὰρ ἄλλων οἱ ἱερεῖς ὑπὲρ οἰκείων καὶ φίλων καὶ πολιτῶν αὐτὸ μόνον εἰώθασι τάς τε εὐχὰς καὶ θυσίας ἐπιτελεῖν ὁ δὲ τῶν Ἰουδαίων ἀρχιερεὺς οὐ μόνον ὑπὲρ ἅπαντος ἀνθρώπων γένους ἀλλὰ καὶ ὑπὲρ τῶν τῆς φύσεως μερῶν, γῆς, ὕδατος, ἀέρος, πυρός, τάς τε εὐχὰς καὶ τὰς εὐχαριστίας ποιεῖται τὸν κόσμον, ὅπερ ἐστὶ ταῖς ἀληθείαις, ἑαυτοῦ πατρίδα εἶναι νομίζων, ὑπὲρ ἧς ἱκεσίαις καὶ λιταῖς εἴωθεν ἐξευμενίζεσθαι τὸν ἡγεμόνα ποτνιώμενος τῆς ἐπιεικοῦς καὶ ἵλεω φύσεως αὐτοῦ μεταδιδόναι τῷ γενομένῳ.

5   Spec. Leg. II.29 (167) (Colson 410): διὸ καὶ θαυμάζειν ἐπέρχεταί μοι, πῶς τολμῶσί τινες ἀπανθρωπίαν τοῦ ἔθνους κατηγορεῖν, ὁ τοσαύτῃ κέχρηται κοινωνίας καὶ εὐνοίας τῆς πρὸς (τοὺς) πανταχοῦ πάντας ὑπερβολῇ, ὡς τάς τε εὐχὰς καὶ ἑορτὰς καὶ ἀπαρχὰς ὑπὲρ τοῦ κοινοῦ γένους τῶν ἀνθρώπων ἐπιτελεῖν καὶ τὸν ὄντως ὄντα θεὸν θεραπεύειν ὑπέρ τε ἑαυτοῦ καὶ τῶν ἄλλων, οἳ τὰς ὀφειλομένας λατρείας ἀποδεδράκασι; cf. also Spec. Leg. I.35 (168–Colson 194), (190–Colson 208); Vita Mosis I.27 (149–Colson 354).

show the closeness between Jews and non-Jews in the correct light and stresses that Jewish prayer stands out by virtue of its selflessness.

Similar observations can be made in Josephus's writings. The Jewish historian remarks with regard to prayer egoism and the service in the Jewish temple, that Jewish prayer takes the well-being of all human beings into account regardless of the difference between Jews and non-Jews. He regarded it as crucial, that the common good must have priority in the prayers over selfish aims and minority interests. According to this he explains with special regard to his pagan readers in his apologia against Apion:[6]

> At these sacrifices prayers for the welfare of the community must take precedence of those for ourselves; for we are born for fellowship, and he who sets its claims above his private interests is especially acceptable to God.

The quoted passage makes clear, that Josephus was familiar with the contemporary philosophical criticism of petitionary prayer and integrated it into his historical writings to defend his religion and his people. In particular, the idea that God considers prayers for the benefit of the general public worthier than those for selfish or for personal interests is a principle that can also be found in philosophical sources and seems to have guided his thinking.

The influence of this thinking will now be proved in the passage of Josephus' historical work that deals with the murder of the famous Choni, who was called in rabbinical texts the 'circle drawer'. Above all the peculiar prayer that Josephus induced Choni to say is of special interest, because it closely corresponds to the model of the philosophical criticism on petitionary prayer. One could even regard Choni's prayer as an example of these ideas. It also characterizes Choni's murderer as morally reprehensible, because of the fact that the pious man was killed on account of the content of his prayer. Josephus begins his account with a short exposition to introduce the events. Accordingly the incident took place about 65 BCE during the civil war between the adherents of Aristobulus and Hyrcanus. Both brothers wanted to seize power in Jerusalem and Hyrcanus formed an alliance with the Arabic king Aretas to out his brother from power. Together with his ally he besieged Aristobulus in Jerusalem, whose forces after an initial defeat partly deserted. The attacker desired to

---

6   Ag. Ap. 2.196–7 (Josephus in nine volumes I *The Life, Against Apion* with an English translation by H.St.J. Thackeray, The Loeb Classical Library 186, [Cambridge 1976] 370): καὶ ἐπὶ ταῖς Θυσίαις χρὴ πρῶτον ὑπὲρ τῆς κοινῆς εὔχεσθαι σωτηρίας, εἶθ' ὑπὲρ ἑαυτῶν· ἐπὶ γὰρ κοινωνίᾳ γεγόναμεν, καὶ ταύτην ὁ προτιμῶν τοῦ καθ' αὑτὸν ἰδίου μάλιστ' (ἂν) εἴη θεῷ κεχαρισμένος.

use the famous Choni and his prayers to request that God deliver divine assistance and decisive victory to him. Josephus characterizes the pious man with words that make Choni's high standing in the eyes of the Jewish population understandable to his readers. He also explains why one pins great hope on Choni's prayers and why Hyrcanus' fighters were convinced that his influence on God could be decisive in winning the war. Thus Josephus calls Choni θεοφιλής[7] and defines with this word his close relation to God,[8] which made his prayer exceptionally successful. But Josephus did not develop this idea further and notes in passing Choni's successful prayer for rain. He confines himself to this brief report and ignores the content and circumstance of the prayer for rain.

However this particular prayer that ended a period of drought won great fame among the Jews. Even centuries later, rabbis related stories about this prayer which was mentioned several times in rabbinical literature.[9] These reports also make clear, why Choni's prayer became famous and was not forgotten for generations after his death. According to the rabbis, Choni dared to pressure God when his prayer did not immediately have an effect. One could even say, that he risked blackmailing God:[10]

> He prayed, but the rain did not fall. What did he do? He drew a circle and stood within it and said before God: Lord of the World, thy children have turned their faces to me, for that I am like a son of the house before thee.

---

7   Ant. 14:2.1 (22), (*Josephus Jewish Antiquities Books 14–15* with an English translation by R. Marcus completed and edited by A. Wikgren, The Loeb Classical Library 489, [Cambridge MA 1998], 14).

8   Cf. O. Betz, 'Der Tod des Choni-Onias im Licht der Tempelrolle von Qumran. Bemerkungen zu Josephus Antiquitates 14, 22–24', in *Jesus: Der Messias Israels, Aufsätze zur biblischen Theologie* (WUNT 42, Tübingen 1987), 59–74, 62; R. Gray, *Prophetic Figures in Late Second Temple Jewish Palestine: The Evidence from Josephus* (New York 1993), 146–7; B. Kollmann, *Jesus und die Christen als Wundertäter. Studien zu Magie, Medizin und Schamanismus in Antike und Christentum* (Forschungen zur Religion und Literatur des Alten und Neuen Testaments 170, Göttingen 1996), 137; K. Wengst, *Jesus zwischen Juden und Christen*, (Stuttgart 1999), 48; M. Becker, *Wunder und Wundertäter im frührabbinischen Judentum: Studien zum Phänomen und seiner Überlieferung im Horizont von Magie und Dämonismus* (WUNT 2:144, Tübingen 2002), 295.

9   A. Büchler, *Types of Jewish-Palestinian Piety from 70 B.C.E. to 70 C.E.: The Ancient Pious Men* (Jew's College Publications 8, London 1922), 199–203, 252; S. Safrai, 'Teaching of Pietists in Mishnaic Literature', *Journal of Jewish Studies* 16 (1965), 15–33, 17–19; E.E. Urbach, 'The Talmudic Sage – Character and Authority' *Journal of World History* 11 (1968), 116–47, 121–2; O. Betz, 'Miracles in the Writings of Flavius Josephus', in L.H. Feldman, G. Hata (eds), *Josephus, Judaism, and Christianity*, (Leiden 1987), 212–35, 219.

10 m.Taan. 3.8 (The text is taken from *Mishnayoth* 'Moed' Ph. Blackman (ed.) (6 vols, London 1952), II, 425. The translation is taken from H. Danby, *The Mishnah*, (Oxford 1954) 198:
    התפלל ולא ירדו גשמים מה עשה עג עוגה ועמד בתוכה ואמר לפניו רבונו
    של עולם בניך שמו פניהם עלי שאני כבן בית לפניך.

Then Choni went a step further and threatened emphatically not to leave the circle before God let it rain. He reinforced this by an oath in God's name:[11] 'I swear by thy great name that I will not stir hence until thou have pity on thy children!' This outrageous action was successful in spite of Choni's provocation of God. It began to rain. Indeed, the rain poured down so hard that one was forced to flee Jerusalem for the Temple Mount. However, Choni's behaviour met with criticism. Above all the rabbis dismissed the contention that with help of the circle Choni was able to force God to react. The important rabbi Simeon ben Shetach allegedly disapproved of Choni's prayer and threatened him with the punishment of excommunication: 'Hadst thou not been Choni I would have pronounced a ban against thee!' The rabbi probably alluded to the magical background of the circle within which Choni was praying.[12] This circle could be a historically reliable tradition, although the stories about Choni are legendary and were reshaped through a long oral transmission.[13] The remark of Simon ben Shetach also makes obvious how uneasy later rabbis were with Choni's way of praying and additionally reveals that his success made them suspicious.[14] But the popular stories about Choni's prayer in a circle were so famous, that the later rabbis could not simply suppress or omit them and therefore they became part of the rabbinical literature. Nevertheless the rabbis diminished Choni's success through the commentary of Simon ben Shetach, which was later part of the stories about his prayer for rain. The reason for this sceptical attitude was probably the magical background of the circle that Choni drew in the ground and stood in while praying. Indeed such magical circles served in many magical papyri of antiquity that hand

---

11 m.Taan 3. 8 (Blackman 425): נשבע אני בשמך הגדול שאיני זז מכאן עד שתרחם על בניך

12 The explanation given by A. Büchler, *Types*, 246 note 2, who interprets the circle as a means to force God to decide and compares it with the behaviour of Popilius Laenas in his negotiations with the king Antiochus IV Epiphanes, Livy 45 12, can be rejected because Choni does not draw this circle around God: cf. W.S. Green, 'Palestinian Holy Men: Charismatic Leadership and Rabbinic Tradition' *Aufstieg und Niedergang der römischen Welt* 2:19, 2, 619–47, 632–3; J. Goldin, 'On Honi the Circle-Maker: A Demanding Prayer', *Harvard Theological Review* 56, (1963), 233–7, 236–7 takes another view.

13 On the later rabbinical traditions of Choni, which regard him as rabbi cf. pTaan 3, 66d, 42–67a, 5; b.Taan 23a; cf. J.-M. van Cangh, 'Miracles de rabbis et miracles de Jésus. La tradition sur Honi et Hanina', *Revue théologique de Louvain* 15 (1984), 28–53, 32–3; W.S. Green, 'Palestinian Holy Men', 641–4; G. Vermes, *Jesus der Jude. Ein Historiker liest die Evangelien*. A. Samely and V. Hampel (eds) (Neukirchen-Vluyn 1993), 57; B. Kollmann, *Jesus*, 138, 140; M. Becker, *Wunder*, 293; H.-J. Becker, 'The Magic of the Name and Palestinian Rabbinic Literature', in P. Schäfer (ed.) *The Talmud Yerushalmi and Graeco-Roman Culture* (Tübingen 2002), III, 391–407, 401–2.

14 W.S. Green, 'Palestinian Holy Men', 636; B. Kollmann, *Jesus*, 138; M. Becker, *Wunder*, 308, 316–17, 320, 328.

down magical rites and incantations as a means for protecting against demons.[15] An important source that makes plain the sense of such a circle comes from Egypt. It is a magical papyrus that contains, among other spells, instructions for causing an eclipse of the sun through the practice of certain rites and incantations. The magician could purportedly use the shadow darkening the sun like an oracle and consult it about the future. During the magical séance the sorcerer needed protection against the demon that caused the eclipse; he used the circle to protect himself. Thus the papyrus contains precise instructions. For protection they recommend a cat's tail[16] and 'magical characters together with the circle upon which you will stand after you have drawn it with chalk.'[17] Accordingly the circle was a method for repulsing demons. This use of the circle remained customary in the Middle Ages and took place in some countries even during modern times.[18] For example the circle was superstitiously regarded as a means of protection against witches and evil spirits. In these circumstances, Choni's circle can be explained as protection against demonic powers who could disturb his prayer and thwart its success.

Josephus was also familiar with the magical connotations of the prayer for rain which will be proved in the discussion that follows. Instead of going into detail, he mentions the prayer for rain in passing and tells nothing about the circle, in which

---

15 Th. Hopfner, *Griechisch-ägyptischer Offenbarungszauber. Mit einer eingehenden Darstellung des griechisch-synkretistischen Daemonenglaubens und der Voraussetzungen und Mittel des Zaubers überhaupt und der magischen Divinition im besonderen* (Studien zur Palaeographie und Papyruskunde 21, Leipzig 1921), I, §239, 56; A. Büchler, *Types*, 246 note 2; I. Abrahams, 'Some Rabbinic Ideas on Prayer', in Studies in *Pharisaism and the Gospels*, (Second Series, Cambridge 1924) 72–93, 74–5; H. van der Loos, *The Miracles of Jesus* (Novum Testamentum Supplement 9, Leiden 1965), 143; W.S. Green, 'Palestinian Holy Men', 634; B. Kollmann, *Jesus*, 138; M. Becker, Wunder, 312–3 cf. also L. Blau, *Das altjüdische Zauberwesen*, (Westmead 1970) (= *Jahresberichte der Landes-Rabbinerschule in Budapest für das Schuljahr 1897–8*, [Budapest 1898]), 33–4.

16 Th. Hopfner, *Griechisch-Ägyptischer Offenbarungszauber. Seine Methoden* (Studien zur Palaeographie und Papyruskunde 23, Leipzig 1924), II, §144, 73.

17 PGM VII 858 (The text is taken from *Die griechischen Zauberpapyri*, trans. and ed. by K. Preisendanz, [compiled by E. Diehl, S. Eitrem, A. Jacoby, Stuttgart 1974] (2. verb. Auflage mit Erg. v. K. Preisendanz u. E. Heitsch durchg. u. hg. v. A. Henrichs), II, 37): οἱ χαρακτῆρες σὺν τῷ κύκλῳ (ᾧ) ἐφεστήξει γράψας κρήτῃ. For the translation see H.D. Betz, *The Greek Magical Papyri in Translation including the Demotic Spells* (Chicago 1986), 141.

18 Cf. Straberger-Schusser, 'Kreis', *Handwörterbuch des Deutschen Aberglaubens V*, 462–78, 465–72; I. Goldziher, 'Zauberkreise', in J. Desomogyi (ed.) *Gesammelte Schriften V* Collectanea 2:5 (Hildesheim 1970) 401–4 (= *Aufsätze zur Kultur- und Sprachgeschichte II* 1916, 83–6), 403; I. Scheftelowitz, *Die altpersische Religion und das Judentum. Unterschiede, Übereinstimmungen und gegenseitige Beeinflussungen*, (Gießen 1920), 73–9; J. Trachtenberg, *Jewish Magic and Superstition: A Study in Folk Religion* (New York 1939), 121.

Choni stood. He instead concentrated on Choni's violent death. The prayer for rain became merely an introduction for the following events, but in Josephus' description of Choni's murder, the magical character of his actions shows through.

Josephus reports that Choni was in hiding and was detained by the adherents of Hyrcanus against his will. They demanded that he curse their enemies, whom they were besieging in Jerusalem. This curse (ἀρά) clearly had magical connotations and is connected with magical spells. It can be compared with a kind of damaging witchcraft that was supposed to weaken the adherents of Aristobulus and paralyze their ability to fight effectively. In the first place, we have to understand the function of curses in warfare during antiquity. This can also explain why Hyrcanus' adherents wanted to use the curse like a weapon, in order to effect a decisive blow to their enemies. It will also be demonstrated that powerful cursing was an age-old tradition in the ancient Near East and the Greco-Roman world that also left its traces in biblical texts. Black magic, specifically intended to harm the enemy, belonged to the art of warfare and had an important place in the preparation of war and in diplomatic deterrence. Most importantly, such curses were designed to discourage enemies of the state merely by intimidation and fear. The curse was regarded as a bodily power that could be projected onto other human beings. It could thereby lessen the vitality of people who were cursed. The words were almost automatically effective.[19] Learned magicians whispered the most powerful incantations. Very impressive examples for the military use of curses come from Egypt and go back in some cases to the 6th and 12th dynasty (i.e. to the Old and Middle Kingdom). From this time come the texts that modern researchers called 'Ächtungstexte'. They were found in several places like Thebes, Giza and Saqqara.[20] In these texts the enemies of the pharaoh were cursed. These combined with such symbolical rites as the smashing of images or vessels with the names of the enemies on it.[21] Such rites allegedly destroyed political opponents as the images and vessels were smashed.[22] In these curses, all princes, who 'rebel' or

---

19 Fr. Pfister, 'Beschwörung' *Reallexikon für Antike und Christentum II*, 169–76, 175.

20 G. Posener, 'Ächtungstexte', *Lexikon der Ägyptologie* I, 67–9, 68; G. Vittmann, 'Verfluchung', Lexikon der Ägyptologie VI, 977–81, 977; A.M. Abu Bakr – J. Osing, Ächtungstexte aus dem Alten Reich 25, *Mitteilungen des Deutschen Archäologischen Instituts Abteilung Kairo* 29 (1973), 97–133, 97; Y. Koenig, 'Les textes d'envoûtemet de Mirgissa', *Revue d'égyptologie* 40, 1989, 113–25.

21 W. Speyer, 'Fluch', *Reallexikon für Antike und Christentum* VII, 1160–1288, 1170; Scharbert, ארר, *Theologisches Wörterbuch zum Alten Testament* I, 437–51, 447.

22 H. Bonnet, 'Fluch', *Reallexikon der ägyptischen Religionsgeschichte*, (2nd unchanged edn, Berlin 1971), 195–6, 195.

'hatch plots' are explicitly threatened with death.[23] Such politically motivated and militarily useful curses were not only known in Egypt. This custom was known in other Near Eastern lands. It was also used for the diplomatic prevention of possible wars by mobilizing the gods against cursed persons. Many treaties on cuneiform tablets can document these occurrences. The curses had their fixed place in the texts of treaties and would become effective in the event that human justice did not prevail.[24] They were designed take effect in the event of disregard, violation, falsification or any alteration of the documents.[25] The fear of such divine punishment guaranteed the respect of the treaties by both parties and prevented war. These documents are very interesting and make Choni's prayer for rain understandable; as a divine weapon, the lack of rain would create a terrible drought, thereby punishing all those who would seek to break the treaty. Examples from Assyrian times were found in the excavations of the Assyrian city of Nineveh.[26] For instance, a treaty between the Assyrian king Samsi-Adad V and the king of Babylon Marduk-zakir-sumi implores the Assyrian weather-god Adad, who is aptly named because of his influence over the rainfall 'canal inspector of heaven and earth':[27]

> May Adad, the canal inspector of heaven and earth, deprive him of rain from the heavens and of seasonal flooding from the underground water; may he destroy his land through famine, roar fiercely at his city, and turn his land into ruins by means of a flood.

The terrifying words of such treaty-curses show without doubt, that either drought or a flood by heavy rain would destroy the kingdom of the ruler who would break the

---

23 K. Sethe, 'Die Ächtung feindlicher Fürsten, Völker und Dinge auf ägytischen Tongefäßscherben des Mittleren Reiches', in, *Leipziger und Berliner Akademieschriften* (1902–34), *Opuscula. Sammlung seltener und bisher nicht selbständig erschienener wissenschaftlicher Abhandlungen* 11, Leipzig 1976 (= Abhandlungen der Preußischen Akademie der Wissenschaften zu Berlin, phil.-hist. Klasse 1926, 5–74), 185–253, 253.

24 Cf. F.Ch. Fensham, 'Malediction and Benediction in Ancient Near Eastern Vassal-Treaties and the Old Testament', (Zeitschrift für die alttestamentliche Wissenschaft 74, 1962), 1–9; P. Maiberger, 'Zur Problematik und Herkunft der sogenannten Fluchpsalmen', *Trierer Theologische Zeitschrift 97*, (1988), 183–216, 196–9; *State Archives of Assyria*. Published by the Neo-Assyrian Text Corpus Project of the Academy of Finland in co-operation with Deutsche Orient-Gesellschaft ed. by R.M. Whiting, Volume II, S. Parpola, K. Watanabe, *Neo-Assyrian treaties and Loyalty Oaths*, (Helsinki 1988), XLII.

25 J. Scharbert, *Solidarität in Segen und Fluch im Alten Testament und in seiner Umwelt, Väterfluch und Vätersegen*, (Bonner Biblische Beiträge 14, Bonn 1958), I, 38.

26 R. Borger, *Assyrische Staatsverträge, Texte aus der Umwelt des Alten Testaments, Rechts- und Wirtschaftsurkunden Historisch-chronologische Texte*, (Gütersloh 1982–5), I, 156.

27 The translation is taken from S. Parpola, K. Watanabe, *Neo-Assyrian treaties*, 5 Line 13–15.

treaty. But such magical practices appear not only in Neo-Assyrian treaties; they survived the decline of the Assyrian and Babylonian states. Traces of similar thinking can also be found in the bible.

Additionally, these ideas directly influenced authors of Greco-Roman times. The Roman historian Abydenos, who lived in the second century CE wrote a history of the Assyrians and Babylonians and can demonstrate this.[28] His source was the historical work of Berossos from Babylon.[29] In the third century BCE this Babylonian priest of Marduk wrote a history in Greek on the rise and fall of the Assyrian and Babylonian states and reported, among other events, on the rule of the famous king Nebuchadnezzar. Berossos based his information about the historical deeds of the kings on older cuneiform sources. The adaptation of Abydenos merely reshaped Berossos' book in accordance with the literary style of Roman times. It also took over from Berossos a prediction of Nebuchadnezzar, who was able to foresee the destruction of his kingdom by the victorious Persians. Nebuchadnezzar hoped to avert the fall of his state by divine intervention. Thus in his prophecy of future disaster he cursed the conqueror, as was the established custom in the cuneiform literature quoted above[30] and called out about the Medes, who formed an alliance with the Persians:

> O would that before he gave up my citizens some Charybdis or sea might swallow him up utterly out of sight; or that turning in other directions, he might be carried across the desert, where there are neither cities nor foot of man, but where wild beasts have pasture and birds their haunts, that he might wander alone among rocks and ravines.[31]

---

28 Cf. P. Kroh, 'Abydenos', *Lexikon der Antiken Autoren*, (Kröners Taschenbuchausgabe, 366, Stuttgart 1972), 1.

29 J. Oelsner, 'Abydenos', *Der Neue Pauly I*, 45.

30 W. Speyer, 'Fluch', 1172.

31 Eusebius PE 9 41, 3 (Eusèbe de Césarée, *La Préparation évagélique*, livres VIII–IX-X, Introduction, traduction et notes des livres VIII et X par G. Schroeder, É des Places du livre IX par É des Places, texte grec révisé des livres VIII-IX-X par É des Places, Sources Chrétiennes 369, Paris 1991, 338–40): ὡς εἴθε μιν πρόσθεν ἢ προδοῦναι τοὺς πολιήτας Χάρυβδίν τινα ἢ θάλασσαν εἰσδεξαμένη ἀϊστῶσαι πρόρριζον· ἢ μιν ἄλλας ὁδοὺς στραφέντα φέρεσθαι διὰ τῆς ἐρήμου ἵνα οὔτ' ἄστεα οὔτε πάτος ἀνθρώπων, θῆρες δὲ νομὸν ἔχουσι καὶ ὄρνιθες πλάζονται, ἔν τε πέτρῃσι καὶ χαράδρῃσι μοῦνον ἀλώνεμον; cf. also: *Die Fragmente der Griechischen Historiker* (F GR HIST) v. F. Jacoby. Dritter Teil, Geschichte von Staedten und Voelkern (Horographie und Ethnographie) C Autoren ueber einzelne Laender Nr. 608a–856 (Erster Band: Aegypten-Geten Nr. 608a–708), Leiden 1958, Fgm. 6, 407. The translation is taken from *Eusebii Pamphili Evangelicae Praeparationis libri XV, Ad codices manuscriptos denuo collatos recensuit Anglice nunc primum reddidit notis et indicibus instruxit*, E.H. Gifford (ed.), (Tomus III pars prior, Oxford 1903), 485.

In this curse, water and desert are playing a key role. These forces of nature would exterminate the invaders, removing them from the earth's surface either by one terrible blow or slowly by famine and thirst. This text, that was probably originally written by Berossos, was for the historian Abydenos so remarkable, that he did not skip it in his book; for this reason it survived in Roman times. But the tradition did not come to an end because Eusebius from Caesarea found this text in Abydenos' writings and included it, among other historical reports, in his collective work *Praeparatio evangelica*. So Nebuchadnezzar's curse became part of Christian literature.

The curse as a means of warfare is also mentioned in the Old Testament, and the biblical texts are often related to the older literature of the Egyptians and Mesopotamians. The magical roots of the curses are obvious. An important biblical example for the curse in warfare comes from the story of the seer Bala'am. Num. 22:1–4 gives a full account of how Israel after leaving Egypt and crossing the desert invades the land of Moab opposite Jericho and pitches camp. In this situation, the king of the Moabites, Balak, feared the fighting power of the invaders and did not risk battle, because Israel had already beaten the Amorites in battle. Thus he sends for Balaam from Pethor at the Euphrates.[32] Balak asks Balaam (Num. 22:6):

> I beg you come and curse this people for me, for they are too mighty for me. We may then be able
>
> to defeat them and drive them out of the country. For this I know: anyone you bless is blessed,
>
> anyone you curse is accursed.

However Balaam blesses Israel on God's command, and did not curse. Several scholars stressed the correspondence between Balaam's curses and the rites mentioned in much older texts for instance from Egypt and Mesopotamia.[33] The magical character of Balak's request is also obvious. Apparently he hoped to banish Israel by use of the curse and deprive it of the strength to fight.[34] The power that could achieve this goal would be contained in Balaam's words[35] that would hinder Israel's fighters during the clash of both armies.

---

32 Scharbert, ארר, 445.

33 W. Schottroff, *Der altisraelitische Fluchspruch*, Wissenschaftliche Monographien zum Alten und Neuen Testament 30, (Neukirchen-Vluyn 1969), 200; B.A. Levine, *Numbers 21-36. A New Translation with Introduction and Commentary* (The Anchor Bible, New York 2000), 150, 169, 213–14.

34 B.A. Levine, *Numbers 21–36*, 138.

35 Sh.H. Blank, 'The Curse, Blasphemy, the Spell, and the Oath', *Hebrew Union College Annual* 23 (1950–1), 73–95, 86.

However the curses mentioned in the Old Testament are not only directed against entire nations merely with the purpose of diminishing their courage and stamina in battle as was planned by Balak. Certain cities were also punished by curse. For example the city of Meroz was cursed[36] according to the book of Judges, because it did not hurry to Israel's aid in its fight against Canaanean kings (Judg. 5:23): 'Curse Meroz, said the angel of the Lord, curse, curse the people living there for not having come to the Lord's help, to the Lord's help as warriors.' This text bears clear similarities to the treaty-curses quoted above, because Meroz did not keep the alliance. The curse would therefore punish the perpetrators of this crime and inflict severe damages on the city and its inhabitants.

Before coming back to Choni's murder during Jerusalem's siege, I want to mention in passing that cursing was also a method of warfare and political fighting among Greeks and Romans. The ritual cursing of the enemies, for instance during a siege, was part of political life. The Romans often asked the gods of the city that they besieged to leave their local temples and offered them in many cases substitute temples in Rome.[37] Through this ceremony of *Evocatio* the Romans sought to undermine the divine protection of the city, readying it to be stormed and depriving it of the support of its deities. Afterwards followed a ritual whose purpose was to award the besieged enemy to the gods of the underworld, thereby leaving him helpless and at the mercy of the Romans. The Romans called this rite *Devotio*.[38] The author Macrobius hands down a formula for *Devotio*, in which the inhabitants of the besieged city were handed over to the *dis inferis*. That is tantamount to a curse.[39] The rite purportedly guaranteed the Romans that the besieged would be carried off by the deities of the underworld during the fighting. In Greece the curse was also mentioned by the sources in cases of political quarrels and warfare. As an example, in Athens, the enemies of the state were officially cursed.[40]

---

36 J. Scharbert, '"Fluchen" und "Segen" im Alten Testament', *Biblica* 39, (1958), 1–26, 6; R.G. Boling, *Judges, Introduction, Translation, and Commentary* (The Anchor Bible, New York 1975), 114.

37 Wissowa, 'Evocatio', *Paulys Real-Encyclopädie der classischen Altertumswissenschaft VI*, 1152–3, 1152; Fr. Pfister, 'Evocatio', *Reallexikon für Antike und Christentum VI*, 1160–5, 1160; H. Versnel, 'Apopompe', *Der Neue Pauly I*, 894; V. Basanoff, 'Evocatio'. *Étude d'un rituel militaire romain*, (Bibliothèque de l'École des hautes Études. Sciences religieuses 61, Paris 1947), 17–41.

38 W. Speyer, 'Fluch', 1211; H. Versnel, 'Devotio', *Der Neue Pauly III*, 493–4, 493.

39 Wissowa, 'Devotio', *Paulys Real-Encyclopädie der classischen Altertumswissenschaft V*, 277–80, 279; cf. also V. Basanoff, 'Evocatio', 30–1, 66.

40 E.g. an Athenian priestess was asked to curse Alcibiades, who was declared enemy of the state. But she refused and declared herself a priestess of prayer and not of curse (εὐχῆς οὐ κατάρας ἱέρεια), Plutarch, Qu. R. 44, 275d (*Plutarch's Moralia in fifteen volumes IV* 263D–351B with an English

The sources of antiquity collected and interpreted so far give a broad historical overview and reach from Egypt to Greece and the Roman Empire; thus, they come from all the peoples, who, over the centuries, dominated politics in the eastern Mediterranean area. The examples given above also prove that peoples of different cultures and religion embraced the cursing of enemies and political opponents. These curses were also an established tradition in the Old Testament; the influence of Non-Jewish ideas cannot be disputed. If one considers these sources, it is also not surprising that Choni was requested to curse the supporters of Aristobulus besieged in Jerusalem. Indeed it suggests itself and was justified by biblical models. Why exactly the besieger came to Choni and did not even hesitate to force him to apply the curse is therefore also easily explained. They were probably aware of a connection between Choni's prayer for rain and the curse and Josephus also knew about it. Thus he explicitly equated the prayer that ended a terrible drought and the curse on military opponents and writes 'ὡς ἔπαυσε τὴν ἀνομβρίαν ... οὕτως ἀρὰς θῇ'. On the first glance these words and especially the formulation 'so...as (ὡς ... οὕτως) seems strange. They also raise the question, why a prayer for rain could be equated or even compared with the effect of a curse. However this becomes understandable if one considers the Assyrian treaties and also Nebuchadnezzar's curse reported by Abydenos. Both texts regard the drought as a divine punishment caused by a curse. From this point of view, the curse and the prayer for rain can be compared and do not belong to two completely divergent spheres. Josephus seemed to be aware of this relationship. Based on this assumption, as the Jewish historian insinuates, Choni was asked to curse the defenders of Jerusalem with a drought. Certainly, the lack of water would weaken their resistance. In accordance with this assumption, the soldiers of Hyrcanus turned to Choni and assumed that he, who prayed successfully for rain, could also stop the rainfall from occurring.

Interestingly enough, this hypothesis is supported by later rabbinical sources. They indicate that Choni refused to stop the rain, when it poured down like torrents and the inhabitants of Jerusalem were forced to flee to the temple mount.[41] The most interesting thing to note is that the rabbinical authors stress that, on another occasion, Choni moderated heavy rainfall by use of his petitionary prayer. Consequently, Choni was able to preordain the quantity of

---

translation by F.C. Babbitt [The Loeb Classical Library, Cambridge MA 1962], 76); cf. F. Graf, 'Fluch II. Griechenland und Rom', *Der Neue Pauly IV*, 573–4, 573.

41 R. Patai, 'The "Control of Rain" in Ancient Palestine. A Study in Comparative Religion', *Hebrew Union College Annual* 14, (1939), 251–86, 283.

rainfall through his prayer.⁴² The same principle — that Choni regulated the rain if required and could therefore also stop it by a curse — was also probably the basis of the request in Josephus's story.

After describing the military situation and the request of Hyrcanus' supporters, Josephus used the curse as the starting point for the events that finally led to Choni's murder. The pious man almost despairingly resisted the demands of the fighters to put the effectiveness of his prayer into their service and use it as a military advantage in the civil war. First he refused to pray (ἀντιλέγων) and than he tried to excuse himself (παραιτούμενον). But the soldiers of Hyrcanus had already brought Choni into their camp and under their control. Nobody could stop them and in the end they put heavy pressure on him. Josephus outlines briefly, how Choni stood in the middle of a furious crowd and was himself besieged from all sides (ἐβιάσθη ὑπὸ τοῦ πλήθους στὰς μέσος αὐτῶν). The bystanders wanted him to intercede with God on their behalf and, one could almost say, to act as the advocate of their case. Finally, Choni found himself compelled to say a prayer. But its content did not at all correspond to the expectations of the surrounding crowd:⁴³

> O God, king of the universe, since these men standing beside me are Thy people, and those who are besieged are Thy priests, I beseech Thee not to hearken to them against these men nor to bring to pass what these men ask Thee to do to those others.

In this prayer Choni preferred to favour neither party. He even went a step further and made their prayers the subject of his own prayer. So he said expressly, that God may neither listen to one side (ἐνακοῦσαι) nor grant the requests of the other side (ἃ οὗτοι παρακαλοῦσιν). He obviously assumed that both groups had already sent their prayers to God without gaining any advantage in the fighting. By considering the prayers of both fighting parties as the subject of his own prayer he thus raised his own prayer to a 'higher level', so to speak. In this act, the influence of principles that were also guiding the contemporary philosophical criticism on prayer become visible. Importantly, Choni had become convinced of God's disregard for selfish and egoistic prayers whose sole objective was the military and political victory of one party or another. Thus he points out that both parties in the civil war, whom he calls 'δῆμος' and 'ἱερεῖς', were specially protected by God and that the wishes of neither group should take precedence over the other. He also

---

42 cf. R. Patai, 'The "Control of Rain"', 282.
43 Josephus Ant. 14:2, 1 (24), (Marcus / Wikgren 14): ὦ θεὲ βασιλεῦ τῶν ὅλων, ἐπεὶ οἱ μετ' ἐμοῦ νῦν ἑστῶτες σὸς δῆμός ἐστι καὶ οἱ πολιορκούμενοι δὲ ἱερεῖς σοί, δέομαι μήτε κατὰ τούτων ἐκείνοις ἐπακοῦσαι μήτε κατ' ἐκείνων ἃ οὗτοι παρακαλοῦσιν εἰς τέλος ἀγαγεῖν.

asks God to remain neutral and not to hear the selfish prayers of both sides. This is a remarkably clear rejection of prayer-egoism and bears some similarities to the prayer for public good of the high priest described by Josephus and Philo. In this situation, Choni's prayer ultimately had the consequence of God not reacting to the prayers of the fighting parties, instead removing himself from earthly affairs. This corresponds with the thinking of many philosophers who shared a similar critical view on petitionary prayer. In the legendary story about king Midas, the orator Maximus tells as a warning example how the disappointed king wanted to turn the ability of transforming everything into gold against his worst enemies.[44] It would harm them, and as Maximus paraphrases Midas' request, 'go away on heads of enemies' (ἀπελθεῖν εἰς ἐχθρῶν κεφαλάς).[45] The utter disappointment of the king who wanted to turn his own disaster against his enemies is a good example for the self-interested prayer that was discredited by Maximus. This reservation was also taken in account by Josephus, when he described Choni's murder. Thus the pious man was ultimately responsible for his own death because his prayer for God's neutrality provoked the fury of the bystanders. They had obviously hoped that he would be the decisive winning factor in the war and that his prayer would bring a quick end to the fighting. Thus they reacted violently and the 'base ones of the Jews' (πονηροὶ τῶν Ἰουδαίων), as Josephus puts it carefully, stoned him to death.

The understanding of these events could be deepened in many respects. But the discussion so far makes plain that Josephus was able to adapt his historical writings to the 'mental horizon' of philosophically educated readers. Because of this form of acculturation Josephus omits all remaining traces of the witchcraft of popular would-be rain-makers.[46] Nevertheless this magical background of Choni's prayer for rain gleams through in later rabbinical traditions and was muted only by soft rebuke. In Josephus'

---

44 On this form of Epipompe cf. W. Speyer, 'Fluch', 1198 and O. Weinreich, 'Primitiver Gebetsegoismus. Ein Beitrag zu Terenz, Andria 232f.', in, *Religionsgeschichtliche Studien*, (Darmstadt 1968), 1–37, 15 (= *Genethliakon. Wilhelm Schmid zum 70. Geburtstag am 24. Febr. 1929* [Tübinger Beiträge zur Altertumswissenschaft 5, Stuttgart 1929], 169–99); O. Weinreich, 'Unheilbannung im volkstümlichen Gebet, Segen und Zauberspruch', in, *Ausgewählte Schriften III 1937 – 1970* unter Mitarb. v. U. Klein hg. v. G. Wille, (Amsterdam 1979), 199–233, 209 (= Universitas 1, 1946, 275–99); O. Weinreich, 'Religiös-ethische Formen der Epipompe', in *Ausgewählte Schriften III 1937 – 1970* unter Mitarb. v. U. Klein hg. v. G. Wille, (Amsterdam 1979), 61–77 (= *Pisciculi*. Studien zur Religion und Kultur des Altertums. Franz Joseph Dölger zum 60. Geburtstage dargeboten von Freunden, Verehrern und Schülern hg. Th. Klauser u. A. Rücker, [Münster 1939], 291–308), 61, 68, 70.

45 Max.Tyr. 5, 1 (Trapp 38, 14).

46 On pagan magical rites for rain-making see W. Fiedler, *Antiker Wetterzauber, Würzburger Studien zur Altertumwissenschaft* (Stuttgart 1931), cf. also Riess, 'Aberglaube', *Paulys Real-Encyclopädie der classischen Altertumswissenschaft I*, 29–93, 42–3.

Jewish Antiquities, Choni becomes the leading exponent of prayer that meets philosophical requirements and stands serenely over the lowly hatred-filled spheres of the civil war of 65 BCE. Furthermore, Josephus reports that, after Choni's murder, God sides against Hyrcanus' supporters, destroys their crops with heavy winds and punishes them with rising food-prices.[47] For this study it is notable that God approved of Choni's unselfish prayer. Therefore, in the Jewish belief system that could be described by Philo and Josephus as a philosophical religion this type of prayer should take precedence.

---

47 Ant. 14:2, 2 (28), (Marcus / Wikgren 16); on this passage cf. M. Becker, 'Wunder', 297.

The Faith of the Translator of the Peshitta: Some Indications in P-Isaiah[1]

Gillian Greenberg

The question of the faith of the Peshitta translator, whether Jewish or Christian, has been intensively discussed. Among the earlier papers, that of Bloch[2] gives a brief summary of the literature up to the early years of the twentieth century. The more recent authoritative work includes discussions by Gelston, van der Kooij, de Moor and Sepmeijer, Morrison, Taylor, Weitzman, Winter, and a forthcoming paper by van Peursen;[3] and in another forthcoming paper, ter Haar Romeny sets out the religious background in second-century Edessa.[4]

In brief, two principal views are held by these authorities. In the one group are those who believe that the Peshitta translator was a Christian and that this faith is evident in the translation of certain verses; there are some passages at which, they

---

1   I am grateful to Drs A. Gelston, S. Brock, W. Smelik and J. Goldingay for their comments on this material during its preparation. I have drawn extensively on the published work of Professor van der Kooij, and on the forthcoming work by Drs J. Goldingay and D. Payne which they have been kind enough to allow me to use at this pre-publication stage; I wish to thank them warmly for their generosity. Reference books: A. Rahlfs, *Septuaginta* (Deutsche Bibelgesellschaft Stuttgart 1979); A. Sperber, *The Bible in Aramaic* (5 vols, Leiden 1962); L. Koehler and W. Baumgartner, *The Hebrew and Aramaic Lexicon of the Old Testament* (Leiden 1994).

2   J. Bloch, 'The Authorship of the Peshitta', *American Journal of Semitic Language and Literature* 35–6 (1918–20), 215–22.

3   A. Gelston, 'Was the Peshitta of Isaiah of Christian Origin?', in C.C. Broyles and C.A. Evans (eds), *Writing and Reading the Scroll of Isaiah* (2 vols, Leiden 1997), II: 563–82; J.C. de Moor and F. Sepmeijer, 'The Peshitta and the Targum of Joshua', in P.B. Dirksen and A. van der Kooij (eds), *The Pehsitta as a Translation* (MPIL 8, Leiden 1995), 129–76; C.E. Morrison, *The Character of the Syriac Version of the First Book of Samuel* (MPIL 11, Leiden 2001), 156–9; M.P. Weitzman, 'From Judaism to Christianity', in A. Rapoport-Albert and G. Greenberg (eds), *From Judaism to Christianity* (JSSSup 8, Oxford 1999), 3–29; *idem., The Syriac Version of the Old Testament* (Cambridge 1999), 237–46; A. van der Kooij, *Die alten Textzeugen des Jesajabuches. Ein Beitrag zur Textgeschichte des Alten Testamentes* (OBO 35, Göttingen 1981); R.A. Taylor, *The Peshitta of Daniel* (MPIL 7, Leiden 1994), 322–4; M. Winter, 'The Origins of Ben Sira in Syriac', *Vetus Testamentum* 27 (1977), 237–53, 494–507 (505–7); W. van Peursen, 'The Peshitta of Ben Sira', (Aramaic Studies, in press).

4   Bas ter Haar Romeny, 'Hypotheses on the Development of Judaism and Christianity in Syria in the Period after 70 CE', in Huub van de Sandt (ed.), *Matthew and the Didaki: Two Documents from the Same Jewish-Christian Milieu?* (Assen forthcoming).

believe, only a Christian would have rendered the Hebrew as has this translator. In addition to these passages which in their view are conclusive, they adduce others as supporting evidence, though acknowledging that in these latter areas the evidence of Christian input is rather less certain. Putting together these two groups of passages, these authorities maintain that the cumulative weight of evidence is sufficient to constitute proof of a Christian translator.

In the other group of authorities are those who believe that the translator was a Jew. While agreeing with those in the first group that there are certain passages at which it can be argued that the difference between Hebrew and Syriac is compatible with a Christian interpretation, they maintain that compatibility is no more than compatibility, and that these passages, even taken all together, do not amount to proof; they accept that there is a considerable number of passages which *can* be interpreted as proof of a Christian translator, but add that there are none or only a minute number which can *only* be interpreted in such a way. The suggestion presented in this paper is another interpretation which is built on the work of these and other scholars.

This interpretation has developed during a study of the translation technique in the Peshitta to Isaiah. Within Isaiah, two obvious areas for study of the faith of the translator are the 'Apocalypse' of chapters 24–7, and the 'Servant Songs' of Deutero-Isaiah.[5] Discussion in the present paper focuses mostly on the 'Servant Songs',[6] with brief reference to supporting material from the 'Apocalypse'. These areas seem to be a propitious area for the investigation of the question, having been so intensively studied both by those who believe that their significance lies in the presence in the Hebrew Bible, and by those who see them as directly relevant to Christianity. A Christian translator of the Peshitta could well have taken the latter view, and this might be detectable in his work. There is, though, a possible paradox: since Christian exegetes have found so much in the Hebrew of these passages to convince them of their importance to Christianity, it could be argued that a Christian translator would not have felt the need to emend his *Vorlage* in any way. Absence of Christian nuance

---

5   The literature on the authorship of these texts, on whether or not they really form a distinct corpus, and on the identity of the Servant, is of course enormous; see for instance the discussions in J.N. Ostwalt, *The Book of Isaiah, Chapters 40-66* (New International Commentary on the Old Testament, Grand Rapids, MI 1998), *passim*; T.N.D. Mettinger, *A Farewell to the Servant Songs: A Critical Examination of an Exegetical Axiom* (Scriptora Minora 13, Lund 1983). For present purposes, however, these problems are not relevant and will not be considered further in this paper.

6   A comprehensive analysis of P-Isaiah from this point of view is in progress, but this paper focuses on passages discussed at the BAJS meeting, University of Durham, July 2003.

would not then suggest a non-Christian translator, but simply a translator who was content with the wording before him.

Perceptions of an input by a Christian translator naturally focus on passages at which there are differences in meaning between the Masoretic text (MT) and the Peshitta (P), so the prevalence of such areas in the Peshitta as a whole is relevant to the present discussion. This prevalence is not high. There is strong evidence that the *Vorlage* from which the translator of the Peshitta worked was close to, though not identical with, the Masoretic Text, and that the translator of the Peshitta almost always strove to preserve the meaning of that Vorlage.[7] Sometimes he failed to understand the meaning of a passage of particularly difficult Hebrew, and made small errors in consequence; often, he made small additions to increase the precision of the text; and analysis of his choice of lexical equivalents suggests the work of a man enjoying the exercise of literary initiative. The balance of evidence, however, strongly suggests that this translator aimed, successfully, to achieve a meticulous rendering of the sense of his *Vorlage*. Throughout the Peshitta to the Servant Songs, the closeness between the Hebrew and the Syriac is indeed remarkable, particularly considering the difficulty of the task of translation. The Hebrew is extraordinarily dense and complex; Baltzer,[8] for instance, writes even of Isa. 42:1, 3 as including terms which in their precise context are 'hardly translatable'.

Nonetheless, there are differences between MT and P, and those discussed below include a number that are compatible with a Christian input.[9] Even in this small corpus, amounting at the broadest definition to hardly more than the length of a single

---

7 See for example, A. Gelston, *The Peshitta of the Twelve Prophets* (Oxford 1987), 111–18, who assesses the evidence suggesting that there were differences between the *Vorlage* of the Peshitta and MT, examining Hebrew variants, passages in which the Peshitta seems to presuppose a different vocalization or word-division of the same Hebrew consonantal text as that of MT, and the evidence of the other ancient versions, and concludes that 'it is hard to avoid the conclusion that the Hebrew *Vorlage* of the Peshitta was very nearly identical with MT'; G. Greenberg, *Translation Technique in the Peshitta to Jeremiah* (MPIL 13, Leiden 2002), 26–31. Clearly, however, the Peshitta is not a slavishly literal rendering; M.D. Koster, 'The Copernican Revolution in the Study of the Origins of the Peshitta' in P.V.M. Flesher (ed.), *Targum Studies*, II, *Targum and Peshitta*, (Atlanta 1998), 15–54, shows for instance that the scribes deliberately introduced certain changes, including some intended to clarify the text, and that other changes entered the text as a result of scribal error. Nonetheless it is nearer the 'literal' than the 'free'; see for instance Weitzman, *The Syriac Version*, 15, who says, 'For the most part, P stands close in sense to the Hebrew of MT'.

8 K. Baltzer, *Deutero-Isaiah* (Minneapolis 2001), 127.

9 For comprehensive discussions of the individual verses to be presented in this paper, see of course A. van der Kooij, *Die alten Textzeugen*; J. Goldingay and D. Payne, *A Critical and Exegetical Commentary on Isaiah 40-55* (Edinburgh forthcoming).

long biblical chapter,[10] there are at least eleven verses which include phrases of interest in the present context.[11] This is a substantial number, particularly bearing in mind the potential paradoxical effect noted above which could tend to reduce the number of passages whose meaning was deliberately modified in translation. The strength of the evidence to be discussed below varies from example to example. There are none in which the evidence of Christian input is beyond question, though some have been by authoritative critics as going far in that direction, and in others taken individually the evidence is suggestive only; the importance of these latter examples lies in their contribution to the cumulative weight of the body of the findings.

The picture is complex. In nine of these eleven passages the Peshitta differs from the MT in presenting a nuance which could be seen to be Christian, or by introducing a messianic theme absent from the MT.[12] In one of this nine, however, the difference seems almost certainly to have been introduced not by the translator but by a later scribe, and its importance here lies in the contrast of its frank anti-Jewish tone with the prevailing subtlety of the differences that may be ascribed to the work of the translator. In the tenth the difference between the Hebrew and the Syriac may give a less, rather than more, anti-Jewish sense. The eleventh example would have provided an excellent opportunity to a translator wishing to introduce a Christian nuance; yet, and arousing much interest in later Syrian commentators, the translator has scrupulously resisted any such temptation, giving a text in which the outstanding interest lies not in any differences between the Hebrew and Syriac but in the similarities.

---

10 Commentators differ, of course, in the boundaries they set on these songs; see for instance C.R. North, *The Suffering Servant in Deutero-Isaiah* (Oxford 1948); Ostwalt, *Isaiah*; Baltzer, *Deutero-Isaiah*. A broad definition is: First Song Isa. 42:1–4, possibly 7–9; Second Song Isa. 49:1–6, possibly 7–13; Third Song Isa. 50:4–9, possibly 10–11; Fourth Song Isa. 52:13–53:12.

11 The eleven selected passages are, in canonical order, Isa. 49:1, 4, 5, 6, 7; 50:10; 53:2, 3, 5, 8, 9. The points of interest in Isa. 49:7; 53:3 are clear but small, and these two passages have been included not primarily for their intrinsic interest but to illustrate the contribution of individually insignificant items to the body of cumulative evidence. The difference between MT and P at Isa. 53:2 is probably due not to the work of the translator but to an error by a scribe, and the passage has been included here to suggest a contrast between the impartial approach of the former and the apparently more partial attitude of those involved at a later time.

12 This is not to imply, of course, that there was no messianic theme in the Hebrew Bible. See for instance W. Horbury, *Messianism among Jews and Christians* (Edinburgh 2003), 5: 'perhaps the major insight of the second half of the twentieth century in the study of ancient messianism [is] a regained recognition that messianic hope belongs to the stream of interpretative tradition which accompanies the Jewish scripture throughout antiquity'.

Given this complexity, it is not surprising that a number of different aspects of the translation feature in the analysis. The eleven verses mentioned above may be grouped as follows:

1. The group of nine passages.

i. The plain meaning of a phrase of clear Hebrew has been reversed: Isa. 49:4;

ii. the choice of lexical equivalent or perception of the root meaning can be seen to introduce a messianic theme: Isa. 49:6; 50:10; 53:5;

iii. the possible change in meaning depends on the perception of punctuation within the verse: Isa. 49:1;

iv. the relevant features are grammatical, together with a possible error at the stage of translation in one: Isa. 49:6 (there is a small grammatical difference between MT and P in his verse, so it should be considered in this group too); Isa. 53:8;

v. the characteristics of the Servant himself are subtly affected, in the first by changing a preposition and giving a Syriac plural for a Hebrew singular, and in the second by the choice of lexical equivalent: Isa. 49:7; 53:3;

vi. a probable, and detectable, scribal error has been allowed to stand in all later extant MSS: Isa. 53:2.

2. An anti-Israelite sense present in the Ktib is eliminated by rendering the Qre: Isa. 49:5

3. The outstanding feature of the translation is its closeness to the Hebrew despite an obvious possibility of introducing a Christian theme: Isa. 53:9

Isa. 49:1, 4, 6; 50:10; 53:2, 5, 8.

1. First the nine verses in which a Christian or messianic nuance appears in P but not in the MT

i. The plain meaning of a phrase of clear Hebrew has been reversed: Isa. 49:4

Clear and apparently intentional divergences from the MT are few in the Peshitta, particularly at passages like Isa. 49:4 where the meaning of the Hebrew ואני אמרתי לריק יגעתי seems to be plain. In the present context, this makes the example all the more interesting: Weitzman, in his discussion of the case for origin of the Peshitta within Christianity, notes that in each of a number of passages sometimes cited in support of such an origin, including Isa. 7:14; 15:9–16:1; 25:6, 7; and Isa. 53:8 which will be discussed below, the original was difficult;[13] here, no such explanation can be seen to apply. The context is the Servant's reference to his call, and to God's statement in the preceding verse עבדי אתה ישראל אשר בך אתפאר, 'You are my servant,

---

13 M.P. Weitzman, 'From Judaism to Christianity', 17, 25–7.

Israel, and in you I will be glorified'. In the MT this is immediately followed by the Servant's lament: 'For I said "I have laboured in vain…"'. In LXX καὶ ἐγὼ εἶπα Κενῶς ἐκοπίασα and Tg ואנא אמרית לריקנו לאיתי this is closely represented; but in the Peshitta ܘܠܐ ܐܡܪܬ ܠܒܪܗ ܕܝܥܩܘܒ ܕܣܪܝܩܘܬܐ ܐܬܠܐܝܬ there is a negative, 'for I did not say[14] I have laboured in vain'; Goldingay and Payne[15] describe this as 'an uncharacteristically frank and confrontational expansion'.

The technique of 'converse translation', discussed for instance by Klein[16] in Targumic tradition, is an unlikely explanation. This technique is occasionally used in the Peshitta for the sake of perceived logic, for instance at Josh. 23:4 where the Hebrew reads ראו הפלתי לכם את הגוים הנשארים, but P renders ܚܙܘ ܕܝܢ ܕܠܐ ܦܠܓܬ ܠܟܘܢ ܥܡ̈ܡܐ ܗܠܝܢ ܕܐܫܬܪܘ, or at Gen. 41:54–5, where the Hebrew reads ובכל ארץ מצרים היה לחם ותרעב כל ארץ מצרים but P gives ܒܟܠܗܝܢ ܐܪ̈ܥܬܐ ܘܒܟܠܗ ܐܪܥܐ ܕܡܨܪ̈ܝܢ ܠܐ ܗܘܐ ܠܚܡܐ ܘܗܘܐ ܟܦܢܐ. Weitzman[17] cites a number of other passages, but Isa. 49:4 is of a different ilk, for here there is no problem in the logic of the Hebrew.

There are at least four reasonable explanations. First, the change was deliberate, introduced by the translator because he found it unthinkable that the Servant should speak of his labours as useless. If he saw the Servant not as a fallible weak human being, but rather as Jesus, the simple addition of the negative would have protected the reader from the dreadful implication that the sufferings had been in vain, and this has been seen by some authorities as a clear demonstration of Christian input. However, as Dr Gelston and Dr Goldingay[18] have commented, other than Christian translators could well have found the implication of the Hebrew difficult to accept.

14 There are no variants in extant MSS at this point: S.P. Brock (ed.), *The Old Testament in Syriac*, Part III, fascicle 1, (The Peshitta Institute Leiden, Leiden 1993). There are other variants in this verse: ܠܒܪܗ ܕܝܥܩܘܒ is present in 7a1 but not 9a1, but this is not strictly relevant to the present discussion; similarly, ܠܒܪܗ appears without the possessive suffix in some MSS, and in some ܡܢܝܐ is followed by the pronoun.

15 Goldingay and Payne, *Isaiah 40-55*.

16 M.L. Klein, 'Converse Translation: A Targumic Technique', *Biblica* 57 (1976), 515–37 (516–29), who gives examples from the Pentateuch of the addition or deletion in translation of negative particles.

17 Weitzman, 'The Interpretative Character of the Syriac Old Testament', in *From Judaism to Christianity*, 55–89 (59).

18 A. Gelston, personal communication, 2002; J. Goldingay, personal communication, 2002.

Second, the negative entered the text as a simple error, occurring either in the translator's reading of the Hebrew ואני, misreading it as ולא, or in a scribe's reading of his Syriac exemplar, giving ܘܠܐ as a corruption of ܘܐܢܐ.[19]

Third, the context may be the stimulus: following God's wonderful and amazing words to Israel in the previous verse, cited above, and preceding God's account of the breadth of the Servant's call, נקל מהיותך לי עבד להקים את שבטי יעקב ונצירי ישראל להשיב ונתתיך לאור גוים להיות ישועתי עד קצה הארץ,[20] perhaps it was unacceptable to the translator that the Servant should be represented as lamenting a failure that had led up to the time represented. Either the failure itself could have been unacceptable, or the fact that the Servant is heard to bemoan the failure.

Assimilation is a fourth possibility.[21] Certainly the translator did assimilate passages, sometimes to texts from other books, sometimes to texts from earlier or later verses in the same book, but not usually if by so doing the meaning was distorted.

In summary, there are a number of more or less convincing explanations of the presence of the negative in P: but it remains true that this dramatic difference between the Hebrew and the Syriac could have seemed, to a Christian translator, essential.

ii. The choice of lexical equivalent or perception of the root meaning may be seen to introduce a messianic theme: Isa. 49:6; 50:10; 53:5.

The idea of 'sprout, offshoot' enters the translation at Isa. 49:6 as the result of an atypical perception of the Hebrew root in this verse. In the MT ונצירי ישראל (Qre ונצורי) the root I נצר 'to watch over, to preserve' is usually perceived, either in the adjectival form of the Ktib, which occurs here only, or in the Qal passive participle of the Qre, referring to the preserved remnant of Israel. This seems to be the understanding shown by LXX διασποράν and Tg גלות. However, P ܘܒܢܬܗ ܕܐܝܣܪܐܝܠ implies that the root was instead II נצר 'sprout, offshoot', as for instance at Isa. 11:1 ויצא חטר מגזע ישי ונצר משרשיו יפרה and gives 'to restore the shoot of Israel'. This

---

19 A. Gelston, personal communication, 2002; S.P. Brock, personal communication, 2002. Dr Brock also notes that the translator could have intended a rhetorical question here, though this in itself would open up the possibility of yet further speculation 'Why'? The use of the rhetorical question in the Peshitta is inconsistent even when such a form is present in the Hebrew *Vorlage*, so its introduction here is at any rate uncertain. 5ph1 is unfortunately illegible at this point.

20 Ktib: ונצירי; Qre ונצורי.

21 van der Kooij, Die Alten Textzeugen, 277–8, points out the closeness of this wording to Isa. 45:19 לא אמרתי לזרע יעקב; Isa. 65:23 לא ייגעו לריק is another possible source.

seems likely to be a deliberate decision: the root נצר occurs elsewhere in Isaiah 10 times, though in Deutero-Isaiah only indubitably here and at Isa. 48:6;[22] the translator understood it well,[23] and rendered it with flexibility and sensitivity.

In Isa. 50:10 the picture is complicated; the presence of a messianic theme not expressed in the Hebrew is interesting but unlikely to indicate deliberate Christian input. The MT is clear: יבטח בשם יהוה וישען באלהיו '…let him trust in the name of the Lord, and rely upon his God' and the parallelism is preserved in LXX πεποίθατε ἐπὶ τῷ ὀνόματι κυρίου καὶ ἀντιστηρίσασθε ἐπὶ τῷ θεῷ. Tg מתרחיץ בשמא דיוי ומסתמיך על פורקנא דאלהיה, however, introduces the theme of redemption in addition to that of trust, as does P ܢܣܒܪ ܒܫܡܗ ܕܡܪܝܐ ܘܢܬܦܪܩ ܒܐܠܗܗ '…let him trust in the name of the Lord, and he will be redeemed by his God'. P does not render the precise parallelism of MT, which would have given a clear indication that the second verbal root was שען 'to support oneself on, to depend on' not ישע in which the theme of 'help' extends to that of deliverance and salvation. In other contexts, P usually recognizes the root שען and translates correctly.[24]

---

22 C.R. North, *The Second Isaiah* (Oxford 1964), 110.

23 There are four possible occurrences of the root I נצר, in the Qal 'to keep watch over' in Deutero-Isaiah, at 42:6; 48:6; 49:6, 8; North, see n. 22 above, notes that only at Isa. 48:6 and 49:6 is the use indisputable. At Isa. 42:6 ואצרך, probably 'I will keep you [in safety]' P uses ܣܘܝ, the denominative verb from the substantive, 'to strengthen, comfort', perhaps having understood either the root I צור, metaphorically 'a refuge, a place of protection' or אזר, 'to gird'; Tg has ואתקנינך 'I will establish you'. LXX καὶ ἐνισχύσω σε may indicate that the Greek translator too read, or understood, something other than the root I נצר. At Isa. 48:6 the sense of MT requires the root I נצר, reasonably rendered by P using the root ܢܛܪ 'to guard, watch, keep' in the passive. At Isa. 49:8 the MT similarly seems to imply the root I נצר, though Koehler and Baumgartner in the *Hebrew and Aramaic Lexicon* note that the root יצר 'to shape, form' is an alternative, and has evidently been perceived by P who gives ܘܓܒܠܬܟ, from the root ܓܒܠ 'to form'. LXX (see Rahlfs, II, 633) has καὶ ἔπλασά σε ; Tg, as at Isa. 42:6, has ואתקנינך. In Isaiah, the relevant verses are 1:8; 26:3; 27:3. At Isa. 1:8 MT נצורה is possibly the Niphal of the root צור, 'to surround, bind', here 'to lay siege to' though the Qal of the root I נצר is a possibility; P has the passive of the root ܨܒܐ, 'to besiege', presumably to be kept watch over in a painful sense, which could have been reached from an understanding of either, though the first seems more likely. LXX πολιορκουμένη and Tg עלה דצירין are along similar lines. At Isa. 26:3; 27:3 *bis*, the root I נצר is clear, and is understood by P, using the root ܢܛܪ. The use of II נצר 'sprout, offshoot' is clear at Isa. 11:1 and 60:21, and at Isa 14:19 it is the only reasonable understanding; at each P gives ܝܘܥܐ 'sprout'. At Isa. 65:4, where the meaning seems to be reached through 'watch over' to 'secret place' P has ܡܥܪܐ, caverns, from the root ܢܥܠ, root-meaning 'to descend into an enclosed valley or into the ground', suggesting influence from LXX σπηλαίοις. J. Morgenstern, 'The Suffering Servant—A New Solution', *Vetus Testamentum* 11 (1961), 292–320; 406–31 (297; 309) translates 'to bring back the scattered ones of Israel', reading the root זרה, 'to scatter' as at Ezek. 6:8; 36:19, at the first of which P has the root ܒܕܪ, and at the second the root ܕܪܐ, both meaning 'to scatter'.

24 P makes the same choice at Ps. 18:19 ויהי יהוה למשען לי where he gives ܣܡܟܐ. This is a particularly interesting example, for at the parallel passage in 2 Sam. 22:19, where the MT ויהי יהוה משען לי is

P to Isa. 24:22 presents a comparable example. The Hebrew spells out the fate of the nobility and the monarch: ואספו אספה אסיר על בור וסגרו על מסגר ומרב ימים יפקדו :they will be gathered together and imprisoned and 'after many days they will be punished' In P. however, the closing phrase differs markedly: ܘܢܬܦܪܩܘܢ ܗܢܘܢ ܐܣܝܪܐ. The prisoners are to be saved, redeemed, rather than punished. The root פקד occurs in 15 other passages in Isaiah, and is always translated appropriatley. The cognate is the usual choice, and indeed the context usually clearly requires this sense; where the meaning is at a further part of the range, other well-chosen verbs are used. LXX is close to the MT: διὰ πολλῶν γενεῶν ἐπισκοπὴ ἔσται αὐτῶν as is Tg ומסגי יומין ייעול דוכרנכון. So on balance this seems like a deliberate and original initiative on the part of the translator.

P to the next verse reinforces this impression. Here God's glory will be evident: מלך יהוה צבאות בהר ציון ובירושלם ונגד זקניו כבוד 'the Lords of hosts will reign in mount Zion and in Jerusalem and his glory will be before his elders. LXX ὅτι βασιλεύσει κύριος ἐν Σιων καὶ ἐν Ιερουσαλημ καὶ ἐνώπιον τῶν πρεσβυτέρων δοξασθήσεται and Tg תתגלי מלכותא דיוי צבאות בטורא דציון ובירושלם וקדם סבי עמיה ביקר are similar. In P, however, the revelation is before God's saints, ܩܕܡ ܩܕܝܫܘܗܝ, not his elders.

P to 53:5 evokes a simlar theme. Here the MT reads ובחברתו נרפא לנו. נרפא is a Niphal perfect, possibly 'we are healed'. LXX τῷ μώλωπι αὐτοῦ ἡμεῖς ἰάθημεν suggests the understanding of a perfect in MT. However, P ܘܒܚܒܪܬܗ ܢܬܐܣܐ and Tg ובדנתנהי לפתגמוהי חובנא ישתבקון לנא both render imperfects, indicating that healing is for the future.

Both emendations, that in Isa. 50:10 and that in Isa. 53:5, are suggestive; yet neither independently introduces a new nuance, for both are close to Tg, and it is possible that both translators were presenting one exegetical tradition.[25] A further complexity is, of course, that this does not prove Jewish rather than Christian

---

almost identical to that in the psalm, P reads ܘܗܘܐ ܠ, ܢܗܪܐ ܕܚܫܘܟܝ. The balance of evidence suggests (G. Greenberg, 'The Peshitta to 2 Samuel 22 and Psalm 18: One Translation or Two?' *Journal of the Aramaic Bible* 2 [2000] 15–23 [19–21]) that the Peshitta to the psalm was written first, and that the rather few differences between that and P-2 Samuel result from light editorial work by the translator of the latter; this is apparently one of the points which he considered needed emendation.

25 See for instance R.R. Rowlands, 'The Targum and the Peshitta Version of the Book of Isaiah', *Vetus Testamentum* 9 (1959), 178–91 (181); S.P. Brock, 'Jewish Traditions in Syriac Sources', *Journal of Jewish Studies* 30 (1979), 212–32; *idem.*, 'A Palestinian Targum Feature in Syriac', *Journal of Jewish Studies* 46 (1995), 271–82 (276); Gelston, *Twelve Prophets*, 189–90.

authorship, for such a tradition might well have persisted after a conversion of the Peshitta school to Christianity.[26]

iii. The possible change in meaning depends on the perception of verse division: Isa. 49:1

The focus here is on the reference of רחוק in the MT. The whole verse reads שמעו איים אלי והקשיבו לאמים מרחוק יהוה מבטן קראני ממעי אמי הזכיר שמי. The MT punctuation, with *athnah* under מרחוק, links יהוה with Isa. 49:1b, and so gives רחוק a geographical meaning; Tg ואציתא מלכון מרחיק is similar; however LXX διὰ χρόνου πολλοῦ στήσεται, λέγει κύριος links רחוק rather with Isa. 49:1a, as does P ܩܕܝܡ ܗ̇ܘ ܕܢܩܘܡ ܐܡ̇ܪ ܡܪܝܐ ܫܡܥܘ ܓ̈ܙܪ̈ܐ, so that in these latter two the term has been understood to refer to distance in time rather than distance in place, and so perhaps to Jesus.[27]

iv. The relevant features are grammatical, together with a possible error at the stage of translation in one: Isa. 49:6; 53:8 (there is a small grammatical difference between MT and P in this verse, so it should be considered in this group too); Isa. 53:8.

In Isa. 49:6 the Hebrew plurals in להקים את שבטי יעקב ונצירי ישראל להשיב are rendered as singulars in Syriac, ܫܒܛܐ and ܢܨܝ̈ܒܗ, again raising the possibility of a reference to Jesus.[28]

In Isa. 53:8 P differs from MT in several grammatical points that might have been intended better to fit the passion narrative, but might simply have been introduced in an attempt to make good sense.[29] The MT מפשע עמי נגע למו 'for the transgression of the people to whom the stroke was due' becomes in P ܘܡܢ ܥܘ̈ܠܐ ܕܥܡܝ ܩܪܒ ܠܗ 'some of the wicked ones of my people touched/approached him'.[30] There may also be an error at the stage of translation; the final verb may have baffled the Peshitta

---

26 Of course this knowledge of Jewish tradition suggests that the translator, if a Christian as I shall argue below, was a Jewish- rather than a gentile-Christian; nor would gentile Christians been likely to have had his competence in Hebrew.

27 Van der Kooij, *Die Alten Textzeugen*, 277 notes that 1 Jn. 1:1; 1 Pet. 1:20, are evoked.

28 Ibid., 278.

29 Weitzman, *The Syriac Version*, 241.

30 See C.F. Whitley, 'Textual Notes on Deutero-Isaiah', *Vetus Testamentum* 11 (1961), 457–61 (459–60), who notes that מפשע עמי implies that God is speaking, but that the context implies first person plural speakers and therefore the phrase is sometimes emended to מפשעינו as in v. 5; M. Dahood, 'Isaiah 53:8–12 and Massoretic Misconstruction', *Biblica* 63 (1982), 566–70 (566) suggests that עמי is an example of the third masc. sing. possessive suffix, as at Mic. 3:5. The difficulty is increased by the problem of the last word: G.R. Driver, 'Once Again Abbreviations', *Textus* 4 (1964), 76–94 (94) suggests למות; Dahood postulates that למו includes a byform for 'water'.

translator,[31] who substituted a translation of נגשׁ 'to approach', which he had already misread for נגשׁ 'to search' in the previous verse: alternatively, he had simply misread his Vorlage as נגשׂ. LXX ἀπὸ τῶν ἀνομιῶν τοῦ λαοῦ μου ἤχθη εἰς θάνατον seems to diverge sufficiently from MT to suggest a difficulty in translation; Tg חובין דחבו עמי עד לותהון ימטי differs too much from MT to be helpful.

v. The characteristics of the Servant himself are subtly affected, in the first by changing a preposition and giving a Syriac plural for a Hebrew singular, and in the second by the choice of lexical equivalent: Isa. 49:7; 53:3

In Isa. 49:7 the MT reads לבזה נפשׁ למתעב גוי לעבד משׁלים 'to him whom man despises, to him whom the nation abhors, to a servant of rulers'. LXX τὸν βδελυσσόμενον ὑπὸ τῶν ἐθνῶν τῶν δούλων τῶν ἀρχόντων is close to MT, as is Tg לדבסירין ביני עממיא לדמטלטלין ביני מלכוותא לדהוו עבדין לשלטונין להון. P however has ܠܕܡܣܠܝܐ ܡܢ ܥܡܐ ܠܗܕܐ ܟܝ ܐܬܐ ܗܐ ܘܠܕܒܥܒܕܐ ܕܫܠܝܛܢܐ, '...to the rejected by the nation, and by the servants of rulers'. The change, achieved by using a different preposition and by giving a Syriac plural for a Hebrew singular, emphasizes the Servant's humble status: everyone may be a ' servant of rulers', but not everyone is 'despised by servants of rulers'.

In Isa. 53:3 a similar effect results from the choice of lexical equivalent. MT reads נבזה וחדל אישׁים: the point of interest is the root חדל, usually 'to cease, forbear, refrain'. Koehler and Baumgartner[32] give the passive 'abandoned' for the form in this passage. P renders ܫܝܛ ܗܘܐ ܘܡܟܝܟܐ ܕܐܢܫܐ 'despised and humble'. Elsewhere in Isaiah, at Isa. 1:16; 2:22: 24:8 where the root is used with the more usual meaning, P uses the root ܒܛܠ, 'to cease, desist', so the root ܡܟ in the passive as here 'humble, meek', is not P's usual approach and may perhaps evoke the use in Mt. 5:5 for those who will inherit the earth. Alternatively, it may simply be a guess at a reasonable translation where the nuance is unusual. Neither LXX ἀλλὰ τὸ εἶδος αὐτοῦ ἄτιμον ἐκλεῖπον παρὰ πάντας ἀνθρώπους nor Tg בכין יהי לבוסרן ויפסיק יקר כל מלכוותא יהון חלשׁין ודוון הא כאנשׁ כיבין ומזמן למרעין are close to the MT, but nor do their interpretations closely resemble P.[33] P's choice may emphasize not the rejection of the Servant by

---

31 Gelston, 'Peshitta of Isaiah', 577–8.

32 *Hebrew and Aramaic Lexicon*, 293.

33 Goldingay and Payne, *Isaiah 40–55*, understand the root חדל 'to cease, cease doing' here, as at Ps. 39:5 אדעה מה חדל אני, taking it to mean 'transient'; in this verse, P understands similarly, using the root

man, but the Servant's presentation of himself, and man's consequent perception of him.

2. An anti-Israelite sense present in the Ktib is eliminated by rendering the Qre: Isa. 49:5

MT reads לשובב יעקב אליו וישראל לא יאסף (Qre לו). The Ktib is difficult, perhaps indicating its originality. Goldingay and Payne suggest 'to stop Israel withdrawing', a reflexive sense as at Isa. 60:20 וירחך לא יאסף. P ܘܠܡܟܢܫ ܠܝܥܩܘܒ ܠܘܬܗ ܘܠܐܝܣܪܐܝܠ is based on the Qre,[34] avoiding an anti-Israel sense present in the Ktib. This understanding is shared by LXX τοῦ συναγαγεῖν τὸν Ιακωβ καὶ Ισραηλ πρὸς αὐτόν and Tg לאתבא דבית יעקב לפלחניה וישראל לדחלתיה יתקרב.

3. The outstanding feature of this translation is its closeness to the Hebrew despite an obvious possibility of introducing a Christian theme: Isa. 53:9

The Hebrew ויתן את רשעים קברו ואת עשיר במתיו is difficult, both word by word[35] and in understanding the sense as a whole. Whitley, for instance, describes Isa. 53:8–9a as 'perhaps the most perplexing passage in Deutero-Isaiah';[36] Goldingay and Payne[37] say of the fourth Song as a whole that the Hebrew is 'a highpoint of unclarity'. This verse is clearly evocative of a Christian theme, but as it stands is no more than evocative. To bring it close to a text which could be used in a Christian context subtle changes are needed, yet what we see in the Peshitta ܘܝܗܒ ܠܪܫܝܥܐ ܩܒܪܗ ܘܠܥܬܝܪܐ ܒܡܘܬܗ is a close rendering: incidentally, this is perhaps a good passage to support the perception of the Peshitta as a translation worked out in very small sections, word by word or phrase by phrase, rather than in larger portions. The Peshitta says' a wicked man gave his grave, even a rich man at his death'. The translator has ignored the Hebrew את, so making the

---

ܗܒ. They also note the possibility that the adjective is turned into a superlative by the subsequent plural.

34 Analysis of P to the 135 Ktib/Qre differences in Jeremiah has shown that it is often impossible to be sure whether or not the translator of that book was influenced by a reading tradition; see Greenberg, *Peshitta to Jeremiah*, 209–17.

35 For instance, ואת עשיר במתיו, where Dahood 'Isaiah 53:8–12', 568 proposes a re-division of the words to עשי ריב 'makers of strife'.

36 Whitley, 'Deutero-Isaiah', 459–60.

37 Goldingay and Payne, *Isaiah 40–55*.

wicked man and the rich man the subjects, but that is all that he has done. Bundy[38] says that the Peshitta version of this verse presented a 'peculiar problematic for those Syrian exegetes who sought to make the Old Testament a Christian book and to that end would use that rendition of the text as a basis for a christological interpretation', and shows how the Syrian commentators were forced by this passage to choose; they could emend the text, they could apply the 'inversion of passages' technique, or they could even invoke scribal error, but they could not base a Christian understanding on the Peshitta text. LXX καὶ δώσω τοὺς πονηροὺς ἀντὶ τῆς ταφῆς αὐτοῦ καὶ τοὺς πλουσίους ἀντὶ τοῦ θανάτου αὐτοῦ is sufficiently different from MT to be unhelpful in this discussion, as is Tg וימסר ית רשיעיא לגיהנם וית עתירי נכסיא דאנסו במותא דאבדנא.

There is a striking contrast between the translator's approach to Isa. 53:9 and the work of the scribes at Isa. 53:2. Here the MT ולא מראה ונחמדהו says of the Servant: 'he had ... no beauty that we should desire him'. In the translation as ܗܠܝܢ ܕܠܐ ܗܘܐ ܠܗ ܚܙܘܐ ܘܠܐ ܗܘܐ܂ we have instead '... and we deceived him'.[39] At first sight, this is a clear anti-Jewish emendation, represented neither in the LXX καὶ οὐκ εἶχεν εἶδος οὐδὲ κάλλος nor in Tg לא חיזו חולא חזויה ולא אימתיה אימת הדיוט ויהי זיו קודשא זיויה דכל דיחזיניה יסתכל ביה. Weitzman has shown, however,[40] that it can readily be explained as a simple scribal error, from ܢܪܓܝܘܗܝ, '(that) we desire him' to ܘܢܛܥܝܘܗܝ, 'we deceived him', and as Dr Gelston has pointed out,[41] 'we deceived him' means little in this context, so this would be an unlikely deliberate emendation. Weitzman's explanation is convincing, but even though the emendation was not introduced deliberately, it may have been deliberately allowed to stand in all later extant MSS, giving a clear anti-Jewish sentiment though in a phrase of such doubtful sense that any careful scribe would have noticed it.

Different scribes took different roles, and modern authorities also interpret their work differently. Koster,[42] who describes so delightfully the development of the text of the Peshitta from egg, hatched by the devoted use of its believers and transcribers into a nice young chicken and then becoming a well-feathered hen, holds that the

---

38 D.D. Bundy, 'The Peshitta of Isaiah and the Syrian Commentators', *Oriens Christianus* 66–7 (1982–3), 32–45 (32).

39 Van der Kooij, *Die Alten Textzeugen,* 277. There are variants in this verse, but none relevant to this particular point.

40 Weitzman, *The Syriac Version*, 243.

41 Gelston, personal communication, 2003.

42 M.D. Koster 'Which Came First, The Chicken or the Egg?' in P.B. Dirksen and M.J. Mulder (eds), *The Peshitta: Its Early Text and History* (MPIL 4, Leiden 1988), 99–126 (126).

basic pattern of the development of the text of the Peshitta, gradually diverging from its Hebrew original, results from an accumulation of haphazard scribal errors.[43] Indeed, there is no lack of evidence of a fairly low level of copyist precision, cited for instance for Genesis and Exodus by Jansma and Koster describing 18b1 and 17a3,[44] by Gelston in his monograph on the Twelve Prophets,[45] by Weitzman on the Psalter,[46] and by Morrison on 1 Samuel.[47]

There is however also evidence that scribes sometimes took considerable responsibility and deliberately introduced emendations, for instance those changes that satisfy the drive for inner logic or Syriac idiom.[48] Gelston's description of the work of Risius, who compared readings in his exemplars and made a judgment in each case[49] as to which to put in the text and which to relegate to the margins shows scribal work in an active development of the text. Lane gives examples of variants that show the importance of study of the history and geography of the MSS: although as he comments the variants themselves may be insignificant, nonetheless analysis shows the scribes exercising responsibility in the selection.[50] Kutscher[51] describes the forces at work on a scribe working on a text written several centuries previously, resulting in his emending the text sometimes consciously, sometimes unconsciously, to bring it into closer accord with the language as he knew it.

The choice of lexical equivalents also suggests that scribes sometimes used their initiative; for instance, in Jer. 20:5 העיר is rendered in 9a1 *fam* with ܪܒܘܬܐ, but in 7a1 with ܩܪܝܬܐ.[52] In Jeremiah, ܩܪܝܬܐ is the preferred term, used to translate עיר in all but two passages other than 20:5, so it seems probable that the original choice of

---

43 *Idem.* 'Translation or Transmission? That is the Question: The Use of the Leiden Old Testament Peshitta Edition' in M. Augustin and H.M. Neimann (eds), *Basel und Bibel: Collected Communications to the 17th Congress of the IOSOT* (Beiträge zur Erforschung des Alten Testaments und des antiken Judentums 51, Bern, forthcoming).

44 The Peshitta Institute Leiden, *The Old Testament in Syriac*, Part I, fascicle I, e.g. 20, 23, T. Jansma and M.D. Koster (eds) (Leiden 1977).

45 Gelston, *The Twelve Prophets*, 22.

46 Weitzman 'The Peshitta Psalter and its Hebrew *Vorlage*', in *From Judaism to Christianity*, 114–29 (119).

47 Morrison, *Samuel*, 82–5; 88–90.

48 Weitzman, *The Syriac Version* 280.

49 Gelston, *The Twelve Prophets*, 28–34.

50 D.J. Lane, 'Lilies that Fester: The Peshitta Text of Qoheleth' *Vetus Testamentum* 29 (1979), 481–90 (487–9).

51 E.Y. Kutscher, *The Language and Linguistic Background of the Isaiah Scroll (1QIsaᵃ)*, (Leiden 1974), 17.

52 Greenberg, *Jeremiah*, 131, 131 nn. 17 and 18.

ܡܕܝܢܬܐ was deliberate, and was later deliberately overridden. P-Isaiah[53] yields other instances of the use of different Syriac roots in different MSS as equivalents. For example, in 49:1 the MT √שמע is rendered with ܨܘܬܝ in 7a1 but with the cognate in a number of later MSS, and in 52:12 √הלך with √ܐܙܠ in 9a1 but with √ܗܠܟ in 7a1. Accepting that there was only one *Urtext*,[54] it seems that different scribes chose different Syriac synonyms or near synonyms.

Weitzman, considering the possibility that copyists of the Peshitta were influenced by LXX, gives an example in Ps. 2:12, where only part of the Peshitta MS tradition agrees with LXX;[55] he cites a further example at P-Qoh. 12:5 where for each phrase the P MSS offer two renderings, one reflecting the Hebrew and one the LXX, but the MSS differ among themselves. There is also evidence of scribal revision in the Peshitta to the parallel passages of 2 Sam. 22 and Psalm 18: here it seems that later scribes made emendations to one passage or the other aimed at bringing the two texts into even closer agreement with one another.[56] Weitzman instances less conclusive evidence after the Hebrew, citing 1 Chr. 26:13–27, 34; Judg. 20:20–1.[57] There is also evidence of scribal revision in the Peshitta to the parallel passages of 2 Samuel 22 and Psalm 18; here it seems that later scribes made emendations to one passage or the other aimed at bringing the two texts into even closer agreement with one another.

So there is a considerable body of evidence suggesting at the least that some scribes, sometimes, used initiative in their work, taking responsibility for a choice of one word rather than another. Scribes who were capable of such work would also have been capable of noticing, and would presumably have wanted to notice, a word which seemed not to fit the context; they could perhaps have seen that a word in an exemplar could have arisen by corruption of another Syriac word which would have better fitted the context.

There are of course many errors by translator or by scribe where, despite the mistake, the Syriac as it stands makes acceptable sense; these are normally only detectable by a reader who has access to a Hebrew text or has very detailed

---

53 See The Peshitta Institute Leiden, *The Old Testament in Syriac*, Part III, fascicle I, S.P. Brock (ed.) (Leiden 1993).

54 Weitzman, *The Syriac Version*, 263; 308–9.

55 *Idem.*, 84–6.

56 Greenberg, '2 Samuel 22 and Psalm 18', 19–21.

57 Weitzman, *The Syriac Version*, 278–9.

knowledge of the Hebrew text, and in such cases there is no reason why a scribe could be expected to correct the error. At 53:2, however, the sense of the Syriac seems sufficiently unclear for a careful reader to notice the problem and to wonder how it arose; yet no extant MS gives evidence that any scribe was sufficiently dissatified with his exemplar to introduce an emendation here. A comprehensive study of passages at which the sense of the Peshitta is imperfect as a result of error by translator or by scribe is in progress, and may permit a grouping of scribes according to whether or not they remedied such readings; at Isa. 53:2, perhaps, the scribes were all content with the clear anti-Jewish sentiment.

In summary, then, the passages discussed above present an inconsistent picture. In eight, the difference between the MT and P is compatible with input by a Christian translator. Added to the other examples instanced earlier by, for instance, van der Kooij, it is possible to argue that the weight of the cumulative evidence is conclusive. This translator read the Old Testament as the fore-runner of the New and he interpreted accordingly, taking many opportunities to insert a Christian nuance into the text before him.

However, in one of the passages discussed above the Syriac text may be less anti-Jewish than the Hebrew; and in one a text which is readily patient of Christianizing has not been so treated by the Syriac translator. This inconsistency makes it less likely that the differences between the Hebrew and the Peshitta that have been discussed here were deliberately introduced, in pursuit of an agenda; and one other point, a clear pervading theme, argues against such a deliberate change: the translator has scrupulously avoided strident anti-Jewish emendations. His approach contrasts markedly with that of certain of the church fathers, who were plainly antagonistic,[58] and possibly with some later scribes, as suggested above. Perhaps his atitude reflects the peaceable multicultural society of the mid-second century CE in Edessa,[59] before

---

58 For instance, even Aphrahat, J. Parisot (ed.) *Aphraatis Sapientis Persae Demonstrationes*, Patrologia Syriaca (Paris 1894–1907) Demonstration 19, *Against the Jews*, col. 864, cites Isa. 2:3 כי מציון תצא תורה ודבר יהוה מירושלם, but uses a verb in the perfect: ܬܠܗ ܗܝ ... ܣܘܡܟ ... ܝܦܢ ܠܐ ܡܢ ܣܗܕܘܬܐ ܦܐܦ ܐܬܐܠܟܐܬ ܡܗܐ ܕܬܗܝ ܠܐ (Syriac). ܟ ... ܐܬܐܝܟ ... ܠܐܘܟܪ ܗܡ ܠܐܘܟܠܐ ... ܣܘܡܟ ... ܟܝ ܐܣܬܝܙܡ ܗܡ ... ܦܐܦ ܐܬܗܝ ... ܐܘܪ The change in tense could be simple error rather than an objective decision, of course, but the insinuation implicit in the elaboration on the phrase seems to be deliberate; and elsewhere in this Demonstration Aphrahat's use of citations from the Prophets is to say the least selective. There are numerous references to Hosea up to and including 13:11, but in this Demonstration there is no mention of the closing verses of Chapter 14. From Amos, similarly, references up to and including 9:8 are given, notably 9:8b, but the later verses of this chapter are not represented.

59 See ter Haar Romeny, forthcoming, 'Judaism and Christianity'.

the anxiety that Jewish Christian might revert to Judaism became a serious force generating anti-Jewish propoganda.

It seems probable that a text of such importance as Isaiah would have been assigned to one of the most distinguished scholars of any school. If the group of colleagues working on these renderings was already Christian, such a man would have been able to make his input completely convincing; working in a group of like-minded people he would have had no need to defend every nuance. Yet no clear and consistent picture emerges; in these passages, the translator appears not show his usual care to preserve the sense of the Hebrew, yet nor does he apparently make a consistent attempt to make a Christian input. Instead we see the scattered examples that have been identified, with an overall impression of randomness.

So the evidence that the translator was a Christian is suggestive but inconclusive; yet if we take the alternative view, that the translator was a Jew, with no Christian themes present in his conscious or subconscious mind, this raises the focal question, that of the cumulative weight of the examples: if this is the work of a Jew with a wholly Jewish background, why are there so many passages where Christian interpretation *may* be perceived, at some of which, for instance the well-known phrase in Ps. 2:11–12,[60] the Peshitta is alone among the ancient versions in opting for a rendering with possible, occasionally probable, Christian overtones?

The inconsistency and restrained nature of the *possible* Christian input could however be reconciled with the presence of Christian nuances if we postulate a Christian translator whose approach to the work was scrupulously honest. He attempted to put his own convictions, and his literary and liturgical background, to the back of his mind, and to play completely fair by the *Vorlage*, but his attention sometimes wandered so that his subconscious thoughts influenced his rendering perhaps without his even being aware of the change he had introduced; and at a few passages perhaps he simply could not resist the temptation to emend the text. To suggest that the translator deliberately modified a biblical rendering to conform to a different religious tradition is a serious accusation, but the suggestion given here does not impugn the integrity of our translator. Rather, it shows him as a well-intentioned, honest, but fallible human being. The cumulative weight of the examples then

---

60   The MT נשקו בר is rendered ܢܫܩܘ ܒܪܐ (in some MSS, including 9a1). A Hebrew phrase difficult in itself is rendered using a Syriac word of similar sound, and the passage could indeed be read as a reference to Jesus. Weitzman, *idem.*, 242 points out that the possibility remains that this is a word-by-word rendering forced on the translator in this difficult passage, rather than a reflection of his conscious beliefs.

becomes significant — we have not a collection of examples where compatibility with a Christian input is arrived at only more or less at random, nor a translation made by a Christian who took such opportunities as he reasonably could to introduce his own themes, but the work of a Christian translator who tried his best to stick to his *Vorlage* but who sometimes failed and let his own beliefs and background show through.[61] Such a man could also have been responsible for the impassioned Peshitta to parts of Chronicles, notably verses included in David's prayer (1 Chron. 29:10–19), joyous in the Hebrew but desperately sad in the Peshitta. Weitzman[62] argued convincingly that the depth of the translator's own grief, his evident participation in the Jewish suffering, is shown by his rendering of parts of Chronicles at which the *Vorlage* was illegible; at these passages the impossibility of reading the Hebrew forced the translator to guess and so to reveal his own attitudes, or at the least loosened the constraint of the text and allowed him to express his own feelings. Our sensitive and scrupulous Christian writer, though, could have put himself in the place of a Jewish author, and written what he judged an exiled Jew would have felt, particularly if he harked back without bitterness to his own Jewish ancestry.

Perhaps such a translator worked at an early stage in the sequence of the work of the Peshitta School: Weitzman noted the difficulty of placing P-Isaiah in his implicational table,[63] and Gelston[64] suggests that this might result from the translation having been made early, outside the canonical order,[65] in response to the needs of the religious community, before the approach to the work had become formalized. An early date for the translation of Isaiah, at a stage when the evangelization of the community in Edessa responsible for the translation had only just begun, would fit well with this care to keep non-Jewish themes out of the work, and contrasts with the more evident mainstream orthodox Christian themes manifest in, for instance, the alterations made to the Peshitta to Ben Sira in the latter part of the fourth century about which Winter has written.[66] As an illustration of the workings of religion in a pluralistic society, this translation is praiseworthy in its careful fairness.

---

61 See de Moor and Sepmeijer, 'Joshua' 176, who describe 'the deliberate self-effacing of the ancient translator'.

62 Weitzman, *The Syriac Version*, 208–10.

63 Ibid., 178.

64 Gelston, personal communication, 1999.

65 See also R. Beckwith, *The Old Testament Canon of the New Testament Church* (London 1985), 309.

66 Winter, 'Ben Sira', *passim*; see also van Peursen who discusses P-Ben Sira against the background of the plurality of both the Jewish and Christian religions of the time.

Approaches to Sacrifice in Early Jewish Prayer

Stefan C. Reif

Introduction

In the various interpretations of Judaism that are now current, practical liturgical responses of various types are offered to the matter of the Temple rituals that were of such central significance to the Jewish people before the destruction of its cultic centre in 70 CE. Prayers for their full, ultimate restoration, together with passages recording all their details, such as are found in Orthodox siddurim, stand at one end of the spectrum, while at the other, represented by the radical Reform practice, there is a reluctance to make any reference to it at all. Not uncommonly in matters liturgical, the Conservative prayer-books opt for a compromise and find ways of making mention of the rites that were once followed in the Temple by simply reciting their details.[1] It should not, however, be supposed that all the traditionalists of the modern period have been content with the role ascribed to the sacrifices in their standard liturgies. Abraham Berliner (1851–1929), who was lecturer and librarian at the Orthodox Rabbinical Seminary in Berlin, founded by Azriel Hildesheimer, was a major supporter of the Adass Jisroel secessionist congregation and had little truck with the Reform movement.[2] Nevertheless, in his scholarly notes on the prayer-book, he railed against those who rattled off the details of the sacrifices in a ritualistic fashion without knowledge of their origins and content.[3]

Where there does, however, appear to be some degree of unanimity among Jewish religious groups of various hues is in the interpretation of the historical relationship between Temple ritual and synagogue liturgy. In this matter, one encounters the well-established and oft-repeated notion that sacrifice was replaced by prayer, and the notion is by no means the exclusive mantra of either the more traditional or the more

---

1   A summary of the overall attitudes to this and similar liturgical customs on the parts of various current interpretations of Judaism, together with details of the relevant prayer-books, are to be found in my volume *Judaism and Hebrew Prayer* (Cambridge 1993), 294–331.

2   I. Wolfsberg, 'Professor Abraham Berliner' in S. Federbusch (ed), *Ḥokhmat Yisra'el Be-Ma'arav Eyropa* (Hebrew; Jerusalem 1958), 101–8.

3   A. Berliner, *Randbemerkungen zum täglichen Gebetbuche (Siddur)* (Berlin 1909), 17.

progressive movements. For the leader of separatist German orthodoxy in the nineteenth century, Samson Raphael Hirsch, the 'present Divine service' is 'only a faint echo of that originally ordained by God in the Sanctuary in Jerusalem' but by that very definition is nevertheless its replacement.[4] The subject of animal sacrifices was of such central liturgical concern to the late Chief Rabbi of the United Hebrew Congregations of the Commonwealth, Lord Jakobovits, that he included an essay on the topic in his edition of the Orthodox prayer-book.[5] As well as arguing for their theological significance and value, and contending that they 'are absolutely central to the very structures of our principal daily prayers', he states categorically that 'prayer...replaced them'.[6] The same idea, though originating and occurring in a different ideology, is given expression in the non-Orthodox camps through their conviction that the synagogue service has replaced the Temple ritual. In the words of Benjamin Szold of Baltimore, 'Therefore we do not unduly lament over the Temple that is destroyed … We mourn not despairingly over the downfall of Jerusalem … Thou hast given us another home in place of that which we lost in the land of our fathers.'[7]

Whatever the theological views of the liturgical practitioners, the question facing the historian of ideas relating to Jewish worship is whether the substitution of the sacrificial system with the recitation of prayers was always seen by the rabbis as a simple and uncontroversial matter. This brief study will attempt to describe and assess the relevant responses on the part of major talmudic and post-talmudic sources during the first millennium of rabbinic Judaism. The material discussed will range from the

---

4   *The Hirsch Siddur: The Order of Prayers for the Whole Year* (E.T.; Jerusalem 1969), 41.

5   On his life and work, see Chaim Bermant, *Lord Jakobovits: the Authorised Biography of the Chief Rabbi* (London 1990) and M. Persoff, *Immanuel Jakobovits: A Prophet in Israel* (London 2002).

6   'Animal Sacrifices in Judaism: Probings into a Psycho-religious Drama' in *The Authorised Daily Prayer Book of the United Hebrew Congregations of the Commonwealth. Based on the original translation of the Rev. S. Singer. Published for the Centenary of the first edition. With a new translation and Introduction to Sections of the prayers under the editorial direction of the Chief Rabbi Lord (Immanuel) Jakobovits* (London 1990), 897–902.

7   *'Avodah Yisra'el: Israelitish Prayer-book for all the Public Services of the Year*, originally arranged by B. Szold, second edition revised by M. Jastrow and H. Hochheimer (Philadelphia 1873), 589. The original German edition was *Israelitisches Gebetbuch für dem öffentlichen Gottessdienst im ganzen Jahre* (Baltimore 1873) and read more stridently: 'Wir klagen nicht, o Gott, um den gefallenen Tempel...Wir klagen nicht über den Sturz Jerusalems, deiner heiligen Stadt...[du] hast uns hier auf dem Boden einer neuen Heimath das Vaterland wiedergegeben, das wir im Lande der Väter für immer verloren hatten.' Part of the passage by Szold is cited by Leon A. Jick, 'The Reform Synagogue' in Jack Wertheimer (ed.), *The American Synagogue: A Sanctuary Transformed* (Cambridge 1987), 90, but without accurate details of the two editions or their interesting variations.

halakhic to the liturgical, the poetic, the mystical and the pietistic, in order to reach a broad understanding of how the topic of the apparently defunct sacrificial system was handled by each generation of rabbinic Jews.

Talmudic-Midrashic Sources

It should be stated at the outset that the documentary evidence for the notion that the Temple rituals were replaced by rabbinic prayer is not found in the Mishnah itself but in the Tosefta and the Talmudim, at times cited within traditions that are identified as tannaitic by amoraim of the third and fourth centuries. When a source is sought for the timing of the *'amidah* prayers of morning and afternoon, it is the daily offering in the Temple that is cited as the precedent. The performance of divine worship that has lost its location on the Temple Mount finds an alternative place in the Jewish heart at prayer. The biblical and Second Temple notion of עבודה ('service') is re-interpreted as עבודה שבלב ('service of the heart') and cultic acts have thus become metamorphosised into spiritualised liturgy.[8]

But a number of other passages indicate that such a view was by no means unanimous. It is alternatively suggested that the daily *'amidot* owes its origin to the biblical patriarchs, Abraham, Isaac and Jacob and verses are imaginatively interpreted to support the idea that each of them instituted one of the three daily *'amidah*. It is also proposed that the inspiration comes from the changing phases of the day. Is it not natural for people to thank God in the morning for having survived the night, to entreat Him at noon to see out safely the remainder of the day, and to express the wish at night that the light of dawn should once more be witnessed?[9] It is perhaps the more ascetically minded of the talmudic teachers who opt for the view that the liturgical act of fasting, leading as it does to a physical contraction of the body fats and fluids, is the equivalent of the burning up on the altar of the corresponding animal products, or the even more radical concept that rabbinically formulated prayer is in fact superior to the sacrificial system once practised in the Temple. On the opposite, conservative side, some rabbis held tenaciously to the view that nothing could ever win divine

---

8   Tosefta, Berakhot 3.1 (Zuckermandel ed., p. 5); PT, Berakhot 4.1 (7a); BT, Berakhot 26b. See also Jubilees 22:6–9.

9   BT, Berakhot 26b; PT, Berakhot 4.1 (7a).

favour more successfully than that system and they promoted the custom of attaching to the mention of the Temple a prayer that it should be speedily restored.[10]

Those seeking a successor that could function no less centrally in rabbinic theology than the Temple had done in the earlier religious infrastructure of the Jews were not restricted to the field of prayer. One of the dominant views is that the study of Torah, especially at night, is the equivalent of every form of sacrifice and incense offered in the Temple and some teachers take this further and argue that it totally removes the requirement for such offerings, that it develops a close relationship between the Torah student and God, and that God actually prefers study to the cult. There is indeed a piece of exegesis relating to 1 Sam. 2:3 and Exod. 15:16 that appears to argue that a reasonable degree of intellectual development is tantamount to the rebuilding of the Temple because in the first of these texts the word דעות ('knowledge') occurs between two divine epithets while in the latter the word מקדש ('sanctuary') does the same.[11]

The talmudic sources indicate that there was some confusion as to whether ritual acts once performed in the temple were continued, either in their totality or to only a limited degree, in the synagogue, or whether they had become effectively obsolete until its future restoration. One interesting view, based on an interpretation of Ps. 118:27, is not only that the species of plants used on the feast of Sukkot can still be brought together ritually by a Jewish individual but that such a person has performed an act that is equivalent to building an altar and offering a sacrifice. Similarly, while the verse in Deut. 27:7 makes a close association between the offering of sacrifices, with its attendant consumption of meat, and the joy of the festivals, there is another verse that advises the Jew how to achieve such a level of joy without the Temple. The advice is based on Ps. 104:15 and promotes the idea that the drinking of wine can bring about happiness on a festival even in the absence of sacrifices. In some talmudic circles the equivalent religious value of the cult was located among various examples of ethical behaviour rather than within any liturgical activity. Humility was regarded as of the same value as offering the whole gamut of sacrifices while charitable deeds were seen as having the same power to effect atonement for Israel's sins as the Temple had once had. Kindness to impoverished scholars was particularly lauded, the

---

10 BT, Berakhot 17a and 32b; Avot de-Rabbi Nathan, Recension A, chapter 4, Schechter ed., p. 20, now republished with additional annotation by M. Kister, *Avoth de-Rabbi Nathan: Solomon Schechter Edition* (New York 1997); BT, Rosh Ha-Shanah 30a.

11 BT, Menaḥot 110a; Avot de-Rabbi Nathan, Recension A, chapter 4, Schechter ed., p. 18; BT, Shabbat 30a; BT, Sanhedrin 92a.

act of granting them hospitality being equated with offering the daily sacrifice and the charity of filling their wine glasses being seen as parallel to pouring a wine libation in the temple.[12] A rather different, and somewhat more mystical view, was destined to have a major impact on the later development of various aspects of rabbinic liturgy. A statement ascribed to God in the course of a conversation with Abraham declared that the passages recording the order of the Temple sacrifices had been divinely ordained so that when God heard them being formally recited He would regard it as if the offerings themselves had been made and would forgive the sins of those who had recited them.[13]

It is not our task in the present context to evaluate the attributions of these above statements, precisely to date their origins and literary evolution, or to assess the degree to which they had an immediate halakhic application. For our purposes, the fact that such views were given expression in the early rabbinic period, and were not suppressed from within the corpora of traditions, is sufficient to indicate that a complex religious debate was taking place that is relevant to our topic. There was a serious interchange of ideas among the talmudic teachers about the future and/or the replacement of sacrifice and its relative theological importance in evolving Judaism. At first, a strong body of opinion contended that there was little or no connection or continuation. Gradually, space appears to have been found for alternative notions that gave sacrifices a continuing liturgical role but, as the following discussion will demonstrate, the transition was not a simple one.[14]

Tractate *Soferim*

One of the most important sources concerning rabbinic liturgical practice in the centuries immediately after the talmudic period is *Massekhet Soferim*. The date and provenance of this 'minor tractate' have by no means been definitively established but we may say with confidence that it reflects customs from the middle of the geonic

---

12 BT, Sukkah 48a; BT, Pesaḥim 109a; BT, Sanhedrin 43b; Avot de-Rabbi Nathan, Recension A, chapter 4, Schechter ed., p. 21; BT, Berakhot 10b; BT, Yoma 71a.

13 BT, Taʿanit 27b.

14 These various talmudic notions have been explained as intellectual, mystical and eschatological responses by J. Neusner, 'Emergent Rabbinic Judaism in a Time of Crisis: Four Responses to the Destruction of the Second Temple', *Judaism* 21 (1972), 313–27.

period and records a substantial degree of Palestinian custom.[15] It will be recalled from earlier remarks that the Talmud itself already laid emphasis on the formal recitation of texts relating to the Temple sacrifices and to the theological value of such a practice. In this connection there are a number of traditions that are documented in *Soferim* and that may therefore be regarded as important developments in the period during which it was compiled. It is laid down that during each festival the biblical verses relating to that festival and, in some instances, to the sacrifices that were originally brought in the Temple on that festival, are to be recited.[16] Another custom mentioned in the tractate is the recitation of specific psalms on particular days on the basis of the tannaitic tradition that this is what was done in the Temple and the conclusion that this is equivalent to building a new altar and making a sacrifice on it.[17]

Reference is also made in *Soferim* to the 175 sabbath readings from the Pentateuch which represented the Palestinian Jewish lectionary (according to its triennial cycle) and, in a somewhat opaque comment, they are equated with the daily burnt-offering in the Temple.[18] That daily burnt-offering is also mentioned in a ruling that requires the recitation of the *qedushah* on Ḥanukkah, New Moon and the intermediate days of Pesaḥ and Sukkot because that offering is specified in the pentateuchal legislation for sacrifices on those days.[19] While these attempts were being made to give a more active role to such cultic matters, it has to be acknowledged that the prayer that is, according to *Soferim*, to be recited on the New Moon and that makes detailed reference to the messianic age, looks forward to rejoicing, glad tidings, Torah study, Jewish independence and the traditional fixing of the New Moon in considerable detail but makes only brief allusion to the rebuilding of the Temple and none to the sacrifices.[20] What we then have in the *halakhah*-oriented guidance provided by *Soferim* is a tendency to give some increased liturgical attention to the Temple ritual but by no means any trend towards restoring it to any central place in Jewish liturgy.

---

15 M.B. Lerner, 'Massekhet Sofrim', in S. Safrai and P.J. Tomson (eds) *The Literature of the Sages. First Part: Mishna, Tosefta, Talmud, External Tractates*, (Assen/Maastricht 1987), 397–400.

16 *Massekhet Soferim*, M. Higger (ed.) (New York 1937), 17.5, 302–3 and 20.8–9 (E.T., I.W. Slotki [ed.], London: Soncino, 1965, 17.11, 296–98 and 20.10–12, 315–16).

17 *Soferim*, Higger (ed.), 18.2, 310–13; Slotki (ed.), 18.1, 299–300.

18 *Soferim*, Higger (ed.), 16.8, 291–2; Slotki (ed.), 16.10, 292.

19 *Soferim*, Higger (ed.), 20.5, 345; Slotki (ed.), 20.7, 313.

20 *Soferim*, Higger (ed.), 19.7, 331–3; Slotki (ed.), 19.9, 307.

Poetic Yom Kippur Ritual

For their part, however, those who were more intensely involved in the development and expansion of Jewish liturgical poetry saw the synagogal references to ceremonials (*'Avodah*) that had been conducted by the High Priest on Yom Kippur in Temple times as fertile ground for cultivating a much richer crop of cultic allusions and for promoting a more staple diet of emotive responses to its loss. Such references had gradually been included in the liturgy in talmudic times but had limited themselves to the unadorned reports originating in the Pentateuch and the Mishnah.[21] The liturgical poets embellished these reports to a considerable extent, as has been succinctly summarised by Ezra Fleischer in his classic introduction to the Hebrew liturgical poetry of the medieval period (in my own translation):

> The details of the Yom Kippur ritual in the Temple follow the traditional pre-classical piyyutic style and are presented in a realistic manner, being treated in a restrained and accurate fashion. The liturgical poems that accompany them, on the other hand, are more emotive and give intense and enthusiastic expression to the feelings that the traditional liturgical poetry attaches to the detailed ceremonial. Here the poets use colourful and exaggerated figures to describe the glorious and beautiful appearance of the High Priest when he performed the ritual, the outstanding joy of the generations who viewed it, and the miserable state of those who did not live at that time but only after the destruction of the Temple.[22]

It may even be the case, as has been argued by Joseph Yahalom, that some of the ideas and descriptions relating to the sacrificial cult and used in these poems have their origins in earlier Jewish traditions that were once valued and transmitted by groups of priests. When the latter's role diminished in significance in the talmudic age, their traditions were relegated to a lower level of use and importance but the situation was reversed during the post-talmudic period. At that stage, the liturgical poets took central stage and, with so many of them belonging to the priesthood, were

---

21 I. Elbogen, *Der jüdische Gottesdienst in seiner geschichtlichen Entwicklung* (Frankfurt-am-Main 1931; reprint, Hildesheim 1962), 217; Hebrew edition, התפילה בישראל בהתפתחותה ההיסטורית, J. Heinemann et al. (eds) (Tel Aviv 1972), 162; English edition, *Jewish Liturgy: A Comprehensive History*, trans. and ed. Raymond P. Scheindlin (Philadelphia 1993), 174.

22 E. Fleischer, *Hebrew Liturgical Poetry in the Middle Ages* (Hebrew; Jerusalem 1975), 175.

able to re-instate the Temple traditions, including detailed accounts of the sacrifices, to an honoured position in Jewish liturgy.[23]

A closer examination of the ideas of these poets will permit a better understanding of how they were attempting to re-absorb the notion of sacrifices into the mainstream of liturgical thought and practice. Particularly through their lyrical embellishments of the *'Avodah*, they stressed that the world's creation had been undertaken by God precisely for the sake of the cult and attempted a rehabilitation of the biblical concept of purification through Temple rituals that had gradually been replaced in rabbinic thought by the idea of individual atonement. While the talmudic rabbis had been at best equivocal about the functions of the priest after the Temple's destruction, the composers of the *piyyuṭim* concerning the *'Avodah* idealized and glorified his role. For them, he was the people's direct contact with the divine presence and able to assure their participation in the ritual drama. Unlike Christianity, they did not lay emphasis on the victim in the sacrificial act but they did make much of the actual details surrounding its offering. What was in effect happening was that the composers and reciters of this liturgy about the cult were using the synagogal setting as a backdrop against which to act out an epic drama of contact between the human and the divine through the sacrificial ritual. In this way they were offering an alternative response, at once both more traditional and more radical, to the various explanations that had been proposed by the talmudic rabbis for the loss of the religious achievements that had been experienced on the Temple Mount in Jerusalem. Perhaps even more significantly for later liturgical developments in the rabbinic prayer-book, this alternative response was characterized by the process of recitation.[24] The poets were picking up and expanding on the talmudic statement, noted earlier, that recitation of the sacrificial details would be counted by God as the equivalent of making the offerings themselves and would thereby bring the forgiveness that those rituals had once promised.[25] By adopting such a position, they were to an extent struggling to wrest back from the rabbinic scholar the religious power that had been

---

23 J. Yahalom, *Priestly Palestinian Poetry: A Narrative Liturgy for the Day of Atonement* (Hebrew; Jerusalem 1996), 56.

24 All this is very well presented and summarized by Michael Swartz, particularly in his two articles 'Ritual about Myth about Ritual', *Journal of Jewish Thought and Philosophy* 6 (1997), 135–55, and 'Sage, Priest and Poet: Typologies of Religious Leadership in the Ancient Synagogue' in Steven Fine (ed.), *Jews, Christians, and Polytheists in the Ancient Synagogue: Cultural Interaction during the Greco-Roman Period* (London 1999), 101–17.

25 See n. 13 above.

granted to him by the talmudic sources primarily because of his halakhic expertise and devotion to study.

Yeṣirah

However early it may be dated, the *Sefer Yeṣirah* was also of undoubted importance to the Hebrew literary tradition and to Jewish thought in the post-talmudic period and reflects the approaches adopted by those who were particularly attracted to mysticism, speculative thought and wisdom literature. These areas, no less than the legal and poetic traditions, exercised an influence on the content of the developing liturgy that was destined to grow in the course of the medieval centuries. What *Yeṣirah* has to say about the Temple cult is therefore of relevance to this discussion of the various understandings of its role in synagogal prayer. Here again, recitation and verbalization are of central significance but in this instance the emphasis is on the intrinsic spiritual value of the language in which they take place rather than on the matter of cultic forgiveness. The letters of the Hebrew alphabet are understood to represent the constituents of the Temple and to have taken over its cosmic function and the power once to be found in the sacrificial system is now located in the Hebrew language. It is that medium that brings together God and the Jewish people, as once did the sacrificial rituals. It is not difficult to see how such a notion would encourage and strengthen the tendency to include in the liturgy the recitation of those passages that detail the rituals once performed in the Temple. Peter Hayman's analysis of paragraph 38 of *Yeṣirah* provides a clear and helpful précis of what that work was trying to say:

> ... the author wishes to transfer from the Temple to the Hebrew language that total symbolic structure which we have found in so many earlier versions of Judaism. Instead of the three Temple courts, symbolising maybe three heavens, we have 'three matrices *Alef, Mem, Shin*'; instead of the *Menorah* and the seven cubit measurements we have 'seven double letters'; instead of the twelve gates of the outer courts we have the 'twelve simple letters'. Instead of the universe being sustained by the Temple cultus, it is now sustained by the power of the Hebrew language on the lips of God and, maybe also, on the lips of men. Once the Temple was the *yesod* (the foundation) now it is the 'twenty-two fundamental letters' (*'esrim ushtayim 'otiyot yesod*).[26]

---

26 P. Hayman, 'Some Observations on *Sefer Yeṣira*: (2) The Temple at the Centre of the Universe', *Journal of Jewish Studies* 37 (1986), 176–82. See also his article 'Was God a Magician: *Sefer Yeṣira* and Jewish Magic', *Journal of Jewish Studies* 40 (1989), 225–37.

Early *musaf* Prayer

It is true that the *musaf* prayer — essentially of course the *'amidah* — differs from the other prayers in that it has a direct precedent among the Temple sacrifices, while they are linked with such sacrifices only by means of rather convoluted exegesis. In addition, it began its life as an exclusively communal act of worship and was only later added to the liturgical obligations of the individual. Nevertheless, the earliest form of the *musaf* appears not to have differed greatly from its *shaharit* equivalent in simply making reference to the hope for a renewal of revelation, and possibly also for a universal knowledge of God, and to God's blessing of Israel through the particular festival on which it is being recited.[27] It was the liturgical innovator and promoter of the early third century, Rav, who appears to have expressed a preference for an additional reference to be inserted into the *musaf* that consisted of details of the sacrifice once made in the Temple on that festival and it was his view that came to dominate the form of the prayer in the middle ages.[28] But the process was not a simple or consistent one as is demonstrated by the evidence of early Genizah texts. One of these still records what seems to have been a simple form of the passage that precedes the concluding doxology of the central benediction:[29]

והשיאנו יי אלהינו את ברכת מועדיך לשלום כאשר אמרת ורצית כן תברכנו סלה כי בישראל עמך בחרת

ואותנו קדשת ונעשה לפניך את חובתנו תמידי יום וקרבן מוסף ב א יי מקדש ישראל ויום צום הכפורים

מוחל וסולח לעונותינו ולעונות עמך בית ישראל ברחמים בעבור שמו הגדול:

It will be noted that, in addition to the theme of God's blessing and sanctification of Israel through the observance of the festival, the final sentence before the doxological conclusion requests that the Jewish people might in the future again be able to perform their obligatory daily sacrifices as well as to make their additional (*musaf*) offering but does not yet specify the details of these sacrifices or cite the

---

27 Elbogen (see n. 21 above), German edition, 264; Hebrew edition, 198; English edition, 207.

28 PT, Berakhot 4:6 (8c): רב אמר צריך לחד' בה דבר. ושמואל אמר א"צ לחד' בה דבר. ר' זעירא בעי קומי רבי יוסי מה (8c):
לחדש בה דבר. א"ל אפי' אמר ונעש' לפניך את חובותינו תמידי יום וקרבן מוסף יצא:

29 Cambridge University Library (henceforth = CUL), T-S 8H23.8. On this fragment, see N. Wieder, 'Genizah Studies in the Babylonian Liturgy', *Tarbiz* 37 (1968), 153–4, reprinted in *The Formation of Jewish Liturgy in the East and the West* (Hebrew; Jerusalem 1998), 31–2; E. Fleischer, *Eretz-Israel Prayer and Prayer Rituals as Portrayed in the Geniza Documents* (Hebrew; Jerusalem 1988), 133, 136–7 and 140 and 'Fragments of Palestinian Prayer Collections from the Genizah' (Hebrew), *Kobez Al Yad* (N.S.) 13 (1996), 134; and S.C. Reif, 'Festive Titles in Liturgical Terminology' (Hebrew) in *Proceedings of the Ninth World Congress of Jewish Studies 1985* (Jerusalem 1986), Division C, 70.

biblical verses that record them. This text would then represent a period before which such additions were made and a context in which there was still doubt about the degree to which the sacrificial cult was again to be given central significance. That the move towards granting it such a significance in this part of the liturgy remained controversial becomes apparent from the close examination of the variant versions of this sentence, as they have been cited by Naphtali Wieder, who has convincingly argued that textual adjustments became necessary because of the new content of the *musaf* prayer:[30]

- The early Palestinian poet, Yannai, has: כי בו תישעה מיד עמוסיך תמידי יום וקרבן מוסף

- Genizah text, Westminster College, Cambridge Arabica I.12 reads: תרצה לפניך תפילת עמוסיך כתמידי יום וקרבן מוסף

- The Persian rite opts for: ותרצה לפניך תפלת בניך כתפילת עמוסיך כתמידי יום [ו]קרבן מוסף

To my mind, what is being reflected in these various versions is the argument about the place of sacrifices in rabbinic prayer. Firstly, Rav suggests that a reference to the future pilgrimage should note the restoration of the relevant sacrifices. The details of these are then expanded, making it necessary to re-justify the original sentence by linking it with prayer. Yannai reflects the views of the poets of Eretz Israel who, as has earlier been argued, were devoted to the idea of the restored sacrificial cult *per se*. According to him, the request is for God to favour the daily and *musaf* offerings being made by his chosen people, the word עמוסיך referring to the people of Israel and their resumed sacrifices, when the cult is again a real event. But according to the Westminster text, which is also represented in the remnants of Palestinian versions that survived in the Italian, French and English versions of the middle ages, God should find favour in the prayer of the chosen people just as he once did, historically, in the Temple cult. In the Persian rite (also linked with that of Eretz Israel), the simile is used again and the subject is prayer and not sacrifice. But in this case, the word עמוסים has been understood as the patriarchs and the plea is that God should find favour in the prayers of today's Jews just as he did with those offices created by the patriarchs, the equivalent of the sacrifices once offered in the Temple. This is a neat way of including both ideas about the origins of the *'amidah* that are recorded in the Talmud, at the same time as giving the central role to prayer.[31]

---

30 Wieder, *Jewish Liturgy* (see previous note), 616–18.
31 See the sources cited in nn. 8 and 9 above.

Torah as Study or as Cult

If the textual variants just cited testify to a counter-attack on the part of those who were adamant that synagogal prayer had replaced Temple ritual as the central experience of Jewish liturgy, there are also indications from the late geonic period that tensions continued in the matter of how precisely sacrifices were to be classified and incorporated within the developing rabbinic liturgy. In Natronai ben Hilai Ha-Gaon's nuclear prayer-book of the ninth century, he lays out instructions for the recitation of various passages in the introductory section of the morning prayers.[32] These include the accounts of the daily offering in the Temple recorded at the beginning of Numbers 28 and the first chapter of the mishnaic tractate *Zevaḥim*, beginning *ezehu meqoman*. Lest it be thought that this is in some sense an idealization of the sacrificial ritual, he makes it clear that at least part of the justification lies elsewhere. He cites the talmudic passage[33] that includes a number of views about the kind of passage before which one is to recite the benediction for Torah study and concludes that the reading of these two cultic instructions is mandated in order to fulfil the all-inclusive view that selections from the Pentateuch and the Mishnah are to be among those that are to be studied for this purpose.[34] For Natronai's successor as the head of the Sura academy, Saʿadya ben Joseph Ha-Gaon, the emphasis is undoubtedly on Torah study through pentateuchal and mishnaic passages, as 'a tradition', but not on the sacrificial ritual as such.[35]

For their part, the Genizah fragments, mostly dating from the late geonic period, testify to a continuing fluidity about the degree to which passages dealing with the sacrificial system are to be given liturgical importance. One set of fragments appears to prefer the priestly benediction, either Num. 6:22–6 or 6:24–6, immediately after the three Torah benedictions[36] and before the mishnaic passage from *Pe'ah* 1:1 recording those kindly deeds that are without legal stipulation as to amounts, and those that bring reward in the after-life as well as in this world.[37] Another set includes both the

---

32 L. Ginzberg, *Geonica* 2 (New York 1909), 109–10 and 114–17.

33 BT Berakhot 11b.

34 Natronai also includes R. Ishmael's *baraita* at the beginning of *Sifra* among the passages to be recited since that is a midrashic text and he has therefore met all the possible obligations listed among the views expressed in the talmudic passage.

35 *Siddur R. Saadya Gaon*, I. Davidson, S. Assaf and B.I. Joel (eds) (Jerusalem1941; second edition, 1963), 358; Wieder, *Jewish Liturgy* (see n. 29 above), 562.

36 See n. 33 above.

37 E.g. CUL, T-S NS 157.15, NS 160.27 and NS 230.90; T-S AS 105.151 and AS 120.95

priestly benediction and the daily offering, usually Num. 28:1–8, but usually with the latter being recited first.[38] There are also those that have the passage about the daily offering immediately after the Torah benedictions but break off at that point, leaving us in the dark as to whether the priestly benediction may immediately have followed.[39] At this juncture in the prayers, it is unusual among the fragments to find the fifth chapter of *Zevaḥim* or R. Ishmael's *baraita*.[40]

On the other hand, another Cambridge Genizah fragment places the matter of the restoration of the Temple cult squarely among those items for which special supplication is made immediately after the recitation of the morning benedictions and which obviously therefore loomed large in the writer's theological wish-list. In an unusual combination of entreaties and benedictions, the text includes a wish for Torah knowledge and adherence to the divine will, a benediction of thanks for the creation of mankind in God's image, and a request for the avoidance of dishonesty.[41] It then continues with a prayer for the rebuilding of Jerusalem and the restoration of the Temple that actually concludes with the benediction used in this connection in the daily *'amidah*, the *haftarah*, wedding benedictions and the grace after meals.[42] The text reads:

כן יהי רצון ורחמים מלפניך י"י אלהינו ואלהי אבותינו שתבנה [עי]רך בימינו ותכונן היכלך בחיינו ותשמחינו בבנין עירך ותעורר ישיני עמך ותחיש קץ הפלאות ותחדש ימינו כקדם ותנחמינו מהרה בבנין בית מקדשך כאשר אמרת והבטחת ברוך אתה י"י בונה ברחמיו את ירושלים:

Later Medieval Developments

If one examines the later medieval rites, and indeed some of their modern counterparts, one encounters two groups of readings, each of which appears to be offering the worshipper the opportunity of reciting biblical and rabbinic texts, including those centred on the sacrificial cult. They are separated by longer or shorter

---

38 E.g. CUL, T-S NS 154.80 and NS 158.2.

39 E.g. CUL, T-S 8H9.15, NS 121.7 and AS 103.63; on the first of these, see Wieder, *Jewish Liturgy* (see n. 29 above), 204.

40 But see CUL, T-S NS 123.11 and NS 123.12.

41 CUL, Add.3160.1; see J. Mann, 'Genizah Fragments of the Palestinian Order of Service', *Hebrew Union College Annual* 2 (1925), 269–338, which requires some minor corrections, as incorporated in the text here transcribed.

42 For sources and discussion of this Jerusalem benediction, see my article, 'Some Notions of Restoration in Early Rabbinic Prayer' in J.M. Scott (ed.) *Restoration: Old Testament, Jewish, and Christian Perspectives*, (Leiden 2001), 293–4.

sets of other material and this separation may have permitted the inclusion of both groups in spite of their similar liturgical aim of meeting the requirement to study a broad selection of Torah. Elbogen identifies the first as consisting of the priestly benediction, the daily offering and the mishnaic passage from the tractate *Pe'ah*, as already detailed above, and the second as the daily offering, the fifth chapter of *Zevaḥim* and R. Ishmael's *baraita*.[43] He offers the tentative suggestion that the former group may have been Palestinian in origin but the Genizah witnesses cited above and the earlier evidence from the talmudic and post-talmudic period may indicate that there was also another consideration in the gradual formulation of such passages. Perhaps there were some circles that wished to lay stress on the practical details of the Temple service, as a way of enacting a form of restoration, while others opted for passages that were less centred on the cult, as a way of encouraging the intellectual aspect of Torah study.

There are two additional pieces of research that would appear to indicate the existence of such a tension at the end of the geonic age and the beginning of the medieval period. Recent manuscript study by Fleischer and Ben-Shammai have added substantially to our knowledge of the special ceremonies, prayers and biblical verses recited by pilgrims on their visits to Jerusalem. The walls of Jerusalem were circumambulated before the Temple Mount was finally reached and specific sets of verses and prayers were recited at each of the gates of the city. Those who inspired and instituted this ritual were the 'Mourners of Zion' who were intensely moved by the references to the Temple and deeply lamented the loss of that institution. What is of particular interest is that these liturgical ceremonials, with their practical manifestations of love for the lost centre, were conducted by both Rabbanites and Karaites, perhaps another indication that the division of custom was not controlled by geographical or sectarian preference but by liturgico-theological concerns.[44]

My own close examination of those benedictions in the *'amidah* that are concerned with the restoration of lost Jewish institutions also appears to be of relevance to the present discussion. Some texts stress the rebuilt city of Jerusalem, the return of the Jews from the exile, the presence of God in Zion and the re-establishment of his rulership over Israel and, indeed, over the whole world. Others

---

43 Elbogen (see n. 21 above), German edition, 90–1; Hebrew edition, 70–1; English edition, 78–9.

44 E. Fleischer, 'Pilgrims' Prayer and the Gates of Jerusalem', in E. Fleischer, M.A. Friedman, J.A. Kraemer (eds) *Mas'at Moshe: Studies in Jewish and Islamic Culture Presented to Moshe Gil* (Hebrew; Jerusalem 1998), 298–327; H. Ben-Shammai, 'A Unique Lamentation on Jerusalem by the Karaite Author Yeshu'a ben Judah', in *Mas'at Moshe*, 93–102.

seem to be more directly concerned with the reconstructed temple of the idealized messianic age, the people's appearance at the pilgrim festivals and the related festive rites, and the details of the sacrificial cult. It should be acknowledged that the texts do not always represent one tendency or the other but often constitute a combination of various themes. At the same time, there does at times seem to be a trend in one direction or the other and such a trend may cease to be easily identifiable as the texts evolve through the ages and borrow elements from each other.[45]

Since mention has briefly been made of the practice to recite the fifth chapter of the mishnaic tractate *Zevaḥim*, a few points should be made about this custom. The earliest codifications of the practice occur in the liturgies of Natronai, Amram and Maimonides, that is to say, in Babylon of the eighth and ninth centuries and followed in Egypt in the twelfth century.[46] Since the manuscripts of the liturgical work of Amram ben Sheshna Gaon often reflect the customs of the European rites of the high middle ages rather than any purer Babylonian tradition, one should generally be cautious about dating its contents to ninth-century Sura.[47] In this case, however, the other two sources appear to indicate that the reading is an authentic one. At this early stage, as is clear from what has been previously stated, the passage may have been either an exercise in re-enacting the temple ritual or the replacement of the latter with an intellectual equivalent by way of textual study.

There is no doubt, however, that later developments were more influenced by kabbalistic notions which encouraged an increase in the liturgical importance attached to sacrificial matters and a consequent expansion of the passages detailing them. Reference was still made to the talmudic passages in *Menaḥot* and *Ta'anit* [48] but the recitation was additionally thought to be of prophylactic value against such disasters as the plague, and the mishnaic chapter was seen as special because it recorded no disagreement between the tannaitic teachers anywhere in its text.[49] The developments of the late medieval and early modern period are, however, beyond the scope of this

---

45 See the article cited in n. 42 above.

46 For Natronai, see n. 32 above; *Seder Raw Amrom Gaan [sic]* (Warsaw 1865), 2; Seder *Rav 'Amram Ha-Shalem*, A. L. Frumkin (ed.) (Jerusalem 1912), 55a (=109); *Seder R. Amram*, part 1, D. Hedegård (ed.) (Lund 1951), Hebrew text, 10, English text, 24; *Seder Rav 'Amram Ga'on*, E.D. Goldschmidt (ed.) (Jerusalem 1971), 7.

47 Wieder, *Jewish Liturgy* (see n. 29 above), 1.53 and 1.163; Reif, *Hebrew Prayer* (see n. 1 above), 185–7; and R. Brody, 'The Enigma of *Seder Rav 'Amram*' (Hebrew) in S. Elizur et al. (eds) *Knesset Ezra: Literature and Life in the Synagogue: Studies Presented to Ezra Fleischer* (Jerusalem 1994), 21–34.

48 See nn. 11 and 13 above.

49 A. Berliner, *Randbemerkungen zum täglichen Gebetbuche (Siddur)* (Berlin 1909), 28; *Bet Yosef* (commentary of R. Joseph Karo) on *Ṭur, Oraḥ Ḥayyim*, section 50.

study. Suffice it to say, in order to bring the argument full circle and to return to the remarks of Berliner which were cited at the beginning of the discussion, that Seligmann Baer is concerned to include in his commentary on the prayers an instruction to read the chapter from *Zevaḥim* with proper understanding of its content. To this end, he even attaches to it the fifteenth-century commentary of R. Obadiah of Bertinoro.[50] Again, the intellectual may be seen to be counter-attacking the mystic.

Summary

There was clearly substantial talmudic discussion about the future and/or replacement of sacrifice and its relative theological importance in rabbinic Judaism. Although there was from the outset a strong body of opinion that there was no connection or continuation, there was also a tendency to seek ways of incorporating details of sacrifices into the prayers, and not simply opting for the view that prayers had wholly replaced sacrifices. This tendency subsequently strengthened in the post-talmudic period and is evidenced in the earliest prayer-books. There was also a major move on the part of the liturgical poets to restore the cult to a central role, especially by way of poetic versions of the *'Avodah* ritual for Yom Kippur, while a belief in the mystical, even magical use of language encouraged the recitation of the relevant passages concerning the cult. The tenth century saw an enthusiastic interest on the parts of both Karaites and Rabbanites in special circumambulations of Jerusalem and in the recitation of connected prayers but, it must be admitted, without any central concern for details of the sacrificial cult. On the other hand, the textual variations in the prayers concerning Jewish restoration from about the same era reflect a tension between different notions of the future of Jerusalem. The Jewish liturgy ultimately incorporated, in conflated format, and not always in a fully logical presentation, two independent trends towards either Torah study or cultic restoration. The kabbalists of the late medieval and early modern periods, for their part, saw a prophylactic value in the recitation of passages concerning the sacrifices and this gave such texts an increased status in the regular prayers. To propose, therefore, that sacrifice was replaced by prayer is undoubtedly a gross over-simplification of a long and complicated liturgical process.[51]

---

50 Baer, *Seder 'Avodat Yisra'el* (Rödelheim 1868), 50.

51 What I have written here is therefore a more nuanced interpretation of the subject than the briefer and less precise comments I offered in *Hebrew Prayer* (see n. 1 above), 138.

The Temple as a Place of Prayer in the Pentateuchal Targumim[1]

Robert Hayward

The Mishnah, Philo's philosophical and exegetical treatises, the writings of Josephus, and a host of other Jewish documents bear witness that the Temple in Jerusalem was thought of as the place for prayer *par excellence*.[2] There were good grounds for this belief; for had not king Solomon, the builder of the First Temple, besought the Almighty to hear his and Israel's prayers directed 'towards this place' (1 Kgs 8:29–30); and had not Daniel, exiled far from the Land of Israel and in mortal danger, prayed three times a day towards Jerusalem (Dan. 6:10)? Furthermore, had not Isaiah the prophet spoken of the Temple as 'a house of prayer for all the nations' (Isa. 56:7)? Granted all this, the ancient interpreters of Scripture faced a serious difficulty regarding the Temple and prayer. It may be expressed as follows. Not once in all the priestly legislation about the Tabernacle and its service set forth in the books of Moses do we have a mention of prayer. No command is given to those taking part in the Service in any capacity to pray, pronounce blessings, or utter words of thanksgiving. The single exception to this state of affairs, the commandment that the high priest make confession of sins over the goat sent out on Yom Kippur (Lev. 16:21), does not alter the general picture.[3] It simply 'proves the rule'. Students of

---

1 The Aramaic Targumim are cited according to the following editions, with relevant abbreviations, as follows: A. Sperber, *The Bible in Aramaic. 1 The Pentateuch according to Targum Onkelos* (Leiden 1959) = TO; E.G. Clarke, W.E. Aufrecht, J.C. Hurd, and F. Spitzer, *Targum Pseudo-Jonathan of the Pentateuch: Text and Concordance* (Hoboken 1984) = PJ; A. Díez Macho, *Neophyti 1 Targum Palestinese Ms de la Biblioteca Vaticana*, vol. 1 Génesis (Madrid-Barcelona 1968) = TN; M. L. Klein, *The Fragment-Targums of the Pentateuch according to their Extant Sources*, (2 vols, Rome 1980) = FT; and M. L. Klein, *Geniza Fragments of Palestinian Targum to the Pentateuch*, (2 vols, Cincinnati 1986) = CG. Translations are mine, unless otherwise stated.

2 See m. Tam. 5:1 for the prayers uttered in the daily service along with the ten commandments, the Shemaʿ, and the Priestly Blessing; Philo, Vita Mosis 2.107; Josephus, Ag. Ap. 2.196–7; and sources cited by A.Z. Idelsohn, *Jewish Liturgy and Its Development* (New York 1972), 16–25; note also New Testament references to prayer in the Temple at Luke 18:10; Acts 3:1. On communal prayer in general in late Second Temple times and its relationship to the Temple, see now Lee I. Levine, *The Ancient Synagogue* (New York 2000), 151–9.

3 Traditionally, the verb רנן at Lev. 9:24 is understood as a reference to prayer within the Temple service: see PJ, FT Ms Paris 110 and Ms Vatican 440, and marginal gloss to TN of that verse; but the verb in

151

Scripture in antiquity, therefore, might be expected to consider whether the Pentateuch might not indirectly state, or at least imply, that the sanctuary was appropriate for prayer.

Elsewhere, I have argued that the Jews of the third century BCE who translated the Pentateuch into Greek, faced with this difficulty, found the solution to this problem in those verses speaking of the sanctuary as the place where God made His Name to dwell, which they explained as meaning the place where God's Name might be called upon, invoked in prayer.[4] The *Meturgemanim*, faced with the same difficulty, adopted a different solution. For them, the Temple is intrinsically associated with prayer because of its location. It is situated on the very spot where Jacob, the ancestor of all Jewish people, had himself prayed and had seen in a vision a ladder linking earth and heaven. The top of this ladder reached heaven; angels were going up and down; and above stood the Almighty Himself (Gen. 28:11–13). Scripture itself reports Jacob's reaction to these things in Gen. 28:17, which the Targumim were to interpret with reference to the Temple and prayer. The Hebrew reads as follows:

ויירא ויאמר מה נורא המקום הזה

אין זה כי אם בית אלהים וזה שער השמים

And he was afraid, and said: How fearful is this place!

This is none other than the house of God; and this is the gate of heaven.

Seven Aramaic versions of this verse have survived. In addition to the three complete Pentateuchal Targums of Onkelos, Neofiti, and Pseudo-Jonathan which translate the whole verse, we possess a translation of the whole verse in Fragment Targum Paris Ms. 110; renderings of parts of it in two marginal glosses to the text of Targum Neofiti; and an interpretation of the latter half of the verse in a Targum fragment from the Cairo Geniza.[5] All these Targumim agree that Jacob received his vision in the very

---

biblical Hebrew means 'give a ringing shout', and the Targumim represent a very definite interpretation of it. For two further references to prayer specifically in the Temple reported by Targumim of the Pentateuch, see TN of Lev. 19:30; 26:2, where the Hebrew verb ירא has provided the meturgeman with the springboard for the exegesis: the other extant Targumim of these verses have no references to prayer.

4   See my forthcoming article 'Understandings of the Temple Service in the Septuagint Pentateuch', in J. Day (ed.), *Temple and Temple Worship in Ancient Israel* (Oxford 2005).

5   The FT Paris Manuscript will hereafter be abbreviated as FTP. On TN's glosses, see S. Lund and J. Foster, *Variant Versions of Targumic Traditions within Codex Neofiti 1* (Missoula 1977), 85; B. Barry Levy, *Targum Neophyti 1. A Textual Study*, (3 vols; Lanham 1986), I, 1–83; and M. McNamara, *Targum Neofiti 1: Genesis* (The Aramaic Bible 1a, Edinburgh 1992), 141. The Geniza fragment belongs to Cambridge University Library MS T-S B 8.4, folio 1r, published by Klein, *Geniza*

place where the Temple would later be built; but the several texts conceive of the link between Temple and prayer in quite differing ways. Indeed, we may categorize the Targumim of this verse into distinct groupings, in the first of which mention of prayer is explicit, while in the second it is either missing or remains implicit.

Targumim with Explicit Mention of Prayer

In this category we may first consider TN, which interpreted Jacob's words as follows:

> How fearful is this place [*vacat*] ... a common [הדיוט] place, but a place prepared [or, made ready,
>
> מזומן] from before the Lord; and this gate is the gate of prayer, prepared [מזומן] up to the top [עד
>
> צית] of heaven.

In this Targum, the Hebrew phrase 'the gate of heaven' is the exegetical stimulus for reference to prayer. If heaven has a gate, then, by definition, it has an entrance through which things might go in. Second Temple writings like 1 En. 9:2 allude to the *gates* of heaven: in this text, indeed, the cries of those on earth ascend to the gates of heaven, while the four great angels Michael, Sariel, Gabriel, and Raphael look down from the sanctuary of heaven and hear them.[6] TN is heir to such ancient ideas, according to which heaven has several gates through some of which the luminaries can pass on their daily journeys.[7] This particular gate for prayer, according to TN, is 'prepared' like the earthly 'place' where Jacob slept. This expansion of the Hebrew suggests that the 'place' and the 'gate' were predestined by God from the days of creation, like the ram offered at the Aqedah as substitute for Isaac (TN Gen. 22:8) and items including the Temple and the Throne of Glory listed in b. Pes. 54a; Ned. 39b,

---

Fragments, I, [37]. This manuscript has been dated between the second half of the eighth and the middle of the eleventh centuries CE: for this, and other details, see U. Glessmer, *Einleitung in die Targume zum Pentateuch* (Texte und Studien zum Antiken Judentum 48, Tübingen 1995), 115–17.

6   See detailed discussion by G.W.E. Nickelsburg, *1 Enoch 1. A Commentary on the Book of 1 Enoch, Chapters 1–36; 81–108* (Minneapolis 2001), 202–3, 205–8.

7   See especially material in 4Q209 (= 4QAstronomical Enoch[b] ar), an Aramaic text which offers explicit reference to the gates [תרעא] in heaven, the same Aramaic form encountered in the Targumim: a good example of this, where the text is undamaged and the ms reading is clear, may be found at 4Q209 fr. 7, col. 2 lines 8, 10. On this text, see further F. García Martínez, 'Aramaic Enoch and the Books of Enoch', in his *Qumran and Apocalyptic. Studies on the Aramaic Texts from Qumran*, STDJ 9 (Leiden 1992), 97–115.

and other sources.[8] Indeed, the same verbal form מזומן we encounter in TN's version of Exod. 15:17, which speaks of God's bringing in Israel and planting her

> on the mountain of the house of Your inheritance, a place prepared [מזומן], the house of the
> Shekhina which You have ordained for Yourself, O Lord, the house of Your Sanctuary, O Lord,
> which your two hands have founded [שכללי יתיה].

The language of this verse will concern us again later. For the present, let us note that the 'place' is here firmly associated in TN's Aramaic tradition with the Divine Presence, expressed in terms of a holy place prepared in advance and *founded* by the Lord Himself.[9]

Like TN, PJ also sees the 'gate' as the point of association between prayer and the place where Jacob lay, but in a very carefully defined manner. In this Targum, Jacob announces:

> How fearful and renowned is this place! This is not an un-consecrated place, but the House of the
> Sanctuary for the Name of the Lord; and this is proper [כשר] for prayers, being directed opposite
> [מכוון כל קבל] the gate of heaven, founded [משכלל] beneath the Throne of Glory.

PJ spells out what TN had left somewhat vague: this particular place is in fact the Sanctuary. The Targum articulates this clearly, and, unlike TN, does not presume knowledge of Exod. 15:17 although, as we shall very soon see, the traditional interpretation of that verse was certainly utilized by PJ. Having established that the place is the Sanctuary, PJ asserts that it is ritually fit for prayer, and gives the reason why: it is directed opposite the gate of heaven. Here the Targum falls in line with the interpretation of Exod. 15:17 found in Mekhilta de R. Ishmael *Shirta* 10, where the Hebrew words describing the mountain of God's inheritance, מכון לשבתך (a habitation

---

8   Thus TN of Gen. 22:8 makes Abraham tell Isaac that 'from before the Lord a lamb has been prepared,
    [אזדמן]', on which see R. le Déaut, *Targum du Pentateuque 1. Genèse* (Paris 1978), 216–17. The
    notion that the Temple is a place 'prepared' or made ready by God was known already in the third
    century BCE to the LXX translators: see their version of Exod. 15:17; G. Bissoli, 'Mâkon – hetoimos. A
    proposito di esodo 15, 17', *Liber Annuus* 33 (1983), 53–6; and A. le Boulluec and P. Sandevoir, *La
    Bible d'Alexandrie 2 L'Exode* (Paris 1989), 176. On the 'seven things created before the world' listed
    in b. Pes. 54a and parallels, see J.L. Kugel, *Traditions of the Bible. A Guide to the Bible as it was at
    the Start of the Common Era* (Cambridge, MA 1998), 54–5.

9   The verb שכלל has the sense of 'found', and means also 'to finish a building that has been started': see
    B. Grossfeld, *Targum Neofiti 1. An Exegetical Commentary to Genesis* (New York 2000), 56–7, 75–6,
    who points out how rich in associations is this word, being used by PJ of Gen. 28:17 to describe the
    gate of heaven; and in one particular form in the same Targum of Gen. 22:13 to speak of Isaac's ram at
    the Aqedah; and with reference to the creation of the universe (TN of Gen. 1:1; 2:22); and of Noah's
    ark with its 'gate' (TN of Gen. 6:16).

for Your dwelling), are vocalized to give the sense as 'directed towards, corresponding to, מכוון Your dwelling'. The Hebrew term used here, and reflected no doubt in PJ's translation, adds an important dimension to understanding the Temple as a place of prayer, since the Mishnah Ber. 2:1 famously requires that a man should direct his heart in praying the *Shema'*; that is, he should pray with intense direction of mind and with full concentration, a state described elsewhere by the term *kawwanah*.[10] Since the sanctuary, according to PJ, has as it were a kind of 'in-built' *kawwanah*, it is indeed truly kosher for prayer.

Furthermore, PJ asserts that this sanctuary, directly opposite the gate of heaven, is founded beneath the Throne of Glory, a matter which again the Mekhilta *Shirta* 10 on Exod. 15:17 makes plain.[11] Only five verses earlier, at Gen. 28:12, PJ had attributed to the angels present at Bethel a desire to go down from heaven to see 'Jacob the pious one, whose likeness is fixed upon the Throne of Glory'. The presence of Jacob's likeness, engraved or depicted on God's Throne, is known from many sources (e.g. Gen. Rab. 68:3; 78:3; Num. Rab. 4:1; Lam. Rab. 2:1.2; b. Ḥull. 91b; PRE 35), and is yet another tradition whose antiquity is attested by a non-Rabbinic text, an allusion to it being recorded in the pre-second century CE text the *Ladder of Jacob*.[12] Its presence in PJ at this point, however, is surely designed to emphasize the rightness of this place of the sanctuary for prayer, since directly above it the likeness of Jacob is to be found, Jacob who himself had prayed in that very place: for like TN and FTP among the extant Targumim of Gen. 28:11, PJ had explained the statement of the Hebrew text that Jacob had 'lighted upon the place', ויפגע במקום, as a reference to prayer, following a well known Rabbinic interpretation of the verb ויפגע as referring to prayer.[13]

---

10 m. Ber. 2:1 states that a man has fulfilled his duty in reading the Shema' if he has 'directed his mind', אם כיון לבו. For fundamental Rabbinic statements on the requirement of *kawwanah* in prayer, see b. Ta'an. 2a; Sifre Deut. 41; and discussion in E.E. Urbach, *The Sages. Their Concepts and Beliefs*, translated I. Abrahams (2 vols, Jerusalem 1979), I, 396–9.

11 For the text of Mekhilta, I have used J.Z. Lauterbach, *Mekilta de-Rabbi Ishmael*, (3 vols, Philadelphia 1933), II, 78, where he translates the whole section as follows: '*The Place for Thee to Dwell In. Corresponding to Thy dwelling place.* This is one of the statements to the effect that the Throne below corresponds to and is the counterpart of the Throne in heaven'. See further Gen. Rab. 68:11, 69:7; Sifre Deut. 352; Pirqe de R. Eliezer 35 (noted below, 162); and other sources and discussion in D. Muñoz León, *Gloria de la Shekina en los Targumim del Pentateuco* (Madrid 1977), 60–1, 396.

12 See *Ladder of Jacob* 1:4, as translated by the H.G. Lunt, 'Ladder of Jacob' in J.H. Charlesworth (ed.), *The Old Testament Pseudepigrapha*, (2 vols, London 1985), II, 407. On the date of this text, see Lunt, 'Ladder', 404–5.

13 See, for example, b. Ta'an. 7b; San. 95b; Sot. 14a; jer. Ber. 4.1.7a; Gen. Rab. 68:9. Note, however, that TO and a marginal gloss of TN to Gen. 28:11 do not follow this line of interpretation, but render the Hebrew simply as 'and he happened upon, lighted upon', Aramaic וערע.

The Fragment Targum preserved in Ms. Paris 110 brings new details to our attention. According to this tradition, Jacob exclaimed:

How fearful is this place! This place is not a common [הדיוט] place, but is directed [מכוון] as/to a

house of prayer [בית צלו]; and this gate is a gate directed [מכוון] up to the top [עד ציח] of heaven.

Like PJ, this Targum stresses the fact that both place and gate are directed: they both possess *kawwanah*, as it were, and on earth are in correspondence with heavenly realities. But FTP's treatment of one particular phrase in the Hebrew original is quite striking: Jacob's reference to 'the house of God' is rendered with the words 'directed as/to a house of prayer'. For this strand of Targumic tradition, proper understanding of God's house is expressed as 'a house of prayer', a phrase rare in the Hebrew Bible, but famously included in Isaiah's prophecy (Isa. 56:7) that God's house, which is His house of prayer (Hebrew בית תפלתי), shall be called בית תפלה, 'a house of prayer', for all the nations. Through this oblique allusion to Isa. 56:7, FTP suggests that Isaiah's prophecy finds its realization in Jacob's awe-struck recognition that this place is so directed towards heaven.

Closely related to FTP are the fragmentary Targum texts represented by the Cairo Geniza fragment and the second marginal gloss of TN:

... but a place prepared [מזמן] as a house of prayer; and this is the gate which is directed [דמכוון]

up to the top of heaven. (CG)

... and this place is not a common place, but is a place prepared [מזמן] as a house of prayer; and

this is the gate which is directed [דמכוון] up to ... (Nmg second gloss).

These two Targumim have managed to include both the notions of 'direction' and 'preparedness', ascribing the first to the 'place' where Jacob slept, and the second to the 'gate' which he had perceived. Once again, the indirect influence of Isa. 56:7 is apparent, but with the distinctive nuance that the place of the 'house of prayer' had already been prepared and made ready by God in the manner of TN, while the 'gate' is directed to heaven in the manner of PJ and FTP.

For all these Targumim, Gen. 28:17 was understood as offering direct Scriptural proof that prayer may rightly be offered in the Temple, which stands revealed as an especially appropriate place for such prayer. Each separate Targum, however, has its own distinctive method of associating the Temple with prayer. For TN, the notion of the 'gate of heaven', along with the sense that the 'gate' and the place where Jacob had slept had been 'prepared' beforehand by God in the manner of the mountain of His inheritance described in TN of Exod. 15:17, is determinative. PJ also sees the importance of the 'gate of heaven', but precisely insofar as the place where Jacob slept — a place kosher for prayers because it is the sanctuary to the Name of the Lord — is 'directed' towards or has correspondence to that heavenly gate. Such a view recalls the explanation of Exod. 15:17 in the Mekhilta, with its mention of the thrones of God below and on high being in direct correspondence with each other. Earlier in commenting on Gen. 28:10, PJ had alluded to Jacob's likeness fixed upon the Throne of Glory, implying yet another reason why the Temple site should be appropriate for prayer. FTP introduced the notion of the 'house of prayer', a Scriptural expression drawn from Isa. 56:7. Here, both 'house of prayer' and 'gate' are envisaged as 'directed' towards heaven; and in all these Targumim which use the language of 'direction' or correspondence between the world below and heaven, we have to do with the business of *kawwanah*, so essential for effective prayer. The 'house of prayer' features again on the expositions of CG and TN's second marginal gloss, both of which adopt the terminology of a place prepared and of the gate directed towards heaven.

Targumim which Omit Prayer or Refer to It Obliquely

The first marginal gloss to TN of Gen. 28:17 contains no reference to prayer. It stands apart from almost all the other Targumim examined to date, and seems concerned solely to establish the correspondence of the earthly Temple with the heavenly. What is preserved of it reads as follows:

> ... this is not an unconsecrated place, but the place of the house of the Lord's Sanctuary; and this is the Temple, directed to/corresponding to the gate of the house of the Sanctuary which is in heaven.

The nearest relation to this Targum is PJ, but only in respect of the opening statement that the place is not unconsecrated (both Targumim use the word חול), but is the place of the house of the Sanctuary. Unless this fragmentary text was once part of a larger exposition which included Gen. 28:11 interpreted as a reference to prayer — a matter on which it is clearly impossible to adjudicate — it would seem that the first marginal gloss of TN had nothing to say about the Temple as a place of prayer in this setting.

We turn finally to TO, which, not unexpectedly, offers the most subtle of all the Targumic interpretations of Gen. 28:17. It also includes a remarkable translation of the Hebrew adjective נורא, 'fearful', as the Aramaic noun דחילו, meaning 'fear, worship, object of reverence', whose oddity Rashi noted in his commentary on this verse.[14] TO may be translated as follows:

> And he was afraid, and said: What an object of reverence is this place! This is not a common place, but a place in which there is good pleasure from before the Lord; and this is a gate opposite heaven.

Unlike other Targumim discussed here, TO has no direct mention of prayer; makes no use of ideas of the 'direction' or 'preparedness' of the place and gate expressed by the verbs כון and זמן; and offers unique translations, first of the adjective 'fearful', and then of the house of God, which becomes 'a place in which there is good pleasure from before the Lord'. Even so, TO's attitude to the place where Jacob slept and the gate of heaven is not so far removed from the other Targumim. Thus the fact that the adjective 'fearful' is rendered as the noun 'object of reverence' may well be intended to mark out this spot as the place of the Temple, where Jews should 'fear before the Lord'. This is also suggested by the fact that TO's translation of this particular verse would recall to the attentive hearer or reader the same meturgeman's interpretation of the phrase 'a hand upon the Lord's Throne', יד על כס יה, in Exod. 17:16 as signifying 'the feared One [דחילא]' whose Shekhina is upon the Throne of Glory'. In the preceding verse (Gen. 28:16), TO had interpreted Jacob's words in the Hebrew, 'surely the Lord is in this place', to signify 'surely the Glory of the Lord is dwelling in this place', thus indicating like TN and PJ of that same verse that the Sanctuary is in view. Then the word הדיוט, 'common', a Greek loan-word, recalls the language of TN, FTP, and the second marginal gloss of TN, all of which stress the sanctity of the spot with their notes about its having been prepared or directed towards heaven, FTP and the second marginal gloss of TN speaking of it furthermore as a 'house of prayer'.

Again, TO's mention of 'a place in which there is good pleasure [רעוא] before the Lord' recalls both the words of Isa. 56:7, where God avers that the offerings in His House of prayer shall be for good pleasure or acceptance (Hebrew לרצון, Targum Jonathan לרעוא) upon His altar; and the words of the Synagogue service with its many petitions that it be the Lord's *will* or *good pleasure*, Hebrew רצון, Aramaic רעוא for such and such a blessing or petition to be granted. In other words, the 'place' under consideration in this verse is a place where both sacrifice and prayer shall be

---

14 See M. Rosenbaum and A.M. Silbermann, *Pentateuch with Targum Onkelos, Haphtaroth and Rashi's Commentary*, (5 vols; New York 1946), I (Genesis), 133–4.

acceptable to God.[15] Finally, the Hebrew expression 'the gate of heaven' becomes in TO 'a gate opposite [קביל] heaven', recalling in some measure PJ's expression at this point that the house of prayer is directly opposite [כל קבל] the gate of heaven. Thus albeit allusively, but economically and elegantly, TO manages to encapsulate much of what the other Targumim have to say.

Final Observations and Conclusions

This brief discussion has shown that six out of the seven extant Targumim of Gen. 28:17 took this Scriptural verse as offering proof from the books of Moses that the Temple was a proper place for prayer to be offered. The failure of the priestly laws explicitly to require prayer in the Temple Service is correspondingly tempered: Jacob, the ancestor of all Jews, had prayed in that very place; and in their several ways the Targumim made use of that fact to show how prayer in the Temple might be supremely effective, because of its geographical location in respect of heaven. Most remarkably, however, not one of these same Targumim reports the tradition that Jacob ordained or instituted ערבית, Evening Prayer, proof for which is most often adduced from Gen. 28:11 and is set out in both Talmuds (b. Ber. 26b; j. Ber. 4.1.7a) and the Midrashim (Gen. Rab. 68:9; Num. Rab. 2:1; Tanhuma מקץ 9; חיי שרה 5; Mid. Teh. 55:2).

Furthermore, the majority of the midrashim which expound Gen. 28:17 make no reference in their interpretations either to prayer or to the place of prayer in the Temple. Thus Gen. Rab. 69:7 and its parallels in Tanhuma ויצא 9 and Sifre Deut. 352 took the verse to mean that the Almighty had shown to Jacob a vision of the Temple built, destroyed, and rebuilt; PR 30:3 presupposes this exegesis, and develops it by personifying a ravaged Jerusalem who despairingly asks Jacob, sent to comfort her, how she can possibly receive consolation from one who said of her אין זה, 'this one is not?' (The midrash arrives at this interpretation by 'atomizing' the Hebrew of the words אין זה כי אם בית אלהים, 'this one is not other than the house of God'.) R. Aha in Gen. Rab. 69:7 tells how the gate of heaven will be opened in the future for righteous ones like Jacob; and Mid. Teh. 81 and PR 39:2 (see also b. Pes. 88a) present God as vowing that because Jacob called the Temple a 'house' before it was built, He will

---

15 See B. Grossfeld, *The Targum Onqelos to Genesis* (The Aramaic Bible 6, Edinburgh 1988), 105 for further arguments founded on m. Maas. Sh. 5:12 and Gen. Rab. 69:7 that TO here is indeed referring to the Temple.

therefore call that house by Jacob's name, a reference to the prophecy of Isa. 2:3 with its description of the Temple as 'the house of the God of Jacob'. PRE 35, however, is an exception to all this, expounding Jacob's words in Gen. 28:17 as follows:

> From this verse you learn that everyone who prays in this place in Jerusalem is as if he prayed
> before the Throne of Glory: for the gate of heaven is there; and it is surely open to hear prayer, as
> it is said: And this is the gate of heaven.

This seeming distance between the Targumim of Gen. 28:17 and most other Rabbinic comments on the verse requires some explanation. Possibly the fact that Targum once regularly featured as part of the liturgy of the synagogue in a way that the surviving collections of midrashim did not may hold a clue: congregations needed to know precisely what rationale for regarding the Temple as a place fit for prayer might be found in the books of Moses, and the Targumim, or at least six out of seven of those extant, supplied the answer. Yet this rather practical and down-to-earth explanation is not really a sufficient account of things. For the fact is that the Patriarch Jacob had prayed on the Temple site when the Sanctuary itself was as yet unbuilt, a point evident in Scripture and assumed by tradition (see, for example, b. Ḥullin 91a); and even in those conditions the spot where he prayed was declared to be have been prepared by the Almighty, directed towards the heavenly world, and a place fit for effective prayer. Whatever date we ascribe to the several traditions out of which the Targumim are composed, in their present form they speak to a Jewish world where the Temple is no more.[16] Like the Patriarch, the Targumim, as well as Midrash Gen. Rab. 69:7 and parallels have seen the Temple built and destroyed. They have yet to see it rebuilt. Six Targumim proclaim in their differing ways that from Jacob's time onwards, the Temple site was a place for prayer, and that it remains so. That is to say: even when the Temple was destroyed, the fundamental significance of its site could not be impaired; and the hope that it may be rebuilt as a place of prayer, which is explicit in Gen. Rab. 69:7 and parallels, seems to me to be latent as a subtext in the Targumic versions of Gen. 28:17. Indeed, the differing phraseologies and nuances which the several Targumim have adopted in their expositions of Gen. 28:17 may not be unrelated to wider discussions and considerations of the Temple as a place

---

16 It will be evident from remarks throughout this essay that individual elements in the Targumic interpretations surveyed are often possessed of ancient lineage: for example, we noted the 'prepared' nature of the Temple site (LXX of Exod. 15:17); the association of the gate of heaven with prayer (1 Enoch 9:2); and the association of Jacob's likeness with the divine Throne (Ladder of Jacob 1:4). But the Targumim in their present written forms date from the time after the Temple had been destroyed; and that fact must be kept in mind in any discussion of their treatments of Gen. 28:17 in particular.

especially fit for prayer, concerns which can be observed in other Rabbinic sources examined elsewhere in this volume by Stefan Reif.[17] It is difficult to imagine how could it be otherwise for the Targumim, associated as they were with a synagogue Service regularly praying for the restoration of the Temple Service, and the divine acceptance of both sacrifices and prayer:

> Accept, O Lord our God, thy holy people Israel and their prayer; restore the service to thy most
> holy house; receive in love and favour both the fire-offerings of Israel and their prayer; and may
> the service of thy people Israel be ever acceptable unto thee.[18]

---

17 See S. Reif, 'Approaches to Sacrifice in Early Jewish Prayer' in this volume.

18 The prayer *'avodah* from the *'Amidah* of the daily synagogue Service, translated by S. Singer, *The Authorised Daily Prayer Book of the United Hebrew Congregations of the British Commonwealth of Nations* (London 5722/1962), 52. According to m. Tam. 5:1, this prayer was uttered in the Temple while it stood; for discussion, see Idelsohn, *Jewish Liturgy*, 105–6. Note that, in the form given in Singer's Prayer Book, God is petitioned to accept, Hebrew רצה, Israel's prayer, and to receive it ברצון, translated by Singer as 'in favour'. The prayer ends with the request that Israel's service 'be acceptable', Hebrew ותהי לרצון. This terminology recalls the language of TO, that the Temple site is one in which the Lord 'finds favour' or 'good pleasure'.

Jewish Liturgy and Magic Bowls[*]

Dan Levene

Introduction

Hebrew prayer shows no trace of magic and incantation, and is free from the vain repetitions in primitive and heathen cults.[1]

This comment by Joseph Herman Hertz, the chief rabbi of the United Hebrew Congregations of the British Commonwealth (1913–46), reflects an attitude that is still common; and is perhaps also suggestive of the feelings and attitudes current to those who express it. Although it is probably true to say that there is not much of the magical that is obviously detectable in the liturgy, it is, nevertheless, also true to say that there is plenty of evidence to suggest that a relationship existed between the two. A denial of such a connection – the wish to disassociate Judaism from the taint of magic – is, however, not surprising, as attested by the sentiments expressed in the statements of influential scholars such as Elbogen:

Likewise, there is no overlooking the fact that Babylonia is the source of every superstition in the world. Some of the amoraim were affected by these errors of their native land, and were subject to fear of demons, nightmares, and witchcraft. The text of the prayers was only rarely affected by these, and remained simple and natural; but the synagogue service was not infrequently touched by

---

[*] Unless stated translations of primary sources are those provided in their respective original publications. Translations of the Babylonian Talmud are, unless stated otherwise, from the Soncino Talmud (*The Babylonian Talmud*, I. Epstein (ed), (London 1935–52)). Translations of the Bible are, unless otherwise stated, from the JPS (*Tanakh, A New Translation of the Holy Scriptures According to the Traditional Hebrew Text* (Philadelphia, New York, London 1985).
    Signs used in the transliteration of the texts: ( ) – uncertain readings; [ ] – restoration of lost writing; < > - omitted by the scribe by mistake; ⌈ ⌉ – only part of the letter is visible; { } – superfluous writing in the text; ^ ^ – written above the line; ↓↓ – written below the line.

1   J.H. Hertz, *The Authorised Daily Prayer Book of the United Hebrew Congregations of the British Empire* (London 1955), xi.

them. Especially in later centuries, when every word in the Talmud was seen as binding, and when people lived in fear of witches and demons, these errors led to sorry consequences.[2]

Others, however, considered these issues in a somewhat different light, as can be seen in a comment made by Trachtenberg who portrays the connections between prayer and magic in a more specific historical context:

> Along with the elaboration of angelology went its practical corollary, the utilization of angels in magic. The Talmud, though speaking often of angelic apparitions, knew nothing of the conjuration of angels as distinguished from the conjuration of demons. At most, there appears to have existed in the Talmudic period the practice of calling upon, or praying to the angels, as intermediaries before God, to intercede in a crisis. Even Geonic mysticism was reserved on this point, but evidently during the later period, which saw so marked a development of angelology, the Talmudic prayer had been transformed into a magical invocation, as the *Aramaic Incantation Texts*, published by Montgomery, and such a work as the *Sword of Moses*, edited by Gaster, indicate.[3]

It is, of course, important to note that the relation between magic and Jewish liturgy has to be considered from a variety of perspectives. There are the elements of magic that are detectable in the liturgy, there are the elements of liturgy that are detectable in magical texts, and, furthermore, there are hymns and prayers that are not part of the liturgy as we know it, but are forms of 'prayer' that occur in the mystical Hekhalot and Merkabah literature.

Indeed, it must also be noted that the relationship between magical incantation and prayer has been discussed at some length by anthropologists as part of the greater issue of magic vs. religion within the context of a wide variety of cultures. One might cite comments such as the following by Frazer:

> If magic be deduced immediately from elementary processes of reasoning, and be, in fact, an error into which the mind falls almost spontaneously, while religion rests on conceptions which the merely animal intelligence can hardly be supposed to have yet attained to, it becomes probable that magic arose before religion in the evolution of our race, and that man essayed to bend nature to his

---

2   I. Elbogen, *Jewish Liturgy, a Comprehensive History by Isamar Elbogen*, trans. Raymond P. Scheindlin. Based on the original 1913 German edition, and the 1972 edition edited by Joseph Heinemann (Philadelphia – New York – Jerusalem 1993), 212.

3   J. Trachtenberg, *Jewish Magic and Superstition* (New York 1939), 72.

wishes by the sheer force of spells and enchantments before he strove to coax and mollify a coy, capricious, or irascible deity by the soft insinuation of prayer and sacrifice.[4]

As well as later observations made by Tambiah who says that:

Rituals exploit a number of verbal forms which we loosely refer to as prayers, songs, spells, addresses, blessings and so forth. .... The fact that such a battery of verbal devices may appear in a single rite should not only give us insights into the art of ritual but also dispel any lingering traces of a Frazarian hangover. Some anthropologists have operated with the concept of 'magic' as something different from 'religion'; they have thought of 'spell' as acting mechanically and as being intrinsically associated with magic; they have opposed 'spell' with 'prayer', which was thought to connote a different kind of communication with the divine. Frazer carried this thinking to an extreme by asserting that magic was thoroughly opposed to religion, and in the interest of preserving this distinction dismissed half the globe as victims of 'confusion and magic with religion'.[5]

These contributions are but snapshots from the great intellectual journey that has been negotiated along the magic vs. religion debate. Nevertheless, what is important to point out, regardless of this debate, is that it must be realized that those who composed, produced and consumed the type of magical incantations in late antiquity that we find in magic bowls, would not have considered the issue in quite the same way as we have done over the past two centuries. In fact, it is quite clear from a number of sources that prayer and magical incantation are the products of the same cultural environment. Furthermore, there is nothing to suggest that those who used prayer and magical incantation were different groups of people. Although distinct in both form, function and context, the evidence indicates that both magical incantation and forms of prayer were not necessarily thought of as contradictory or even totally exclusive of each other.

Prayer in Early Mystical Literature

Before looking at a sample of what can be found in the bowl texts themselves in terms of connections with established forms of prayer, it is important to understand something of the principle which in itself relates these two forms of expression, and to which reference has already been made by Trachtenberg's quote above. I am,

---

4 G.F. Frazer, *The Golden Bough, a Study in Magic and Religion* (New York 1947), 55.
5 S.J. Tambiah, *Culture, Thought, and Social Action* (Cambridge 1990), 18–19.

incidentally, reminded in this context of a comment made by Rabbi Louis Jacobs in a Talmud class I attended some years ago. He said that the difference between magic and prayer was that the first was about taking while the latter was concerned with giving. Although a simplification, the implication contained in this remark is useful for there are points where both magical incantation and prayer operate on the same level.

Joseph Dan's concise description of the mechanics of magical incantation in the early Jewish mystical traditions is much the same as is found in the magic bowls:

> Underlying the Hekhalot and Merkabah Literature is the view (which is also found in the talmudic-midrashic literature), that the knowledge of secrets is power, and knowledge of secrets of the upper world grants the individual with that knowledge power, and influence over them. One who knows the names of the supreme angels and their specific tasks can utilize that knowledge in order to gain a certain mastery over them and force them, by means of magical incantation, to do his will. The incantation is generally composed of a statement which includes secret names (which are on occasion the secret names of God Himself, which the angels must obey), and secret actions - potions, mixtures or the use of other physical means, sometimes at a clearly defined time.[6]

What this means (as the diagram below schematically illustrates) is that it was believed humanity had the possibility of affecting its fate by interacting with the celestial population, namely the angels and God himself. The notion that demons and spirits also constitute a section of the supernatural inhabitants and shared this ability to affect a person's being, is attested in both the Talmudic literature and the magic bowls.[7]

Indeed, early Jewish mystical literature is useful to our debate, as within this material

God

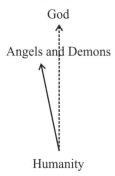

Angels and Demons

Humanity

---

6   J. Dan, *The Ancient Jewish Mysticism* (Tel-Aviv 1993), 18.

7   See, for instance, a discussion of Ashmedai the king of demons: D. Levene, 'A Happy Thought of the Magician, The Magical Get', in R. Deutsch (ed.), *Shlomo: Studies in Epigraphy, Iconography, History and Archaeology in Honor of Shlomo Moussaieff* (Tel-Aviv Jaffa 2003), 175-84.

the line between magic and religion, prayer and incantation, is often so blurred that it is, at times, difficult to distinguish.[8] In bḤul. 91b we find a clear expression of the performative function of prayer in the greater scheme of things:

ואין מלאכי השרת אומרים שירה למעלה, עד שיאמרו ישראל למטה

the ministering angels do not begin to sing praises in heaven until Israel have sung below on earth.

This is a notion that is illustrated more graphically in Hekhalot Rabbati 3:3[9] where we find a theatrical depiction of monumental proportions that depicts the three daily ministrations of the Prince of the countenance:

גאוה מופלאה ושררה משונה, גאוה של רוממה ושררה של זיהיון של מלאך הפנים, מתנהג בה שלשה פעמים בכל יום ויום בבית דין של מעלה כשהוא הולך ובא על הרקיע שעל ראשי הכרובים ושעל ראשי האופנים ושעל ראשי חיות הקדש. והכרובים והאופנים וחיות הקדש חבושים ועומדים תחת כסא הכבוד, וכיון שרואים כל מי שבמרום כשהוא הולך ובא על ערבות רקיע שעל ראשי הכרובים ושעל ראשי האופנים ושעל ראשי חיות הקדש, מרתיעין ומתבהלין ומתעלפין ונופלין לאחוריהן. כי במאה ושמונים וחמשת אלפים רבבות פרסאות אין כל בריה יכולה ליגע לאותו מקום מפני זוחלי אישות שטורדין ויוצאין מפי הכרובים, ומפי האופנים ומפי חיות הקדש, שפותחין פיהן לומר קדוש בשעה שישראל אומרים לפניו קדוש, כדבר שנאמר קק"ק ה' צבאות

...three times every day in the law courts of above when he (the Prince of the countenance) goes and comes upon the heaven that is above the heads of the cherubim and above the heads of the ofanim and above the heads of the holy hayot. And the cherubim and ofanim and holy hayot are detained and standing under the throne of glory. And as they see all who are in the height as he comes and goes upon the Aravot heaven that is above the heads of the cherubim and above the heads of the ofanim and above the heads of the holy hayot, they tremble and are afraid and they faint and fall backwards. For in the 185,000 myriads of parsangs there is no being that can approach that same place due to the rivers of fire that flow and come out from the mouths of the cherubim, and the mouths of the ofanim and the mouths of the holy hayot, who open their mouths to say 'Holy' at the time that Israel say before Him 'Holy'. As it is said 'Holy, holy, holy The Lord of Hosts' (Isaiah 6:3).

Here we see how Israel's recital of its daily order of prayer, the liturgy, has a pivotal function in the greater, cosmic, scheme of things. It is, in fact, required for it to be

---

8   As discussed in the scholarship of, for instance, R. Elior, 'Mysticism, Magic and Angelology', *JSQ* 1, (1993), 3–53 and M. Shwartz, *Scholastic Magic* (Princeton, New Jersey 1996), 18–22.

9   P. Schäfer in Zussamenarbeit mit Margarete Schlüter und H.G. von Mutius, *Synopse zur Hekhalot-Literatur* (Texte und Studien zum Antiken Judentum; 2, Tübingen 1981), 100§–101§. The translation of the text is my own.

complete; the celestial beings need Israel's prayers to fulfil their own ministrations of the Godhead. In contrast, we can cite a bowl incantation opening formulae such as:

אסותא מן שמיא ל X בת/ת Y

Salvation from heaven for X son/daughter of Y.[10]

Or:

בישמך מרי אסואתא אסיא רבא דרחמי אסירא וחיתמא ומחתמא כולה קומתיה ובית משכביה דהדין X בר Y

In Thy name, O Lord of salvations, the great saviour of love. Charmed and sealed and countersealed is the whole person and the bed chamber of X son of Y[11]

Such formulae convey the personal, almost intimate, quality of these incantations that were, in fact, produced and sold as commodities tailor-made for individual clients, each with their own specific problems and requests. The contrast between these amulet formulae and the grandiose descriptions of the cosmic function of Israel's prayers is stark. However, the portrayal of the liturgy and incantation in such contrast can be misleading; there is overlap. Consider the passage in bSan. 44b in which all the elements discussed above are presented, as it were, as part of one package:

<div dir="rtl">אמרה <u>רוח פסקונית</u> לפני הקדוש ברוך הוא רבונו של עולם אם יבואו אברהם ושרה ויעמדו לפניך אתה אומר להם ומכלים אותם (משלי כה) ריבך ריב את רעך וסוד אחר אל תגל'</div>	**The intercessory spirit** said before the Holy One, blessed be He, 'Sovereign of the Universe! If Abraham and Sarah came and stood before Thee, wouldst Thou say [this] to them and put them to shame?' Debate thy cause with thy neighbour, but reveal not the secret of another! (Prov 25:9)
<div dir="rtl">ומי אית ליה רשותא כולי האי אין דאמר רבי יוסי ברבי חנינא שלש שמות יש לו פיסקון איטמון סיגרון</div>	**But has he so much license?**— Yes, For R. Jose son of R. Hanina said: He has three names: Pisakon, Itamon, and Sigaron.
<div dir="rtl">פיסקון <u>שפוסק דברים כלפי מעלה</u> איטמון</div>	Pisakon, **because he argues against**

---

10 Montgomery's bowl numbers 11, 12, 16 and 24, to list but a few of many examples, start with this formula (J.A. Montgomery, *Aramaic Incantation Texts from Nippur* (Vol. III.: University of Pennsylvania. The Museum, Publications of the Babylonian Section, Philadelphia 1913 (Henceforth AIT)).

11 AIT 19, but similar examples are AIT 7 and 27.

שאוטם עונותיהן של ישראל סיגרון כיון
שסוגר שוב אינו פותח (איוב ל"ו)

the Most High; Itamon, because he hides the sins of Israel; Sigaron, because when he concludes a matter, none can reopen it. (Job 36:19)

היערך שועך לא בצר אמר רבי אלעזר

Hadst thou prepared thy prayer before thy trouble came? R. Eleazar said:

לעולם יקדים אדם תפלה לצרה שאילמלא (לא)
הקדים אברהם תפלה לצרה בין בית אל ובין העי
לא נשתייר משונאיהן של ישראל שריד ופליט
ריש לקיש אמר

One should always offer up prayer before misfortune comes; for had not Abraham anticipated trouble by prayer between Beth-el and Ai, there would not have remained of Israel's sinners a remnant or a survivor. Resh Lakish said: **He who devotes his strength to**

כל המאמץ עצמו בתפלה מלמטה אין לו צרים
מלמעלה

prayer below, has no enemies [to overcome] above.

This intercessory spirit of the Talmud (רוח פסקונית) is another designation of Metatron (מטטרון), the chief angel and hero of *Enoch III*, known also as AHYW PSQTYH (אהיו פסקתיה) in the *Sword of Moses*.[12] This is the angel whose notoriety is acknowledged both in the Talmud (bḤag. 15a), where we are told he was severely lashed for giving the impression that 'Perhaps, — God forefend! — there are two divinities!', as well as in the Geniza (c. eleventh century) and magic bowl materials (c. seventh century) where the division between God and Metatron could be construed as unclear.[13] Thus, even without looking at the evidence found in amuletic texts one can find sufficient reference to the nature of the connection between Jewish prayer and incantation in late antiquity.

The Liturgy

One might note, before pointing out a couple of the more obvious magical fragments that are found in the liturgy, that the synagogue, at least, was no stranger to the presence of

---

12 For the identification of AHYW PSQTYH as Metatron in the *Sword of Moses* see D. Levene, *A Corpus of Magic Bowls* (London 2003), 112–13.

13 See P. Schäfer, 'Jewish Liturgy and Magic', in H. Cancik, H. Lichtenberger and P. Schäfer (eds), *Geschichte-Tradition-Reflexion* (Tübingen 1996), 551 for the occurrence of this ambiguity of Metatron in Geniza material , *Corpus*, 111 concerning Moussaieff 155:4–6 in which it seems that Metatron is credited with the act of creation.

magical activities and their products. Indeed, a number of amulets that were found within synagogues attest, at the very least, to a physical presence.[14] The introduction to the Gaonic *Havdala de-R. Aqiva* includes a recommendation that that piece of 'magical liturgy' should be performed in 'a pure place or the synagogue' (במקום טהור או בבית כנסת).[15] Although not specifically in the synagogue, there are at least three occurrences in the *Sword of Moses* that require magical rituals to take place during particular parts of the daily liturgy.[16] In fact, the use of liturgical forms in various passages within these two texts is blatant, consisting for the most part of a variety of forms of borrowing and modification.[17] A fine example is 'the prayer to the magician' (התפילה לקוסם) in the *Sword of Moses*, concerning which Bar-Ilan suggests it is likely the author took the daily prayer he was acquainted with and combined it with magical prayer.[18] The liturgy itself is, of course, a different issue, in that it would be difficult to determine what magical elements might have been interwoven into the daily and seasonal order of prayers prior to the Gaonic period, from which our earliest editions originate. There are, nevertheless, at least two references in the liturgical corpus that can be considered as obviously associated with magical traditions. The first is the *Shema' 'al ha-mittah*. Though not an incantation, the claim that it protects against demons is well known from bBer. 5a; a passage that is noted already in the Amaram's order of prayers.[19] The

---

14 As for instance Amulets two and three from Horvat Kanaf (J. Naveh and S. Shaked, *Amulets and Magic Bowls*, (Jerusalem 1987), 44–54) and Amulet 16 from Horvat Marish (J. Naveh and S. Shaked, *Magic Spells and Formulae*, (Jerusalem 1993), 43–50).

15 G. Scholem, 'The Havdala De R. Akiva, a Source for the Jewish Tradition of Magic in the Gaonic Period הבדלה דר' עקיבא, מקור למסורת המאגיה היהודית בתקופת הגאונים', *Tarbiz* 50 (1980–1), 250. (My translation.)

16 Harari (Y. Harari, *חרבא דמשה: מהדורה חדשה ומחקר* (Jerusalem 1997), 92, n. 49) points these out as occurring in XX/22–3, XXIII/20–2 and a fragment found on p. 144 of his edition. To give an example, the last of these references states: והכן יעביד יטבול בנהרא מן רמשא ויצלי מן בא"י אלהינו וכן בצפרא וכן במנחתא כן יעביד תלתא יומין ואימת מצלי הדין צלותא בתר עושה שלום And thus he shall do: he shall bathe in the river from the evening and (then) pray from 'Blessed be art Thou YHWH our God', and so in the morning, and so in the afternoon. Thus he shall do three days and when praying this prayer after 'make peace'. (My translation.)

17 For the *Sword of Moses* see Harari, *Sword*, 92–101 and M. Bar-Ilan, *The Mysteries of Jewish Prayer and Hekhalot* (Ramat-Gan 1987), 110–12.

18 Bar-Ilan, *Mysteries*, 111.

19 E. D Goldschmidt, *סדר רב עמרם גאון* (Jerusalem 1971), 55. The relevant section in bBer. 5a is as follows: כל הקורא קריאת שמע על מטתו מזיקין בדילין הימנו שנאמר (איוב ה') ובני רשף יגביהו עוף ואין עוף אלא תורה שנאמר (משלי כ"ג) התעיף עיניך בו ואיננו If one recites the *Shema'* upon his bed the demons keep away from him. For it is said: 'And just as sparks fly upward'. The word 'fly' refers to the Torah, as it is written: 'You see it then it is gone'. This part of the liturgy also includes Zech. 3:2, that is one of the most common verses in magic bowls, and the *Hashkivenu* that is a plea for protection against a variety of

second is a much later incantation, probably eighteenth century, and not as well noted an addition to the liturgy that occurs only in Sephardic Mahzor for Shavuot after the Akdamot. Although a late addition, it is clear from its style and content that much of its origins can be traced to late antiquity (see appendix for the text of this incantation and some comments regarding early precursors).

Magic Bowls

Like the Hekhalot and Merkabah mystical literature and other magical material from the early medieval period found in the Geniza, the bowls have a number of telltale signs in the form of small expressions that betray connections with liturgy. The most obvious is the common use of the expression 'amen amen selah' (אמן אמן סלה) though, there are others like 'Blessed art Thou Lord the God of Israel (ברוך אתא יהוה אלהי ישראל)[20] and 'Blessed art Thou our Lord the King of the world' (ברוך אתה יהוה אלהינו מלך העולם)[21] whose origin is clearly liturgical. Other expressions include: 'Blessed art Thou the Lord our God, King of the universe, the great, mighty, revered, wondrous and lofty' (ברוך אתה יהוה אלוהינו מלך העולם האל הגדול הגיבור והנורא והמופלא והמ(ע)(ולא)[22] that is almost identical to the first benediction: ברוך אתה יי אלוהינו ואלהי אבותינו אלהי אברהם אלהי יצחק ואלהי יעקב האל הגדול הגבור והנורא אל עליון; and: 'The Lord reigned the Lord reigns the Lord will reign for ever and ever' (יהוה מלך יהוה מאלך יהוה ימלך לעולם ועד)[23] that is a response in the *Yehi Khevod* prayer. The two expressions just noted occur in their respective bowls, in a manner wholly characteristic of these incantations, as parts of invoked holy names.

Another similarity that the bowls have with liturgy is their extensive use of verses that seem, in many cases, to have been used on account of their prominence in liturgy,[24] suggesting the possibility that they might have been culled from the order of prayers rather than from the

---

calamities, such as enemies, pestilence, swords, famine, sorrow and the adversary the like of which are usually found in magical incantation.

20 Gordon bowls E/F:5 (C. Gordon, 'Aramaic Magic Bowls in the Istanbul and Baghdad Museums', *ArOr* 6 (1934), 331).

21 Naveh and Shaked's Bowl 12b:13 (Naveh and Shaked, *Amulets*, 193).

22 Moussaieff 102:10 (Levene, *Corpus*, 44-5).

23 Moussaieff 156:11 (Levene, *Corpus*, 115-16).

24 Naveh and Shaked, *Magic*, 22.

Bible itself. It might be noted that a survey of a sample of twenty bowls containing seventeen verses revealed that all but two were found in the weekly order of prayers.[25]

A verse that occurs in a number of places in the bowls is Deut 6:4: 'Hear O Israel! the Lord is our God, the Lord alone' (שמע ישראל יהוה אלהינו יהוה).[26] Indeed, it is just as likely that this verse was borrowed by these incantations directly from the Bible, the mezuzah or the tefillin, rather than from the liturgy. However, a pair of duplicate bowls from the Berlin Museum suggest otherwise.[27] These bowls (see appendix for full text) contain much more than Deut 6:4; they include the first two groups of verses of the *Shema'*, Deut 6:4–9 and 11:13–21, as well as the response 'Blessed is the name of His glorious kingdom for ever' (ברוך שם כבוד מלכותו לעולם ועד) after Deut. 6:4 that distinguishes this excerpt as liturgical. The absence of the third part of the *Shema'*, Num. 15:37–41, in the Berlin bowls is specifically consistent with the way the *Shema'* was recited in the *Arvit*, the daily evening prayer, as we know from mBer. 2:2 and bBer. 13a.[28] The *Shema' 'al ha-mittah* is yet another variation of this theme that is regarded to have special protective qualities against demons (see n. 19 above). In more recent times, in accordance with the stipulations in the Babylonian Talmud, only the recitation of the first section of the *Shema'* (Deut.6: 4-9) was required.[29] We do, however, know from R.

---

25 The bowls that were used for this little survey are the bowls from the Moussaieff collection that appear in Levene, *Corpus*. To date I know of no other survey or study of the occurrence of verses in the bowls; such an enterprise could prove useful.

26 AIT 26:1, BM117878, De Menil bowl III:3 (C. D. Isbell, 'Two New Aramaic Incantation Bowls', *BASOR* 223 (1976), 18), and at least three unpublished bowls that I have collated.

27 D. Levene, 'Heal O Israel: A Pair of Duplicate Magic Bowls from the Pergamon Museum in Berlin', *JJS* LIV, no. 1 (2003), 104-21.

28 אמר רבי יהושע בן קרחה ... ויאמר אינו נוהג אלא ביום R. Joshua b. Korhah said: … whereas [the section] 'and the Lord said' is applicable only to the day. According to Elbogen there is evidence to show that in Palestine the third part was omitted right up until the ninth century (Elbogen, *Jewish*, 23). In some traditions, as in the *Sephardi*, it is still omitted from the evening prayer. Further evidence suggesting that the third section was not always read can be found in mBer. 1:5: מזכירין יציאת מצרים בלילות אמר ר' אלעזר בן עזריה הרי אני כבן שבעים שנה ולא זכיתי שתאמר יציאת מצרים בלילות עד שדרשה בן זומא שנא' (דברים טז) למען תזכור את יום צאתך מארץ מצרים כל ימי חייך כל ימי חייך הימים כל ימי חייך הלילות וחכ"א ימי חייך העולם הזה כל ימי חייך להביא לימות המשיח The exodus from Egypt is to be mentioned [in the *Shema'*] at night-time. Said R. Eleazar b. Azariah: behold I am about seventy years old, and I have never been worthy to [find a reason] why the exodus from Egypt should be mentioned at night time until Ben Zoma expounded it: for it says: that thou mayest remember the day when thou camest forth out of the land of Egypt all the days of thy life. [Had the text said,] 'the days of thy life' it would have meant [only] the days; but 'all the days of thy life' includes the nights as well. The sages, however, say: 'the days of thy life refers to this world; all the days of thy life' is to add the days of the messiah.

29 BBer. 60b הנכנס לישן על מטתו אומר משמע ישראל עד והיה אם שמע On going to bed one says from 'Hear, O Israel' to 'And it shall come to pass if ye hearken diligently'.

Asher's commentary to bBer. 9 (no. 29), who cites a tradition in the name of R. Hananel[30] that it was customary to read the second section of the *Shema'* Deut. 11:13–21 at least as far back as the tenth century.[31] If the Berlin bowls were to be considered as having been derived from the *Shema' 'al ha-mittah* then it would confirm yet an earlier date to this practice. Another interesting aspect of this bowl, which reinforces its connection with the liturgy, is the presence of a description of God pushing pharaoh's chariot into the sea that immediately precedes the citation of the *Shema'*. The mention of the exodus of Israel from Egypt is reminiscent of the rabbinical stipulation found in tBer. 2:1[32] that this event be recounted with the *Shema'*.

Moussaieff 108 is another bowl text whose use of verses is strongly suggestive of the liturgy.[33] The bowl starts with a short opening formula that states the incantation's purpose and the name of the client who commissioned it. This is followed by the seven verses that are introduced as a magical name, i.e. 'in the name of (בשום). The verses, which are quoted in full, are: Zech. 3:2; Pss 89:53, 106:48, 72:18 and 19, 104:31 and 106:47. The first verse, Zech. 3:2, is commonly found in magic bowls and has the distinction of being included in all versions of the *Shema' 'al ha-mittah*. Whether its frequent use in magical texts influenced its incorporation into this part of the liturgy, or, conversely, its reputation as liturgy that is effective against demons made it a natural choice for incantation writers is, as yet, impossible to ascertain. Of the other six verses, all from the Psalms, five can be found in *Seder Amram*'s version of the evening prayer as part of the community's prescribed response following the *Haskivenu*. It is of considerable interest to note that they occur in our bowl in the same order of sequence as they appear in the liturgy.

	M108	Seder Aram
Zech. 3:2		
Ps. 89:53	✓	✓
Ps. 135:21		✓
Ps. 106:48	✓	
Ps. 72:18	✓	✓
Ps. 72:19	✓	✓

---

30 The reasoning that is given is the fact that these verses include within them the words 'when you lie down and when you rise up' (ובקומך בשכבך).

31 Codex Turin 51 (fol. 45a, p. 91 of copy) וכשקורא ק"ש על מטתו אומר פרשה ראשונה ופרשה שניה שמע והיה אם שמע (J. Mann, 'Geniza Fragments of the Palestinian Order of Service', *Hebrew Union College Annual* II (1925), 289, n. 51).

32 הקורא את שמע צריך להזכיר יציאת מצרים ... וקריעת ים סוף One who reads the *Shema'* is required to recall the exodus from Egypt ... and the splitting of the Red Sea.

33 Levene, *Corpus*, 71–4 and 190.

Ps. 104:31	✓	✓
Ps. 113:2		✓
Ps. 94:14		✓
1 Sam. 12:22		✓
1 Kgs 18:39		✓
Zech. 14:9		✓
Ps. 33:22		✓
Ps. 106:47	✓	✓

The only difference is that the bowl's second psalm is 106:48 whereas in *Seder Amram* it is Ps 135:21. There is, indeed, a precedent to the sequence in the bowls that might explain the variance therein, namely a tradition noted in tTan. 3:8 and *Seder Olam Rabbah* 30 that cite psalms 106:48, 72:18 and 19 as having been recited in succession at the Temple. Indeed, the *Arvit* comes just before the *Shema' 'al ha-mittah* in which Zekh. 3:2, which is also the first verse in the Berlin bowls, is cited.

The evidence shown above suggests that the verses in Moussaieff 108 were not compiled independently of the liturgical context. Rather, it seems that this formula was, at some point, chosen by the magician from the well-rehearsed daily service that was known by all to have protective power over the dangers of the night; a natural choice indeed. Furthermore, if we consider Elbogen's opinion that dates the composition of the fourth section of the *Arvit*, starting with *Hashkivenu*, to the 'post-talmudic period, specifically the Saboraic period'[34] — a time that coincides well with the general dating of magic bowls — then surely Moussaieff 108 should be considered as the oldest fragment of this prayer.

To conclude, I would just say that it is my impression that the connection between the incantation found in the magic bowls and prayer is not incidental. It is my belief that bowl incantations represent a creative period of this genre of composition and that further investigation into its connection with prayer will shed more light on to the process of its composition. And, maybe even more significantly, it could also advance our understanding of the place of such magical practices in the life and culture of the Jews in general.

---

34 Elbogen *Jewish*, 88.

Appendix 1

The incantation that occurs in Sephardic Mahzor for Shavuot, which was slotted in for reasons that are not apparent to us after the *Akdamot* is rather late.[35] It is prefaced with a caption stating that it was taken from the eighteenth century *Sefer Avodat ha-Qodesh*, which is the work of Hayyim Yoseph David Azulai. The incantation is meant to protect against the evil eye.[36] What is of interest in this incantation is the fact that it preserves much of the archaic form that we find already in magic bowls. Also noteworthy is the fact that another version of this incantation[37] ends with the liturgical formula: 'For you hear the prayer of every mouth. Blessed are you God who hears prayer'[38] (כי אתה שומע תפלת כל פה. ברוך אתה (י"י) שומע תפלה), that categorizes this incantation as a form of prayer. Variations of this incantation seem to have enjoyed a wide circulation in Eastern Europe.[39] Its text, a translation, and some notes follow:

משביע אני עליכם כל מין עינא בישא. עינא (1	I adjure you every type of evil eye. The black
אוכמא, עינא צרובא, עינא תכלתא, עינא (2	eye,
ירוקא, עינא ארוכא, עינא קצרה, עינא (3	the burnt eye, the purple-blue eye, the green eye,
רחבה,	the long eye, the short eye, the wide eye, the
עינא צרה, עינא ישרה, עינא עקומה (4	narrow eye, the straight eye, the crooked eye, the
עינא עגולה, עינא שוקעת, עינא בולטת, (5	round eye, the sunken eye, the bulging eye, the
עינא רואה, עינא מבטת, עינא בוקעת, (6	seeing eye, the looking eye, the eye that breaks
עינא שואבת, עינא דדכורא, עינא דנוקבא, (7	through, the absorbing eye, the male eye, the
עינא דאיש ואשתו, עין דאשה (8	female eye, the eye of a man and his wife, the eye
ובתה, עין דאשה (9	of a women and her daughter, the eye of a
וקרובתה, עין דבחור, עין (10	women

---

35 The version that I am quoting is taken from *The Torah CD-ROM Library* version 9.0, published by D.B.S. Computers Ltd.

36 For a history of the 'evil eye' motif see J.N. Ford, '"Ninety-Nine by the Evil Eye and One from Natural Causes":KTU² 1.96 in its Near Eastern Context', *Ugarit-Forschungen* 30 (1998), 201–78.

37 Naveh and Shaked, *Amulets*, 133

38 My translation.

39 See Ford, *Ninety*, 241, n. 136 who cites a number of variants. I would like to thank Eric Pellow who referred me to a number of other occurrences of this incantation and references to it that attest its wide use. Of particular interest is the mention of this incantation in *Petah Hadevir* of Hayyim Benjamin Pontremoli, addendum to sec. 299:1, fol. 324c, where it is mentioned in the context of a discussion about the *Havdalah* incantation in *Seder Rav Amram*. The author distinguishes between this adjuration and others, such as that employed by the cantors, and argues (against his father!) that it is permitted because it doesn't explicitly refer to, or name, the angels.

11) דזקן, עין דזקנה, עין

and her relative, the eye of the young man, the eye

12) דבתולה, עין דבעולה, עין

of the old man, the eye of the old women, the eye

13) דאלמנה עין דנשואה, עין

of the virgin, the eye of the non-virgin, the eye of

14) דגרושה, כל מין עינא בישא

the widow, the eye of the married woman, the eye

15) שיש בעולם שראתה והביטה

16) ודברה בעין הרע על (פ"ב

of the divorced woman, every type of evil eye that

17) פלונית) גזרנא ואשבענא

there is in the world that has seen and looked and

18) לכון בההוא עינא עילאה, עינא קדישא,
עינא

has spoken in the evil eye upon (NN son/daughter

19) חדא, עינא חורא, עינא דאיהי חור גו

of (name of mother)), I have decreed and adjured

20) חור, עינא דכליל כל חור, עינא

you by that supreme eye, the holy eye, the single

21) דכלא ימינא עינא פקיחא, עינא

eye, the white eye, the eye that is white within

22) דאשגחותא תדירא, עינא דכלא רחמי, עינא

white, the eye that includes all white, the eye that

23) דאיהי רחמי גו רחמי עינא דכליל כל

is all the right (hand), the eye that is open, the eye

24) רחמי, עינא דלית עלה גבנוני,

of constant care, they eye that is all love, the eye

25) עינא דלא אדמיך ולא נאים,

that is love within love, they eye that includes all

26) עינא דכל עיינין בישין אתכפיין

love, the eye that has got no blemishes upon it, the

27) ואתטמרן גו כיפין מן קדמוהי, עינא

eye that does not fall asleep and does not sleep,

28) דנטיר לישראל כדכתיב הנה

the eye that all the evil eyes get upset and hide

29) לא ינום ולא יישן שומר ישראל

themselves in rocks from its presence, the eye that

30) וכתיב הנה, עין יהוה (יאהדונהי) אל

protects Israel as it is written: 'See the guardian of

31) יראיו למיחלים לחסדו:

Israel neither slumbers nor sleeps'; and it is

32) בההיא עינא עילאה, גזרית ואשבעית עליכון

written: 'Truly the eye of the Lord is on those

33) כל מין עינא בישא

who fear him, who wait for His faithful care'.

34) שתסורו ותערקו ותברחו

By that supreme eye, I decree and adjure you

35) ותרחיקו מעל (פ"ב

every type of evil eye.

36) פלונית) ומעל כל בני

That you remove yourselves and flee and run

37) ביתו (לנקיבה ביתה), ולא יהיה

away from (NN son/daughter of (name of

38) לכם כח לשלוט

mother)) and from all the members of his

39) בפ"ב פלונית ובכל

household (for female her household), and may

40) בני ביתו (לנקיבה

41) ביתה), לא ביום ולא בלילה לא

42) בהקיץ ולא בחלום, לא בשום אבר

43) מרמ"ח אבריו, ולא בשום גיד משס"ה גידיו,

44) (לנקיבה לא בשום אבר מאבריה ולא

45) בשום גיד מגידיה) מהיום

46) ולעולם אמן נצח סלה ועד:	you not have the power to control NN
47) (ג"פ) אתה סתר לי	son/daughter of (name of mother) and all the
48) מצר תצרני	members of his household (for female her
49) רני פלט תסובבני סלה:	household), not in the day and not in the night not
50) (ג"פ) סלה תסובבני	in waking and not in dream, not in any limb of his
51) פלט רני תצרני מצר	248 limbs, and not in any sinew of his 365
52) לי סתר אתה:	sinews,
53) כל זה יאמר ג' פעמים:	(for female not in any limb of her limbs and not
	in
	any sinew of her sinews) from this day and
	forever amen eternity selah and eternity.
	(Three times) 'You are my shelter;
	You preserve me from distress; You surround me
	with the joyous shouts of deliverance. Selah.'
	(Three times) 'Selah. You are my shelter; You
	preserve me from distress; You surround me with
	the joyous shouts of deliverance.'
	All this one should say three times.

Notes

The line numbering that has been given to this text is merely for the convenience of the notes below. An amulet with an almost identical text is provided in Naveh and Shaked, *Amulets*, 133, and is referred to in the notes below as B, whereas the text above is referred to as A. These notes include only some of the differences between the two texts in order to illustrate the kind of variance that commonly occurs in magical incantations. The variance is a testament to the diverse traditions that developed over time and a reflection of the variety of types of corruption that can occur during the process of transmission.[40]

1) The opening adjuration משביע אני עליכם is a common legal formula that is used extensively in the Mishna in the tractate Shevuʿot (Oaths). Though the Hebrew form, as we have it here, does not occur in magic bowls, the Aramaic משבענא לכון is very common. The evil eye (עינא בישתא) is reasonably common in the bowls, though the

---

40 For a study of the variance in duplicate texts within magic bowls see Levene, *Corpus*, 24–30.

variety of types of eye are not as numerous.[41] Similar lists of evil eyes can be found in Syriac amulets such as the following:

ܐܣܘܪ ܠܝ ܐܝܣܝܪ ... (Syriac text)

You are bound by me, and I bind you, and excommunicate you, and destroy you, O Evil Envious Eye, eye of the seven evil and envious neighbours, eye of all kinds, the eye that woundeth and pitieth not, the eye of the father, the eye of the mother, the eye of the foreigner, the eye of the gentile (the eye of the foreigner), the dark-grey eye, the jealous eye, the cerulean eye (the eye of the far off), the eye of the wicked men, the eye of man and woman, the eye of old men and old women, the eye of evil and envious men, the eye of the infidel…[42]

As well as in Mandaic:

ʿzhʾ wʿtʾzhʾ ʾynʾh wkʾbyštyʾ wʾynyʾ zrwqtyʾ wʾynʾ brwqtyʾ wʾynʾ qbyštyʾ wʾynyʾ qlyqtyʾ wʾynʾ ʿhyltyʾ

Tremble! Be scared off, Evil Eye and Dimmed (or blinded) (Eye) and Blue Eye and Eye with white cataract, and shut Eye and Eye with a film on it, and Corroded Eye!

ʾynʾ d̠ʾbwk bsʾnʾ wʾynʾ d̠šybʾbyʾ byšyʾ bybnʾywn wʾynʾ d̠ʾzlʾ wʾynʾ d̠ʾtyʾ wʾynʾ d̠rʾhyqyʾ wʾynʾ d̠qʾrybyʾ wʾynʾ d̠d̠ʾyrdyqwnyʾ wʾynʾ d̠d̠ʾrdyqwnyʾtʾ wʾynʾ d̠zʾnʾy wʾynʾ d̠zʾmʾr wʾynʾ d̠kwlh tybyl wʾynʾ d̠mhʾtʾ

The contemptuous eye of your father and the eye of evil neighbours and their sons and the eye of those who go and the eye of those who come and the eye of those who depart and the eye of those who approach, and the eye of the boys and the eye of the girls and the eye of *zanai* and the eye of *zamar* and the eye of all the earth and the Eye which struck …

---

41 In AIT 30:3,4 we find the following: עינאנא דיכרא נקבתא עינא חאסדניתא עינא דחזי אף בית ליבא Eye of man (or) woman; the Eye of the contumely; the Eye which looks right into the heart. In BM 103357:7, 8: עינא בישתא וחוסמתא the evil and envious eye (J. B. Segal, *Catalogue of the Aramaic and Mandaic Incantation Bowls in The British Museum* (London 2000), 85). Furthermore, in the bowls the evil eye is usually bound (אסיר) or sealed (חתים) except for one instance that I have found in an unpublished bowl, Moussaieff 116:1, 2 (forthcoming by the current author).

42 H. Gollancz, *The Book of Protection Being a Collection of Charms* (Amsterdam 1912), §19 codex C, 86–7.

wʾynʾ dᵈrʾhyqyʾ wʾynʾ dᵈqʾrybyʾ

the eye of those who depart and the eye of those that approach …

ʿsyrʾ wsdymʾ ʾspʾr wnywʾl ʾynʾ zrwqtyʾ ʿsyrʾ wsdymʾ ʾynʾ mṣwṣtyʾ ʿsyrʾ wsdymʾ ʾynʾ
qlyqtyʾ ʿsyrʾ wsdymʾ ʾynʾ ʿkwmtyʾ ʿsyrʾ wsdymʾ ʾynʾ qdwrtyʾ ʿsyrʾ wsdymʾ ʾynʾ qbwrtyʾ
ʿsyrʾ wsdymʾ ʾynʾ hlwtyʾ

Bound and confined and cut out and tormented is the Blue Eye; bound and confined and cut out and tormented is the Dried-up Eye; bound and confined and cut out and tormented is the Whitened Eye; bound and confined and cut out and tormented is the Darkened Eye; bound and confined and cut out and tormented is the Cut-out Eye; bound and confined and cut out and tormented is the Buried Eye; bound and confined and cut out and tormented is the Hollow Eye…[43]

.וכל מין דבר ומגפה ושדין ורוחין ולילין :After: כל מין עינא בישא B has

2) B has the more likely צהובה, yellow, rather than צרובה.

9) After: ובתה B has the additional: עינא דאשה ואחותה.

11) B is lacking: עינא דזקנה.

13, 14) B is lacking: עין דגרושה.

15–17) Whereas A has: שראתה והביטה ודברה בעין הרע על (פ"ב פלונית) in B we find: שרוצה
לשרוף בהביטם איתם בתגבורת יסוד אש מצד מזרח מערב דרום וצפון.

18) B is lacking: עינא קדישא.

20–23) Where in A there is: עינא דכלא ימינא in B there is only: עינא ימינא. Where in A we have: עינא

עינא דאיהי רחמי גו :in B there is עינא דאשגחותא עינא חדוא. B is lacking דאשגחותא תדירא
רחמי עינא דכליל כל רחמי.

This section has the equivalent: חוור בגו חוור וחוור דכליל כל חוור, that occurs several times in the Zohar (Part III, 129b and 130a).

25) B is lacking עינא דלא אדמיך.

27) Where in A there is: גו כיפין מן קדמוהי in B there is only: מן קדמוהי גו כיפין.

29) B is lacking Ps. 121:4.

32–37) The following selections of extracts from magic bowls illustrate the close similarities between them and the formula found in this section of the incantation: Ellis 1:7–8:[44]

---

43 E.S. Drower, 'Shafta d Pishra d Ainia, A Mandaean Magical Text', *JRAS* (1937), sections 1–10, 150–70 and 350–60.

44 This text is presented as a parallel to AIT 11 and was corrected by Epstein (J. N. Epstein, *Studies in Talmudic Literature and Semitic Languages* (Jerusalem 1983), 340). The translation here is taken from

ופוקו וקדחו ועירוקו ואיזילו מן ביתה ד

go out and break through and flee and go from the house of ;

AIT 7:15–16:[45]

בטילו ופוקו מין ביתיה ומין דירתיה ומין כוליה פגריה דהדין יזידאד בר איזנדוך ומין מירדוך איתתיה בת
באנאי ומין בניהון ומין בנתהון ומין כל אינשי ביתהון דלא תיחבלון בהון כל חבאלא בישא ולא תישנון יתהון
ולא תידרכון ולא תיחטון בהון ולא תיתחזון להון לא בחילמא דליליה ולא בשחרתא דיממא מן יומא דנן
ולעולם אמן אמן סלה

Desist and go forth from the house and from the dwelling and from the whole body of Yezidad son
of I. and from Meriduch his wife daughter of B., and from their sons and daughters and all the
people of their house, that ye injure them not with any evil injury, nor bewilder, nor amaze them,
nor sin against them, nor appear to them either in dream by night or in slumber by day, from this
day and forever, Amen, Amen, Selah…

and Gordon H:13–14:[46]

מומינא לכון ומשבענא לכון דתתזעון ויתפקון מיניה מאתן ארבעין ותמני הדמי קומתיה לא תקומון במיקמיה
ולא תשכבון בבית מישכביה מן יומא דנן ולעלם

I adjure you and make you swear that you depart and go forth from him (yea from) the two
hundred and forty-eight members of his body. May they not stand in his standing (place) nor lie
in his sleeping chamber, from this day unto eternity.

Where in A we find: (פ"ב פלונית) עליכון כל מין עינא בישא שתסורו ותערקו ותברחו ותרחיקו מעל
in B there occurs: עלך עינא בישא דכל מין דבר ומגפה שמבהלין ומעל כל בני ביתו (לנקיבה ביתה)
ומפחידין לאדם בהביטם אותו שתסורו ותרחקו ותעדון ותערקון ותברחון מין הדין ביתא ומן הדין מחוזא
ומן כל מאן דדר בה.

Appendix 2

VA 3854

‏אסותא מן >ש<מיא דתיהוי לה לאיסאלבאב (2) בת רימנא ותיתסי בירחמי שמיא (3) מן אישתא ומן עריתא ומן (1)
עינא {בי} (4) בישתא ומן זיקא בישא ומן סטנא (5) בישא ומן רוחא בישא ומן מרוביא (6) בישא ומן מלויתא
בישתא ומן {לילי} (7) ליליתא בישתא דיכרא וניקיבא (8) ומן כל רוחין (9) וזיקין ומ(ז)יקין בישין (.ין) (10) בין
דיתכיר (11) שמיהון ובין דלא אי (12) תכיר שמיהון כולכון ואסירי(תון) (13) וחתימיתון מיניה בעיזקת(יה) (14)

M. Sokoloff, *A Dictionary of Jewish Babylonian Aramaic* (Ramat-Gan, Baltimore and London 2002),
983a.

45   Corrected by Epstein, *Studies*, 335.

46   C. Gordon, 'Aramaic and Mandaic Magic Bowls', *ArOr* 9 (1937), 87–8.

דאילשדי {בעיזק} (15) ובעיזקתיה דישלמה בר (16) דויד מלכה(.) דישראל דיחתימין (17) בה תלת (18) מאה

ושיתין ושיתה ^שידין דחתמי<ה>^ אדם {לש} (19) לשית בריה אנה גיוין ומחין על כפי (20) דאינוש לא יעול

עלוהי לביש {ביש}

(21) כסי לטורא דאינוש לא יעול {על} (22) עלוהי לביש בישמיה דיה ביה (23) יה יה יהי יה יהו (24) יה יהוה

צבאות שמו (25) דעבד אתין ותמהין במצרים (26) ועבד בישין בגו ימיניה ודחק (27) {ו}מרכבתיה דפרעה בגו ימא

(28) דסוף אמין אמין סלה הללויה (29) שמע ישראל יהוה אלהינו (30) יהוה אחד ברוך (31) שים כבוד מלכותו

לעלם (32) ועד ואהבתה {א}(ת) (33) את {יתיה}[47] {(א)(ית)} יהוה אלהיך {ב} (34) (ב) בכל לבבך ובכל נפשיך (35) ובכל

מאדיך {והיו} (36) והיו הדברים האלה אשר (37) אנכי מצויך היום {על} (38) על לבביך ושיננתם לבני(ך) (39)

ודברת בם בשבתיך בבת(ך) (40) ובליכתך בדרך (41) ובשכבך ובקומיך {וקש} (42) וקשרתם לאות על ידיך (43)

והיו לטוטפות בין עיניך

(44) וכת{ם}בתם על (45) מזוזות ביתיך {ובי} (46) ובישעיריך והיו אם (47) שמע תישמעו איל {מ} (48)

מצוותי אשר אנכי מצוה (49) (א)תכם היום לאהבה את {יהו} (50) יהוה אלהיכם (.)ולעובדו בכל לבבכם (51)

ובכול נפשכם ונ{נ}תתי מטר ארצכם (52) בעיתו יורא ומלקוש ואספתי דגניך {תי} (53) תירשיך ויצהריך ונתתי

עשב בשדיך {לב} (54) לבהימתיך ואכלת ושבעתה הישמרו {לכ} (55) לכם פן יפתה {יה} (56) לבבכם וסרתם

ועבדתם אילוהים אחירים {ו} (57) והישתחויתם להם וחרה אף יהוה בכם ועציר (58) את השמים ולא יהיה מטר

ו<ה>אדמה לא תיתין את יבול<ה>

(59) ואבד{ם}תם {מ} (60) מהירה {מ} (61) מיעל הארץ (62) הטובה אשר (63) יהוה אלהיכם נותן (64) לכם ושמתם

את {ד} (65) דברי אלה על לבבכם {ו} (66) ועל נפשכם וקשרתם אתם (67) לאות על ידכם {והיו על ידכם {68}

והיו לטוטפות בין עיניכם {ולמדת} (69) ולמדתם אתם {ו}את בניכם לדביר {ב} (70) {בם} בם בם בשבתיך <בביתיך>

ובליכתך בדרך (71) ובשכיביך ובקומיך ו{כ}כתבתם על (72) מזוזות ביתיך ובשעריך {ריך למ} (73) למען ירבו

ימיכם וימי בניכם על (א.) האדמה

(74) (in the centre on either side of the figure) (75) למען (76) ירבו ימיכם (76) ימיכם וימי (77) בניכם (78)

וימי (79) וימי בניכם (80) על האדמה (81) אשר

(82) {אדמה אשר (ני)}(ני)<שבע> יהוה < לאבותיכם לתת (starts to the left of the figure outside the circle)

להם כימי השמים על הארץ>

(83) (above the figure) אשר (84) (.ו.) (85) (in the skirt of the figure) יהוה יה

Translation VA 3854

(1) Healing from heaven - that it may be for Aysal(hu)bab (2) daughter of Rimna. May she be healed by the

mercies of heaven (3) from fever and from shivering and from the evil (4) eye and from the evil blast and

from the evil (5) prosecutor and from the evil spirit and from the evil (6) educator and from the evil

(female) companion and from (7) the evil Lilith - male and female, (8) and from all evil spirits (9) blast

---

47 Could also read יהוה.

181

demons and harmers. (10) Whether their names were recalled (11) or whether their (12) names were not recalled. All of you, you are bound (13) and sealed from her by the signet ring (14) of Elshadai, (15) and by the signet ring of Solomon son of (16) David the king of Israel by which are sealed (17) three hundred (18) and sixty six demons which Adam sealed (19) for Seth his son. He placed bodies and they slapped his hands (20) so that no human might come near him for evil.

(21) He covered the mountain so that no human might come near (22) him for evil. By the name of YH by YH (23) YH YH YHY YH YHW (24) YH YHWH Sabaoth is his name. (25) (He) who performed signs and wonders upon Egypt, (26) and performed bad things by the agency (31) of his right hand, and pushed (27) pharaoh's chariot into the Red (28) Sea. Amen amen selah hallelujah. (29) Hear O' Israel YHWH our God (30) YHWH is one. Blessed is (31) the name of His glorious kingdom for ever (32) and ever. You shall love (33) the Lord your God (34) with all your heart, with all your soul, (35) and with all your might. (36) And these words (37) which I command you this day (38) shall be in your heart. You shall impress them upon your children, (39) and you shall speak of them, when you sit at home (40) and when you go on a journey, (41) when you lie down and when you rise up. (42) And you shall bind them for a sign on your hand, (43) and they shall be as ornaments between your eyes.

(44) And you shall write them on the (45) door-posts of your house (46) and upon your gates. Now, if you will (47) carefully obey (48) My commandments which I command (49) you today: to love the (50) Lord your God, and to serve Him with all your heart (51) and with all your soul, then I will provide rain in your land (52) in its proper time, the early and the late rains; and I will gather in your corn, (53) your new wine and your oil. And I will provide pasture (54) for your cattle; and you will eat and be satisfied. Beware (55) lest your heart be (56) lured away, and you turn aside and serve other gods, (57) and bow down to them. For then the Lord's anger will blaze against you; He will restrain (58) the heavens so that there will be no rain; the ground will not yield its produce,

(59) and you will soon (60) perish (61) from the good (62) land which (63) the Lord is giving (64) you. Therefore store these (65) words of Mine in your heart (66) and in your soul; bind them (67) for a sign on your hand, (68) and let them be as ornaments between your eyes. (69) Also teach them to your children, and speak (70) of them when you sit (at home), and when you go on a journey, (71) when you lie down, and when you rise up. And write them on (72) the door-posts of your house and on your gates, (73) so that you and your children will live long in the land

(74–79) so that you and your children will live long (80) in the land (81) that (82) the Lord <swore to your forefathers to give them, for as long as the heavens are above the earth.> (83) that (84) (YYY) (85) Y(H)WH Y(H)

Moussaieff M108

(2)⁴⁸ הדין קמיעה למיסר שידי דיוי וסיוטי וסטני מן הדין ביתיה דאדיב בר בתשבתה (3) בשום ויאמר יהוה אל הסטן

יגער יהוה בך הסטן יגער יהוה ב(ך ה)בחר בירושל(י)ם (4) הלוא זה זה אוד מוצ'ל מ'אש ברוך יהוה לעולם אמן

>ו<אמן ברוך יהוה (5) אלהי ישראל מהעולם ועד העולם ואמר כל העם אמן הללויה (6) ברוך יהוה אלהים אלהי

ישראל עושה נפלאות לבדו (7) וברוך שם כבודו לעולם וימלא כבודו את (8) כל הארץ אמן >ו<אמן (9) יהי כבוד

יהוה לעולם ישמח יהוה במעשיו (1) הושיעינו יהוה אלהינו וקבצינו והצילנו מן הגויים להודות לשם קדש(ך)

↓להש↓ת(ב)ח בת(הי)לתיך↓

Translation of Moussaieff M108

(2) This amulet is for the binding of demons, dews, frights and satans from this house of Adib son of Bat-Šabbeta. (3) In the name of: 'But the Lord said to the Accuser, "The Lord rebuke you, O Accuser; may the Lord who has chosen Jerusalem rebuke you! (4) For this is a brand plucked from the fire"'. (Zech. 3:2) 'Blessed is the Lord forever; Amen and Amen'. (Ps. 89:53) 'Blessed is the Lord, (5) God of Israel, from eternity to eternity. Let all the people say, "Amen". Hallelujah'. (Ps. 106:48) (6) 'Blessed is the Lord God, God of Israel, who alone does wondrous things. (7) Blessed is His glorious name forever; His glory fills the (8) whole world. Amen and Amen'. (Ps. 72:18-19) (9) 'May the glory of the Lord endure forever; may the Lord rejoice in his works!' (Ps. 104:31) (1) 'Deliver us, O Lord our God, gather us and deliver us from among the nations, to acclaim Your holy name, to glory in Your praise'. (Ps. 106:47)

Bibliography

Bar-Ilan M. 1987. *The Mysteries of Jewish Prayer and Hekhalot.* (Ramat-Gan)

Dan J. 1993. *The Ancient Jewish Mysticism.* (Tel-Aviv)

Drower E. S. 1937. 'Shafta d Pishra d Ainia, A Mandaean Magical Text', *JRAS*, 611–589

Elbogen, I. 1993. *Jewish Liturgy, a Comprehensive History* by Isamar Elbogen, trans. Raymond P. Scheindlin. Based on the original 1913 German edition, and the 1972 edition edited by Joseph Heinemann (Philadelphia - New York – Jerusalem)

Elior R.1993. 'Mysticism, Magic and Angelology', *JSQ* 1, 3–53

Epstein, J.N. 1983. *Studies in Talmudic Literature and Semitic Languages* (Jerusalem), 329–74

Ford J.N. 1998. '"Ninety-Nine by the Evil Eye and One from Natural Causes":*KTU*² 1.96 in its Near Eastern Context', Ugarit-Forschungen 30, 201–78.

---

48 Unlike most bowls whose text spirals from the centre of the bowl to its rim, this one spirals from the rim to the centre. A closer examination of it reveals that line 1, consisting of Ps. 106:47, was added at the beginning of the text as the scribe miscalculated the room he had to write on the surface of the bowl. As he reached the centre of the bowl and ran out of space he simply added this last verse at the beginning of the text where there was still some free space to write (for more see Levene, *Corpus*, 71–4 and 190).

Frazer, G.F. 1947. *The Golden Bough, a Study in Magic and Religion.* (New York)

Goldschmidt E.D. 1971. ‏סדר רב עמרם גאון‎ (Jerusalem)

Gollancz H. 1912. *The Book of Protection Being a Collection of Charms.* (Amsterdam)

Gordon C. 1934. 'Aramaic Magic Bowls in the Istanbul and Baghdad Museums', *ArOr* 6, 319–34

—— 1937. 'Aramaic and Mandaic Magic Bowls', *ArOr* 9, 84–106

Harari Y. 1997. ‏חרבא דמשה: מהדורה חדשה ומחקר‎ (Jerusalem)

Hertz, J.H. 1955. *The Authorised Daily Prayer Book of the United Hebrew Congregations of the British Empire.* (London)

Isbell C.D. 1976. 'Two New Aramaic Incantation Bowls', *BASOR* 223, 15–23

Levene D. 2003. 'A Happy Thought of the Magician, The Magical Get', in R. Deutsch (ed.), *Shlomo: Studies in Epigraphy, Iconography, History and Archaeology in Honor of Shlomo Moussaieff* (Tel-Aviv Jaffa), 175–84

—— 2003. *A Corpus of Magic Bowls.* (London)

—— 2003. 'Heal O Israel: A Pair of Duplicate Magic Bowls from the Pergamon Museum in Berlin', *JJS* LIV, no. 1, 104–21.

Mann J. 1925. 'Geniza Fragments of the Palestinian Order of Service', *HUCA* II, 269–388

Montgomery, J.A. 1913. *Aramaic Incantation Texts from Nippur* (Vol. III.: University of Pennsylvania. The Museum, Publications of the Babylonian Section, Philadelphia

Naveh J. and S. Shaked 1987. *Amulets and Magic Bowls.* (Jerusalem)

—— 1993. *Magic Spells and Formulae.* (Jerusalem)

Schäfer P. 1981. in Zussamenarbeit mit Margarete Schlüter und H. G. von Mutius, *Synopse zur Hekhalot-Literatur* (Texte und Studien zum Antiken Judentum; 2, Tübingen)

—— 1996. 'Jewish Liturgy and Magic', in H. Cancik, H. Lichtenberger and P. Schäfer (eds), *Geschichte-Tradition-Reflexion* (Tübingen), 541–56

Scholem G. 1980–1. 'The Havdala De R. Akiva, a Source for the Jewish Tradition of Magic in the Gaonic Period ‏הגאונים‎', ‏'הבדלה דר' עקיבא, מקור למסורת המאגיה היהודית בתקופת‎, *Tarbiz* 50, 243–81

Segal J.B. 2000. *Catalogue of the Aramaic and Mandaic Incantation Bowls in The British Museum* (London)

Shwartz M. 1996. *Scholastic Magic* (Princeton, New Jersey), 18–22

Sokoloff M. 2002. *A Dictionary of Jewish Babylonian Aramaic* (Ramat-Gan, Baltimore and London)

Tambiah S. J. 1990. *Culture, Thought, and Social Action* (Cambridge)

Trachtenberg, J. 1939. *Jewish Magic and Superstition* (New York)

The Four-fold Structure of the Passover Haggadah[1]

Jeremy Schonfield

In memoriam David Britt, 1939–2002

The Passover Haggadah, the home liturgy for the eve of Passover, includes the instruction that participants should imagine that they themselves had experienced the Exodus.[2] On other festivals participants are assumed to identify with the relevant narrative dimensions, but on this occasion alone empathy with past events is explicitly required. The reason given in the same liturgical passage is that the liberation recalled at Passover lies not merely in the past, but is the source of each participant's present freedom. Other texts suggest that it will be the model for a 'future Passover': the coming of the messiah.[3] This theme becomes dominant only later in the liturgical proceedings, and is expanded in liturgical hymns commonly included in European Haggadot only since the fourteenth century.[4]

The Haggadah contains a variety of prose texts and poetry designed apparently to help participants experience the Exodus in this way, some describing the events themselves and others reporting on the celebration of Passover at later periods. The recital of these texts is accompanied by symbolic foods and is followed by a festive family meal which completes the work of identification, carrying the narrative from the verbal onto the sensory plane.

In view of the need for emotional immediacy, the sections of the Haggadah preceding the meal might be expected to fulfil an introductory and expository role, to outline the themes of the festival and recount the events associated with the Exodus in order to help participants empathize with those events. Yet although each text involved is clear in itself and in most cases is attested in early rabbinic literature, the

---

1   An earlier version of this paper was presented at the Conference of the British Association of Jewish Studies, Hatfield College, Durham, on 16 July 2003.

2   E.D. Goldschmidt, *The Passover Haggadah: Its Sources and History* (Jerusalem 1960) [Hebrew], 125. Sephardi versions differ little in content from this standard Ashkenazi edition.

3   Ibid., 118, also in the poem comparing the Exodus with the present, culminating in the messianic advent, 99–101.

4   Ibid., 97, 140. It is assumed in the petition for the restoration of Zion on 136.

sequence is collectively so lacking in clarity that it appears to form little more than a loose anthology. This apparent aimlessness has attracted little adverse comment (presumably because rabbinic readers are tolerant of digressions and allusiveness, especially in liturgical contexts). The Passover Haggadah is consequently treated as an inexplicit backdrop for free-ranging discussion on the Exodus. The present paper proposes a novel reading of these introductory sequences of the Haggadah, which suggests that far from being a selection of loosely linked passages, they are clear in structure and function and actively contribute to the task of making the events comprehensible.[5]

The Haggadah as it is used today[6] begins with Kiddush and the drinking of wine, as do other Sabbath and festival eves. But when wine is drunk on Passover-eve, uniquely, participants lean as though at ease after liberation. Such a blessing over wine is generally followed on Sabbaths and festivals by a blessing over bread, but on Passover-eve the celebrant instead first distributes a bitter herb dipped in saltwater and then displays a *maṣâh*. This wafer is broken in half, part being set aside to be eaten later, and part replaced with two others before him.[7] At this festive meal, therefore, not only is bread absent, but the *maṣâh* substituted for it is pointedly not eaten after the blessing over wine. It is merely shown to those present and then withdrawn and concealed. The celebrant next recites a statement of the symbolic principles of Passover — *Ha' laḥma' 'anya'*, 'This is the bread of affliction' — identifying the link between the dry wafers just seen and the events commemorated at Passover.[8] The bitter herbs and the salt water in which they are dipped, as participants will discover, similarly symbolize suffering.

These unfamiliar rituals set the scene for four liturgical questions to be asked by the youngest person present, highlighting the absence of bread, the eating of bitter herbs, the dipping and the practice of leaning. This is the only time in the Jewish year that a participant's reaction forms part of the liturgy, that a question-and-answer sequence forms part of a ceremony and that a ritual is reserved for a youngest participant. The rest of the Haggadah is conventionally assumed to provide a response

---

5 A preliminary version of this idea appeared as Jeremy Schonfield (ed.), *The Rothschild Haggadah: A Passover Compendium from the Rothschild Miscellany* (London 2000), 12–13.

— 6 Some of the earliest known redactions, of the geonic period, differ in relatively minor detail from those now in use. Four early versions are presented in parallel in Shmuel and Ze'ev Safrai, *Haggadah of the Sages: The Passover Haggadah* (Jerusalem 1998) [Hebrew], 260–84.

7 For the number of wafers used see E.D. Goldschmidt, *Die Pessach-Haggada Herausgegeben und Erklärt* (Berlin 1936), 14.

8 Goldschmidt, *The Passover Haggadah*, 117.

to these ritual questions. But, as has been noted, its fractured surface offers no clear message, leaving the explicit challenge of the questions apparently unresolved.

The Structure of the Haggadah in the Talmud

The fact that early rabbinic writers did assume that the Haggadah would clarify the Exodus narrative emerges from two *Mishnayot* and their related talmudic remarks, devoted to the child's questions and to the father's response.[9] The first *Mishnah* spells out a version of the four questions,[10] which is provided in case a child is unable to frame the questions unaided. This suggests that intellectual challenge forms part of the ritual itself and that information is withheld specifically in order to arouse curiosity.[11] The father should reply to these according to the child's ability to understand, 'beginning with shame and concluding with praise [of God]', designed to encompass the passage from slavery to freedom. After this response he should recite, for the benefit of all those gathered, a text identified by the pentateuchal citation, *'Aramî 'obed 'abî*, commonly translated either as 'My father was a wandering Aramean...', or as 'An Aramean sought to destroy my father...',[12] drawn from the pentateuchal ceremony of presenting firstfruits at the Temple after the Israelites' arrival in Canaan. It is included here apparently as a normative version of the Exodus narrative.

The *Gemara* on this *Mishnah* explores the statement that the father should 'begin [his response to the questions] with shame and end with praise', and identifies two versions from which he may choose to do so, each being associated with a different Babylonian rabbinic school. That of Rav (Abba Arikha), the first to be mentioned in the talmudic text, is described as beginning with the words *Mithilâh 'obdê 'abodâh zarâh hayû 'abôtenû*, 'At first our fathers were idolators...', and the second, that of Samuel (Mar Shemuel, Rav's friend and rival), with the words *'abadîm hayinû*, 'We were slaves...'. There is no indication of their content beyond these opening words. Texts beginning in this way appear in the Haggadah as it is now used, but without

---

9   BT. Pesaḥim 116a–b.

10   M. Pesaḥim 10:4.

11   The desire to stimulate childrens' interest is confirmed elsewhere by references to games involving the snatching or withholding of *maṣâh* (T. Pesaḥim 10:6; B. Pesaḥim 109b), or the distribution of nuts (B. Pesaḥim 108b–109a)

12   Deut. 26:5; Rashi prefers the second interpretation, treating *'obed* as a tentative *po'el*, 'sought to destroy', and Ibn Ezra and Rashbam the first.

typographical distinction or any indication of their relationship to each other or to adjacent texts. That of Samuel comes first,[13] followed, after a number of paragraphs, by the beginning of Rav's version,[14] and then, after several more paragraphs, again without being marked in any way, by the opening words of the normative narrative of the Exodus mentioned in the talmudic discussion, now prefixed with the summons *ṣe' û-lemad*, 'Go and learn…' and a midrashic introduction.[15]

The second *Mishnah* points to an element supplementary to the three already mentioned. Rabban Gamliel is reported as saying that 'Whoever does not mention three things on Passover has not discharged his duty, namely the paschal offering, unleavened bread and bitter herbs…',[16] items which the text then outlines briefly. The *Mishnah* does not specify whether Rabban Gamliel's formulation is designed itself to be recited, or whether it is intended as a checklist of subjects to be discussed at some point during the evening, but a version does appear in the Haggadah, introduced by the mishnaic statement that this a view expressed by Rabban Gamliel.[17] The mishnaic discussion next describes how participants should identify with the experience of the Israelites and praise God for the rescue, statements which similarly appear in the Haggadah and conclude the expository part of the liturgy.[18] They introduce *Hallel*, the liturgical name of Psalms 113–18 recited in the Temple, although only Psalms 113–14 are recited before the meal. The mishnaic discussion next gives a text introducing the theme of thanks, an idea which dominates the liturgy after the meal. Rival versions of a blessing beginning *'ašer ge'alanû*, 'who redeemed us,' are attributed to Rabbi Tarfon and Rabbi Akiba.[19] The remainder of *Hallel*, reserved for after the grace, points towards the messianic themes explored later in the evening.[20]

The Haggadah's response to the youngest person's questions concerning ritual therefore falls into four parts. The two introductions associated with the schools of Rav and Samuel are followed by an apparently normative version and, lastly, by a separate treatment attributed to Rabban Gamliel, all of them culminating in the *Hallel*

---

13 Goldschmidt, *The Passover Haggadah*, 117.
14 Ibid., 119.
15 Ibid., 120.
16 M. Pesaḥim 10:5, BT. Pesaḥim 116a–b.
17 Goldschmidt, *The Passover Haggadah*, 125.
18 Ibid., 125–6.
19 Ibid., 126.
20 Ibid., 131–2. The messianic theme emerges on 136 with the petition for the return to Zion, later amplified in the Ashkenazi concluding hymn by the eleventh-century poet Joseph ben Samuel Tov Elem, *Ḥasal siddûr pesaḥ*, 'Ended is the order of service for Passover', see 97.

and a group of associated concluding texts. It remains unclear how many of these formulations are essential to the ceremony or whether any one of the first three would be sufficient to enable one to 'begin with shame and conclude with praise', before the psalms of *Hallel*. The mishnaic formulation implies that only one of the two introductory versions need be used, and that whether that of Rav or of Samuel is employed, it is to be followed by the 'normative' third sequence. Rabban Gamliel's statement might have been merely a mnemonic listing of items to be mentioned, implying the author's view that the Haggadah consisted of a free discussion of the Exodus which must nevertheless include references to certain issues. But the fact that it is followed by the concluding statement, *Hallel* and the redemption blessing, all of which are presumably to be recited liturgically, suggests that it was indeed designed to form part of the ceremony, as it still does in the Haggadah.

The traditional Haggadah contains all four of these texts, but their origins and original contexts are recalled, in ceremonial contexts, only by the learned, if at all. The view that the structure suggested in the mishnaic and talmudic sources is of historical interest only and that it is irrelevant to the meaning of the Haggadah as a text, however, is in need of revision.

The Four Haggadah Narratives

The mishnaic and talmudic discussions outlined above mention only the introductory terms of each unit, leaving it unclear whether the longer versions appearing in the Haggadah today were familiar to talmudic writers. Evidence for the development of the Haggadah before the gaonic period, when it was redacted, is thin, but little change has taken place since then, making it likely that the present arrangement reflects earlier editorial traditions. The view that the introductory clauses and their subsequent paragraphs are associated is supported by the fact that the themes suggested by openings are echoed in what follows each of them in the traditional Haggadah.

Samuel's Haggadah

The first exposition in the Haggadah, which begins with the words *'abadîm hayinû...*, 'We were slaves...',[21] attributed to Samuel, explores the relevance of servitude to each participant, as is emphasized by the first-person-plural in the opening words. The

---

21 Ibid., 117.

opening paragraph states that if the Israelites had not been rescued their descendants would still be in captivity, and adds that no matter how 'wise, understanding, old or knowledgeable' one is, it is still necessary to discuss the rescue, 'and the more we do so the better'. The idea that this duty extends to scholars continues in the second paragraph, beginning with the words *Ma'aseh berabbi' Eli'ezer...*, 'It is told of Rabbi Eliezer...', which describes how famous rabbis, even in the absence of their students, became so engrossed in debate that they had to be interrupted for morning prayer.[22] The third paragraph, which begins *'amar rabbi El'azar ben 'Azaryah...*, 'Rabbi Eleazar ben Azayah said "I am like one who is seventy years old..."', similarly records a debate in which rabbinic seniority is an issue and concludes that neither youth nor age are barriers to engaging intellectually and emotionally with the Exodus. That event is so significant that it will be discussed even after the coming of the messiah.[23]

These brief portraits of scholars are followed by a doxology, *Barûk ha-makôm...*, 'Blessed be the All-present...', introducing a study-text in the form of a midrashic description of four children, characterized as 'wise, wicked, simple and incurious', each of whom responds differently to the story of the Exodus.[24] The questions they ask, or fail to ask, and the answers they receive echo in number the four questions asked earlier by the youngest present, to which they are perhaps related in origin. The last paragraph in this sequence also takes the form of questions and answers, and narrows down the correct time and place for discussing the Exodus to a moment at which the 'unleavened bread and bitter herbs [both symbolizing poverty] are before you'.[25] It is clear that the sequence of Samuel ends here because the next paragraph opens with the first words of the Haggadah according to Rav. In this way Samuel's narrative traces the passage from slavery in Egypt to the here-and-now of the family table, preparing the ground for the psalms of *Hallel*. If these were to appear here the

---

22 Ibid., 118. This survives only in the Haggadah, but may be compared to T. Pesaḥim 10:12, see 19–20 and Safrai, *Haggadah of the Sages*, 117.

23 Goldschmidt, *The Passover Haggadah*, 118 and the discussion on 20–1, identifying its source as M. Berakhot 1:5. See also Safrai, *Haggadah of the Sages*, 117–19. Professor Raphael Loewe has pointed out in a personal communication that this is possibly a tacit refutation of Paul's 'Christ [is now] our passover' (1 Cor. 5:7).

24 Goldschmidt, *The Passover Haggadah*, 118. The term *banîm*, literally 'sons', is translated inclusively here as 'children' by analogy with *benê Yisra'el*, conventionally 'Children of Israel'. The sources are compared below.

25 Ibid., 119, and discussed 29. See also Safrai, *Haggadah of the Sages*, 124.

Passover theme spanning shame to praise would be neatly encompassed, but they are instead delayed.

Rav's Haggadah

The opening words of the version talmudically attributed to Rav — *Mithilâh 'obdê 'abodâh zarâh hayû 'abotenû*, 'At first our fathers were idolators ...' — follow without interruption.[26] This version of the Haggadah, as the initial words suggest, focuses not only on physical slavery and the Exodus, as did the previous one, but on the interplay between idolatry and the service of God. All these ideas are represented by the word *'abodâh*, literally 'service', used in the previous paragraphs chiefly in the sense of 'slavery', but here as part of a more complex debate.

The opening paragraph cites the post-Exodus book of Joshua's description of the Israelite past from Abraham's election until Israelite slavery,[27] ending with a comparison between Esau's possession of a national territory and Jacob's descent into Egypt, as though to imply the paradoxical nature of Israel's privilege, apparently compromised by exile. The second paragraph opens with a doxology, *Barûk šomer havṭaḥato...*, 'Blessed be He who kept His promise ...', similar to the praise which introduced a study-session in the section attributed to Samuel.[28] In this case the study-text is the pentateuchal promise that Abraham's descendants would be enslaved and rescued, a passage which again spans sacred history, but this time from covenant to fulfilment. The next paragraph, *Vehî' še 'amdâh...*, 'This is [the promise] which has stood...',[29] asserts that Abraham's promise is indeed being kept, despite the exile alluded to in the last words of the first paragraph. It concludes with the statement 'in each generation there are those who rise up against us to destroy us, but the Holy One, Blessed be He, rescues us from their hands', again responding to the themes developed since the opening words of this version and concluding in the here-and-now of the family gathering, as is emphasized by the first-person plural. Survival is celebrated by raising the wineglass while reading that final paragraph, and exile recalled by setting it down undrunk. This marks the end of the present version, to judge by the fact that it is followed by the beginning of the 'normative' text mentioned in the mishnaic discussion. In this way these paragraphs complete a

---

26 Goldschmidt, *The Passover Haggadah*, 119.

27 Josh. 24:2–4.

28 Goldschmidt, *The Passover Haggadah*, 120. On the dating of these paragraphs see Safrai, *Haggadah of the Sages*, 125–6.

29 Goldschmidt, *The Passover Haggadah*, 120.

sequence in which the emphasis is on the awareness of vulnerability and of the privilege of survival, rather than on slavery and its scholarly discussion, as was the case in the first version.

The 'Normative' Haggadah

The third version of the narrative, the one referred to previously as 'normative', begins *Ṣê' ûlemad*, 'Go and learn…', words which seem to invite participants to take a more independent approach than did the previous formulations.[30] Its emphasis is indeed on the narrative itself, rather than on any specific aspect of events, and opens with a midrashic analysis of four biblical verses cited from the firstfruits ceremony. This text which, like that from Joshua in the previous sequence, narratively postdates Israelite liberation, implicitly emphasizes the themes of arrival and security. In style it differs from the previous versions. It aligns each clause with a scriptural parallel, demanding considerable critical acumen to disentangle. The intertextual implications of the juxtaposition justify the challenge suggested in the opening words of this sequence.

Following this midrashic text, but still within the same version of the Haggadah, comes a series of texts believed to be later in date, but not post-gaonic. These include an enumeration of the Ten Plagues, first in full and then in the form of a mnemonic abbreviation, and lastly by three paragraphs in which these are multiplied to a total of 500.[31] This proliferation either reduces the plagues to meaninglessness or magnifies their impact, but medieval commentators noted the near equivalence of the numerical value of the letters in the mnemonic and of the three totals produced by their multiplication, amounting to 501 and 500 respectively, suggesting that Egyptian suffering is similar however it is viewed, be it heavy or light.[32] This preoccupation with the weight of divine punishment may relate to a more general reluctance to rejoice in the downfall of enemies, an idea made explicit in a number of midrashic texts.[33] The hymn, *Dayyenû*, which concludes this sequence shows an analogous

---

30 Ibid., 120. Derived from M. Pesaḥim 10:4.

31 Ibid., 47–8, 123. See Safrai, *Haggadah of the Sages*, 144–50.

32 Menachem Kasher, *Hagadah Shelemah* (Jerusalem 1967) [Hebrew], 52 n. 287 [text section].

33 An awareness of Israelite vulnerability emerges in Rashi on Exod. 14:19, where the possibility they might be drowned is contemplated, and on Deut. 28:60, where they fear the Egyptian plagues. Triumphalism is minimized in the Haggadah by excluding the Song of the Sea, Exodus 15. A brief citation (Exod. 14:31; Goldschmidt, *The Passover Haggadah*, 123) includes a belittling reference to Moses whose name is otherwise absent from the Haggadah. For the silencing of the angels who wished

ambivalence about how one is to understand the coherence of the Exodus, for the poem breaks the entire process down into separate events, each of which might have been 'enough!', as the refrain states, as though the Exodus itself might have been seen as excessive and out of control.[34] This impression of ambivalence about what happened is augmented by the inclusion of two versions of the same hymn, one in verse and the other in prose, the second concluding with the only explicit reference to sin and the fall of the Temple in the Haggadah, since it thanks God for having 'built the chosen house, in order to atone for all our sins'.[35] This brings the reader once again into the here-and-now of exile, thereby preparing the ground for the 'praise' of *Hallel*, adjusting the sense of joyous arrival without cancelling it. Again praise might follow this return to reality, but does not.

Rabban Gamliel's Haggadah

The fourth and last version of the Haggadah includes the mishnaic formulation attributed to Rabban Gamliel, which does introduce the concluding statements and the *Hallel*.[36] The assumed audience is here neither a scholar nor an independent thinker, but someone almost pre-literary, whose attention needs to be gained by means of sight, hearing and taste. The celebrant points, describes and invites participants to taste the symbolic foods, addressing the here-and-now experience of one unable to grasp complex ideas. Each symbolic item is introduced by a formal question — '…what does this mean?' — emphasizing the value of questions as such, and linking these to symbolic foods able to make the tastes of Exodus available. This Haggadah concludes with a statement of the need to identify with the Exodus, which is followed by an introduction to *Hallel*, both of which relate to all the versions of the narratives.[37]

In summary, therefore, each of the four versions included in the Haggadah is distinctive in approach, but concludes in the here-and-now reality of the family gathering. Each differs in approach and even in subject-matter. Samuel's emphasizes slavery and freedom and the intellectual problems these raise, Rav's focuses on the

---

to sing a song of triumph see Louis Ginzburg, *Legends of the Jews* (7 vols, Philadelphia 1909–34), III, 32–3, VI, 12 n. 60.

34 Goldschmidt, *The Passover Haggadah*, 124 and the discussion on 48-51, as well as Safrai, *Haggadah of the Sages*, 150–5 for the possibly gaonic dating of this text.

35 Goldschmidt, *The Passover Haggadah*, 124–5.

36 Ibid., 125.

37 Ibid., 125-6, and the discussion on 53–8; Safrai, *Haggadah of the Sages*, 157–61. The first part appears only in the Haggadah and the second in the *Mishnah* discussed above.

difficulty of survival, the 'normative' sequence addresses the narrative itself and ethical issues raised by triumphalism, while Gamliel's formulation is sensory and non-narrative. These collectively enable the celebrant to take different approaches to the problem of engaging the interest of those present, varying the exposition, arguably, according to their age group, level of understanding and commitment. All are in this way enabled to identify with the experience of survivors and to celebrate their liberation, even though those who are recalling these events are themselves in exile.

This analysis adds a further group of four to those already known to appear in the Haggadah — the four ritual questions, cups of wine and verses analysed in the third version of the Exodus. The number four represents in Hebrew thought the widest possible range of variables, as in the biblical expression 'four corners of the earth',[38] so it may be argued that the four-fold Haggadah is designed to be similarly comprehensive in relating to the needs of different hearers. As such, the closest parallel is with the midrashic description of the four children in the first version of the Haggadah, a text which is similarly concerned with four different modes of understanding the Exodus.[39] This will now be examined for evidence of overlap between the children in that paragraph and the assumptions behind each of the Haggadah narratives.

The Text of the Four Children

The midrashic account of the four children is based on the existence of four separate pentateuchal texts describing how a parent explains the meaning of Passover to a child, in three cases in response to a question and once unprompted.[40] Since it is axiomatic in rabbinic thought that nothing biblical can be superfluous, and because each query and explanation is different, it was concluded that four different kinds of child are intended, each distinguished by character or intelligence. The terms by

---

38 The recurrence of the number four on Passover is viewed rabbinically as derived from the four verbs for rescue in Exod. 6:6–7, followed by the statement that Israel will 'know', in the sense of intimate understanding of the experience of liberation. Biblical texts in which the number four suggests a comprehensive range of possibilities appear in Isa. 11:12 and Jer. 49:36.

39 Goldschmidt, *The Passover Haggadah*, 118.

40 They are derived — in order of their appearance in the Haggadah — from Deut. 6:20, Exod. 12:26, 13:8, 13:14 and again 13:8; the second and third citations are both related to the second child.

which they are referred in this description amount to a crude four-fold typology of a kind familiar in rabbinic thought.[41]

Versions of this reading appear in Mekhilta de Rabbi Ishmael and Talmud Yerushalmi,[42] of the third and fifth centuries respectively, and in the Haggadah, which reached its present form around the ninth century. This last version is juxtaposed with a doxology which is gaonic in date.[43] In Yerushalmi it is attributed to the late-second-century Rabbi Hiyya, Rav's uncle, a contemporary of Yehudah Hanasi and, one may also note, the father of two sons and two daughters.[44] Each version refers to four children, but their characteristics vary, as do the biblical verses related to them. In no case do the biblical verses appear in the same order as in the source, and even questions and answers juxtaposed in the biblical text are redistributed apparently at random rather than related to the same child. Mekhilta lists the children as wise, foolish, wicked and incurious respectively, while Yerushalmi reverses the order of the middle two, mentioning wise, wicked, foolish and incurious children. The Haggadah follows the second order, but replaces the term 'fool' with the gentler one conventionally translated as 'simple', resulting in a cast, familiar since the Middle Ages in manuscript and printed illustrations, of wise, wicked, simple and incurious children respectively.[45]

Certain elements do remain constant across all versions. Taking the paragraphs in the order in which they conventionally appear in the Haggadah, the 'wise' child is associated in all versions with Deut. 6:20, in which an Israelite father, before the entry into the land, is told how to respond to a son who asks what laws were proclaimed by

---

41 See, for instance, M. Avot 5:12–18, and the discussion in Goldschmidt, *The Passover Haggadah*, p. 26 n. 12; Safrai, *Haggadah of the Sages*, 122 n. 11.

42 Goldschmidt, *The Passover Haggadah*, 22–9, Kasher, *Hagadah Shelemah*, 120–1 and Safrai, *Haggadah of the Sages*, 120–4, transcribe and discuss the versions to be found in Mekhilta de Rabbi Ishmael, *Bo* 18, Jacob Lauterbach (ed.) (3 vols, Philadelphia 1949), I, 166–7 (second half of the third century, according to G. Stemberger, *Introduction to the Talmud and Midrash* [Edinburgh 1996], 255) and J. Pesahim 10:4 (first half of the fifth century, see Stemberger, 171). A briefer version is to be found in *Mekhilta de Rabbi Shimon bar Yochai*, David Hoffman (ed.) (Frankfurt am Main 1905), 36.

43 The midrashic passage cannot be shown to have entered the Haggadah earlier. Goldschmidt, *The Passover Haggadah*, 22 and Safrai, *Haggadah of the Sages*, 120, identify the doxology in *Tanna de-bei Eliyahu*, chaps 16 (Friedmann [ed.], 79) and 24 (Friedmann [ed.], 137) and a shorter form in the earlier *Sifrei Deuteronomy* 308 (Finkelstein [ed.], 324). It contains four references to blessing, matching the number of children, see Kasher, 19 [text section]. It appears in the versions of Amram Gaon and Natronai Gaon, but not in those of Saadya Gaon or *Ginzei Schechter*, included in Safrai, 268. It is absent from the Holy Land version also in Safrai, 286–9.

44 BT. Sukkah 20a; BT Yevamot 65b–66a.

45 For instance, Goldschmidt, *The Passover Haggadah*, plate xxxix.

'the Lord our God to you'. Awareness that such a question might eventually be asked and that it requires a clear answer suggests an interest in planning the management of communal memory.[46] The form of the question suggests an interest in detail and fine distinctions, since it distinguishes between 'testimonies, statutes and judgements', the first of which is particularly academic, since it is concerned with ideas rather than with ritual. In none of the midrashic versions is the same response given to this enquiry as in the biblical narrative, however. The latter describes how the father is to respond that 'we were slaves to Pharaoh in Egypt'. In Mekhilta and the Haggadah the question receives a non-biblical answer, the father informing the child in detail of the ritual laws of Passover, ending with the principle that one does not adjourn casually for amusements after the meal. But Yerushalmi quotes Exod. 13:14, stating that 'God brought us out of Egypt and the house of slavery with a strong hand', a text which is addressed in the Haggadah to the 'simple' son and implicitly reflects approval. The biblical response to this question is not employed at all in this text, perhaps because it is the opening sentence of the Haggadah version attributed to Samuel, of which this paragraph forms part.

The question of the second child — 'what is this service to you?' (Exod. 12:26) — which refers in the biblical context to the pascal sacrifice, is attributed in all versions to a child said to be 'wicked'. The biblical answer interprets that offering as a reminder of the smiting of the Egyptian firstborn, but this response is not included in the midrashic paragraph. These writers instead took the words 'to you' as evidence that the child does not feel included, and juxtaposed it with a biblical text which states that 'it' (which is left indefined) is 'because of *this* [an emphasis which suggests anger or a violent gesture] which God did for me in bringing me out of Egypt' (Exod. 13:8). In their biblical context these words are related to the eating of *maṣâh* on Passover rather than to any interaction, let alone an emphatic one of this kind. Each version of the midrash then adds the non-biblical gloss that 'had he been there he would not have been saved', enlarging on the apparently exclusively second-person form of the question by stating that it was because of what God 'did for *me* in bringing *me* out of Egypt'. Commentators argued that the questioner's indifference was evident from the facts that the child merely '*says* [these words] to' the father rather than 'asks' him,[47] and omits God's name from the question.[48] But the evidence against this child remains ambiguous, for the word '*avodah*, literally 'service', could

---

46 See Rashi on Deut. 6:20 and Exod. 13:14.

47 Kasher, *Hagadah Shelemah*, 23 n. 116.

48 Ibid., 23 n. 122. God's name is omitted also from the question of the third child.

mean either the 'service [of God]', which would relate to the Passover ritual as it seems to be in the original, or '[Egyptian] servitude', in other words national slavery, which is the chief association of the *maṣâh* which prompts the biblical response.[49] The editors of the Yerushalmi version suggest that the ritual is the subject, since they expand the opening question to refer to the inconvenience of celebrating Passover. In their view the child is referring to the tiresome annual 'service' in which each is expected to participate, suggesting an unwillingness to participate in social activities. But the other versions imply that the question relates to the relevance of slavery and the Exodus to later generations, in which case the child would be challenging the central Jewish idea that the narrative has permanent validity. In either case, the child would be rejecting a fundamental social value, an idea highlighted by the midrashic writers' choice of response.

The third child, referred to as 'simple' in the Haggadah, but as a 'fool' in Mekhilta and Yerushalmi, asks the same question in each version, 'What is this' (Exod. 13:14), words derived from the same passage as the response to the previous child. The answer in Mekhilta and the Haggadah is the same as in the biblical text, the only biblical exchange kept intact in this way. This states that 'God brought us out of Egypt with a strong hand', emphasizing the first-person plural in contrast to the first-person singular in the answer to the 'wicked' child. But Yerushalmi gives the 'fool' the non-biblical legal response offered in the other versions to the 'wise' child, either reinforcing the view that the question is a good one which deserves a careful response, or because there was no alternative since the 'strong hand' response had already been allocated to the 'wise' child.

The last child, described in all versions as 'one who does not know how to ask', is defined in this way because one biblical answer is prompted by no question. Every version agrees that 'you should broach the matter to him', or more literally 'should open him up', and explain that Passover is celebrated 'because of this which God did for me in bringing me out of Egypt' (Exod. 13:8), a statement unrelated to an inquiry. Rabbinic ambivalence towards this child is clear from the fact that the same answer was given to the 'wicked' child, evidence of a lack of clarity about the nature of the characterization.[50]

---

49 Ibid., 23 n. 118.

50 The use of the feminine imperative in the instruction to 'open him up' is common in early rabbinic writings, and does not suggest the involvement of the mother, see E.D. Goldschmidt, *Die Pessach-Haggada* (Berlin 1936), 44 n. 1.

Rabbinic writers clearly had difficulty defining the psychological types they identified in the four biblical texts, a circumstance which has inspired a number of suggested explanations. Since the 'wicked' child is the only one distinguished ethically rather than according to ability, it has been concluded that the inventory originally consisted of three and that this was a later addition.[51] Attempts have been made to argue that the four children represent different levels of intellectual sophistication, perhaps related to age. But inconsistencies remain, most obviously the admitted intelligence of the 'wicked' child.[52] The Vilna Gaon highlights the uncertainty of the typology by arguing that the children form two pairs of opposites, the first and last distinguished by intellectual ability, and the second and third by virtue. He suggests that the expected order of the questions was disrupted in order to ensure that the listing did not conclude with the 'wicked' one, a position which might imply approval.[53] John Rayner has helpfully suggested that the children are ranked in descending order according to their possession of intellect and virtue, the 'wise' child having both, the 'wicked' and 'simple' one characteristic each, and the 'incurious' neither. He compares this in structure to other rabbinic typologies, including one which categorizes people according to their learning and good deeds.[54] But these solutions fail to resolve all the questions raised by the texts referred to or their arrangement.

Rereading the Four Children

The first child, referred to as 'wise', appears to be as ambivalent about the festival as the 'wicked' one, to judge by the inclusion in the question of a reference to what was 'commanded to *you*'. Attempts have been made to explain the use of this pronoun as an attempt to distinguish between those, like the father, who were present at the revelation, and those, like the child, who were not.[55] Others have pointed out that the 'wise' child adds that these matters were commanded by 'our God', contradicting the

---

51 For a suggested reconstruction of the development see Goldschmidt, *The Passover Haggadah*, 24–9.

52 Abudarham, *Abudarham Hashalem* (Jerusalem 1963), 224, cited in Kasher, *Hagadah Shelemah*, 20 n. 94.

53 See *Sidur Ishei Yisra'el* (Jerusalem n.d.), 519. The juxtaposition of the 'simple' and 'wicked' children is noted in Job 9:22. Cited in John Rayner, 'Die Kinder des Seder', in E.W. Stegemann and M. Marcus (eds) *'Das Leben leise wieder lernen': jüdisches and christliches Selbstverständnis nach der Schoah. Festschrift für Albert H. Friedlander zum siebzigsten Geburtstag* (Stuttgart 1997), 153–63.

54 Ibid., citing M. Avot 5:13–18 and Lev. Rab. 30:12.

55 Kasher, *Hagadah Shelemah*, 21 ns 101, 103.

apparent self-exclusion implied by the pronoun *lakem*, 'to you'.[56] Some liturgical editors — including Mekhilta and Yerushalmi — found it so problematical that they silently changed the scriptural citation to the first-person plural, tacitly admitting the weight of the evidence against this child.[57] The Haggadah retains the incriminating pronoun, which is presumably one of the reasons for which the father's response opens with the emphatic *'ap 'attâh*, 'You must not let this pass, but...', suggesting impatience or even anger.[58]

An additional reason for the father's anger might lie in the questioner's exclusive concern with legalities. The father responds to this child's question by comprehensively surveying the laws of the festival, and concludes by focusing on a detail which involves the withholding of pleasure. The only ruling he mentions is the prohibition against *'afikoman*, a ritual which even 'wise' talmudic rabbis found obscure and which appears towards the end of the tractate devoted to Passover.[59] Since this appears to refer to after-dinner entertainments prohibited on Passover, the answer emphasizes solemnity, even though the child had openly expressed no interest in any amusement.[60] This reason for disapproval is in keeping with the biblical response to this child's question, which ignores the questioner's procedural preoccupation and insists 'We were slaves to Pharaoh in Egypt', as though recalling the need to experience slavery and the Exodus personally. The Haggadah amplifies the implied biblical argument into a rebuke for the child's apparent indifference to slavery, suggesting the father's awareness that the question reflects a misunderstanding of the festival.

The 'wicked' child may similarly be misnamed, for although the father's response opens with the reinforcing word *'ap* as had that of the 'wise' child, there are again grounds for ambivalence. Had this child spoken only as a complacent outsider, unwilling to engage with the values of the family or their ceremonies (as the Yerushalmi suggests), there would indeed be grounds for anger. But the question might rather reflect the child's desire to speak to an older person who had witnessed the Exodus first-hand, an explanation previously offered in mitigation of the 'wise' child's reference to 'you'.[61] Equally the child might be inquiring into the nature of the

---

56 Ibid., 21 n. 99.

57 Ibid., 121–2; Safrai, *Haggadah of the Sages*, 123. It has been suggested that the rabbinic sources reflect an earlier form of the scriptural text, but the ambivalence survives in the Haggadah.

58 Ben Yehuda, *Thesaurus* I, 336–8.

59 M. Pesahim 10:8, BT Pesahim 119b.

60 BT Pesahim 120a.

61 Kasher, *Hagadah Shelemah*, 21 n. 100.

father's experience of Passover, and therefore initiating a debate on the nature of involvement in history and its symbolic representation. Whether the question means 'What is this [divine] service to you?' or 'What is this slavery to you?', therefore, it could represent a child's invitation to a father to describe how Jews still benefit from the Exodus and share a common fate.[62] The father's answer in the midrashic paragraph responds only to the question of the relevance of the slavery, however, perhaps because the theme of ritual was dealt with in the response to the 'wise' child. There the father wished to downplay the importance of ritual, while here he confirms its relevance. The father perhaps feels that focusing again on the slavery would be disruptive to others, so emphasizes instead the need for children to be aware of the historical continuity linking them to their parents and to previous generations. The instruction to 'blunt [this child's] teeth' seems to address the child's complacency and to be designed to 'wipe the smile off his face'.[63] At least this child has recognized the possibility of empathy, however, an idea which seems not to have occurred to the 'wise' one.

It is even possible to see the questions and answers of the 'wise' and 'wicked' children as continuous and sequential, since that of the 'wise' child in the biblical source, concerning the ritual of Passover, receives the answer with which Samuel's Haggadah begins: 'We were slaves ['abadîm] to Pharaoh in Egypt'. The question of the 'wicked' child, 'What is this service/slavery ['abodah] to you?', seems to address that response and to ask what it might mean. The demand that one transcend intellectual detachment and engage with the sacred narrative inspires the 'wicked' child to ask how this can be done.[64]

The third child, who asks merely 'What is this?' is referred to as *tam*, traditionally translated as 'simple' or 'unsophisticated', since the question was taken to reveal merely naive curiosity and little capacity for reflection. Rashi compares the generality of this child's enquiry with the detail in that of the 'wise' child and criticizes this one for 'closing the matter'.[65] But the Hebrew word *tam* also means 'pure', 'straightforward' or 'wholehearted',[66] which would suggest this child's emotional if not intellectual superiority both to the so-called 'wise' and 'wicked' ones. In

---

62 Amos Schonfield, aged eleven, saw that this might reflect a spirit of genuine inquiry about the meaning of the Exodus.
63 See Jer. 31:29 and Ezek. 18:2 for the effect of sour grapes on teeth.
64 Kasher, *Hagadah Shelemah*, 20 n. 94 acknowledges the 'wicked' child's intelligence.
65 Rashi on Exod. 13:14.
66 Ben Yehuda, *Thesaurus* XVI, 7784, it can also mean 'innocent' or 'unblameworthy', see 2 Sam. 15:11, 1 Kgs 22:34.

responding to this question the father can focus freely on the detail of the Israelites' suffering and rescue and the Egyptians' punishment. The child seems able to engage with the narrative, so needs no corrective manoeuvre.

The fourth and last child, 'who does not know how to ask', enjoys such low parental esteem that the father's response uses the same text as for the 'wicked' child, saying how God 'brought *me* out of Egypt', as though to exclude the child from the Exodus. It is less harsh here, since the introductory words of reprimand, *'ap attâh*, are omitted, but the implied critique remains. Almost any question, the name of this child suggests, is better than no question at all, suggesting that the questioner may not be young and pre-verbal, but merely indifferent. The father accordingly explains the story from the outset, presumably pointing to the rituals which inspired the questions of the youngest child earlier, in the hope that this one's curiosity will similarly be aroused.

Four Haggadot for Four Children

Behind the superficial characterization provided by the names allocated to each type, therefore, is evidence of ambivalence about the children's qualities, and even subversion of the terms used to describe them. The behaviour of the 'wise' child is criticized for its limitations, while that of the 'wicked' child is potentially approved, the 'simple' child found praiseworthy, and the incurious one subtly criticized. Each child requires a different narrative approach if it is to be helped to understand the Exodus, this paragraph suggests, and the father's responses summarize the optimal narrative strategies in the briefest form. A fuller and more complex delineation of the responses may be found in the four narratives in the different versions of the Haggadah, however, each of which, as will be seen, relates to the needs of a different child in the midrashic paragraph and appears in the same order as those children.

The Haggadah of the 'Wise' Child

A link between the question of the first child and Samuel's Haggadah is suggested by the first sentence of this version, 'We were slaves to Pharaoh in Egypt...', which is the biblical response to the 'wise' child's question.[67] Just as this child's bookishness and ritual preoccupation leave no room for empathy, so the first paragraph of this

---

67 Deut. 6:20–1.

version of the Haggadah seems to address a detached intellectual reluctant or unable to empathize with the experiences of Israelites. The assertion that even scholars need to discuss the Exodus is followed by examples of rabbis who did so, one group talking the night through even though they were not in the company of their students, and others, introduced by a reference to seniority, debating the post-messianic significance of the Exodus. In the Mekhilta the paragraph is followed by a discussion of how the learned should study the Exodus for its own sake, even if they are alone.[68]

The term 'wise' is saved from being ironic only by the fact that the midrash of the four children itself appears in this version of the Haggadah. This juxtaposition of texts suggest that analytic ability need not totally preclude empathy and may even be essential if the nature of empathy — the subject of the rest of the Haggadah — is also to be understood.[69]

The Haggadah of the 'Wicked' Child

The needs of the 'wicked' child, who threatens to disrupt the attempts of others to empathize, seem to be addressed by the second version of the Haggadah, attributed to Rav. The opening passage of this sequence employs the Hebrew word for 'service' with the same ambiguity as did the question of the wicked child, in the sense both of 'slavery' and 'divine service', while the second paragraph moves to a discussion of the historical continuity from Abraham to the present. The recognition that the historical process affects everyone, and that each person is lucky to be alive, seems calculated to 'wipe the smile' off the face of one who doubts the relevance of Passover. Since exile is compared in rabbinic thought to servitude, moreover, sympathy for the slaves can be equated to solidarity with other Jews.

The Haggadah of the 'Simple' Child

Since the third child seems already engaged with the narrative of the Exodus and in no need of corrective narratives, the father can tell the story without delay. The version of the Haggadah apparently responding to this child's needs therefore recounts the slavery and redemption sequentially and without preamble. But because this child's 'simplicity' is far from naïve, its response is the least 'simple' so far. The

---

68 *Mekilta de-Rabbi Ishmael*, Lauterbach (ed.) I, 167.

69 Titian's 'The Vendramin Family' (1543–7), a typological painting including an older character who looks at the viewer and is the only one with insight into the whole, is discussed by John Drury, *Painting the Word: Christian Pictures and Their Meaning* (London 1999), 25–8.

prooftexts in the midrashic core of this Haggadah transform the four biblical verses into a multilayered exposition ranging over the whole of the sacred narrative,[70] the complex tiering of text and prooftext suggesting an audience capable of sophisticated thought.

An example of this are the words 'a drawn sword in his hand stretched out over [i.e. against] Jerusalem', which is equated exegetically with God's 'outstretched arm' at the Exodus. The prooftext is drawn not from the account of the Exodus, but from that of the plague sent to punish David for having carried out a census of the people, itself paradoxically commanded by God, which was halted by an angel holding an outstretched sword in the way the verse describes. The site on which it stood was declared to be the site of the Temple, and was purchased by the king.[71] This juxtaposition of texts points to the idea that arrival in the Promised Land will not end suffering. Also, the fact that the census was divinely ordained alludes to the way Egyptian slavery, far from being punitive, was predicted to Abraham as part of the divine scheme of history.[72]

In a further complication, the firstfruits ceremony from which the verses are cited takes place only after the participants had completed the Exodus narrative and arrived in the Promised Land, so the chronology in this version reaches far later than the descent to Egypt which is the concluding event in the father's account to the 'wicked' child. Indeed, the supplementary paragraphs appearing after the midrashic survey of these verses carry the narrative forward to the present exile, relating this child more closely to the experience of Jews in every generation than the previous versions.

The Haggadah of the 'Incurious' Child

The version of the Haggadah apparently designed for the child who 'does not know how to ask' contains no narrative as such. The father in the midrashic passage begins his explanation by directing the child's attention verbally to 'this', presumably meaning the ceremonial setting of the family gathering. Rabban Gamliel relies on a sensory language of taste and sight, primary media in the relations between parents and children, and on the act of pointing. The absence of the ability to inquire or challenge is suggested by the way each verbal description is introduced by a question, as though to awaken the inquisitorial instinct which seems so alive in the other

---

70 John Schechter, 'A Still-Wandering Aramean: A Solution to the Haggadah's Prooftexts', *Conservative Judaism* (2000), 52–62, discusses an approach to these sources.

71 1 Chr. 21:16.

72 Gen. 15:13–14.

children. Although this one's incapacity to relate to stories may be due to its young age, the father's use of the same response as for the 'wicked' child, in the midrashic paragraph, suggests that in this case the incuriousness may be a matter of emotional disposition.

Conclusion

The overlap between the midrashic description of the interactions between a father and four children and the four versions of the Exodus narrative appearing in the expository parts of the Haggadah seems too great to be wholly coincidental. But the lack of historical evidence for the development of the Haggadah means that one cannot trace the development of these parallel structures. It can therefore only be regarded as possible, or even probable, either that the editors who finalized the midrash of the four children had the quadrupartite structure of the introductory sequence of the Haggadah in mind, or that the editors of the Haggadah adjusted their work in the light of that midrash. It is even possible that both are the case. In the absence of proof of editorial engagement with these ideas there can be no certainty.

Reading the midrashic passage of the four children in the context of the Haggadah in this way suggests a fresh reading of the structure of each. It would seem that the editors wished to draw attention to an ascending scale of involvement in social thinking, from the detachment of the 'wise' child, via the potential engagement of the 'wicked' one, to the fulsome response of the one referred to as 'simple' and the ability of the last child to taste the symbols of slavery and freedom as though history can be experienced in the present. The first three, who use only language, are increasingly successful in attaining empathy with those who witnessed the Exodus, while the last transcends language altogether by employing symbolic foods for sensory tale-telling. Paradoxically, however, their success is in inverse proportion to their verbal ability. The 'wise' child's question is the most fluent, the 'wicked' one's less so, while the third may have been dubbed 'simple' in part because of the colourless nature of the question. The last dispenses with the verbal medium altogether, turning from language to sense perceptions.

Just as the four versions of the Haggadah offer a pedagogic model for initiating different psychological types into the nature of symbolic thought, so they delineate steps through which the celebrant's own thinking must pass, from the abstract to the sensory, in order to communicate the Passover narrative. The four-fold structure of the Haggadah shows how the celebrant must understand why certain people resist socialization or fail to acknowledge historical values, and must approach or respond to them appropriately. The celebrant does not answer the questions of the first two children as such, but reacts to the emotions that gave rise to them, leading the children towards a deeper understanding of precisely that aspect of the festival which they appear so far to have missed. Only in the case of the last two does the celebrant use story-telling and symbolic foods to generate a real sense of the past. The ability to initiate children in this way involves more than the skill to instruct, since its success depends on the capacity to respond appropriately to resistances such as those of the 'wise' or 'wicked' children. Overcoming their sense of independence from the world around them and its history would require them to unlearn habits of emotional detachment developed while growing up, acquired partly as a result of parental success in 'containing' their emotions as part of the process of socialization.[73] The father must therefore first stimulate independent questioning, and then mediate between the desire for independence and the demands of society.

The text of the four children therefore offers a microcosm of the problem of communicating cultural awareness between generations, problematizing historical memory while examining this as well as the difficulty of constructing group identity in the course of a liturgical and ceremonial sequence. The relevance of parenting to Passover emerges not only from the intense involvement of children in the Haggadah, but from the rabbinic idea that the Exodus reflects the beginnings of a relationship between God and Israel that is commonly described metaphorically as a marriage. The Song of Songs, which is read on Passover and forms the basis of a number of liturgical poems for the first day, is viewed rabbinically as a record of their early attraction to each other, following Israel's discovery of independence after the Exodus.[74] A concern with maturation and the ability of children to form new family units is therefore central to this festival, and the account of the four children, and the four versions of the Haggadah apparently related to them, demonstrate some of the ways this maturation can be promoted.[75]

---

73   R.D. Hinchelwood, *A Dictionary of Kleinian Thought* (London 1991), 420–1, 460–1.

74   One source for this metaphor is Jer. 2:2. See Rashi on Song 1:1. The theme is dominant also in the poems for the first day of Pesach, see Arthur Davis and Herbert M. Adler (eds) *Service of the Synagogue: Passover* (London 1909), 165–71, 175–86; Avie Gold (ed.) *The Complete Artscroll Machzor:Passover* (New York 1990), 566–78, 276–323.

75   This model of a relationship is discussed in Jeremy Schonfield, 'The Jewish Year: Vignette of a Marriage', *The Jewish Year Book 2004* (London 2003), xiii–xix.

'From the Source of *Rahamim*': Graveside Prayer in Habad Hasidism

Naftali Loewenthal

From its earliest generations, the Hasidic movement is noted for its spiritual intensity as regards prayer and other aspects of Judaism, and also for its recognition of 'holy men', the Hasidic Tzaddik or Rebbe. While the focus in most branches of Hasidism is on relationship with a living Rebbe, there remains in the background the kabbalistic heritage of experiencing a connection with a Tzaddik who has passed away, most tangibly at his graveside. In some branches of Hasidism, such as Braslav and now contemporary Habad, where there is no living Rebbe, the graveside relationship is paramount. Investigating this topic raises the more general question of the function of a Hasidic Rebbe in relation to his followers. Let us try to define this in terms of 'opening the door to the spiritual'. We find ourselves in a physical world, and beyond are boundless reaches of spirituality, expressing G-dliness. The individual seeks to enter these realms of the spiritual and draw closer to the Divine. As understood in Hasidism, this is facilitated by the Hasidic leader, whether through personal contact, studying his teachings, following his guidance, or coming to his grave, often called an *'ohel*, 'tent' and connecting with his soul.

Let us begin by considering a few ways in which the Hasidic Rebbe 'opens the door to the spiritual'. The most obvious context of the quest for the spiritual is prayer in the synagogue. The various branches of Hasidism have differing approaches to prayer. For the Habad follower, contemplative prayer entails a sense of the boundless spiritual realms, the *'olamot* described by the Kabbalah, which constitute the inner reality beyond the surface of existence. Focusing on these realms as a kind of ladder towards the infinity of G-dliness, or as a flow of Divine radiance *from* the infinity of G-dliness into the world, means that each Hebrew word of the prayer becomes a vehicle for a sense of contact with the Divine, with the accompanying response of self-surrender, which might be expressed by heartfelt, enthusiastic feeling, expressing love and awe of the Divine, or silent, immobile meditation. Various aspects of the different systems of contemplative prayer in Habad have been explored by Louis Jacobs,[1] Rachel Elior[2] and others.

However one point that has not been considered is the role of the Hasidic leader in this process. It has been pointed out that the first scholars investigating Hasidism were uncomfortable with the too obvious centrality of the role of the Hasidic leader in their own time, and were happy to locate areas of early Hasidic practice where the leader seemed healthily irrelevant. However, this approach may have left some gaps in the full picture. Joseph Dan has made the claim that the role of the Hasidic Zaddik at the beginning of the movement needs re-evaluation.[3]

Let us attempt a beginning of this task by suggesting a model for certain aspects of the role of the Hasidic leader. To illustrate it we will quote a brief passage from a much-discussed early Hasidic text, the *Iggeret Hakodesh*, 'Sacred Letter', of Rabbi Yisrael Baal Shem Tov (d. 1760), generally seen as the founder of Hasidism. The basic substance of the letter is considered authentic by most scholars in the field. There are several versions of the letter, with differences which have been extensively discussed over the past few decades. However, a version of this passage occurs in all of them. The Baal Shem Tov is experiencing an 'ascent of the soul'. He enters a trance-like state, and is conscious of his soul ascending to higher worlds. However, this is a dangerous process. Hence the Baal Shem Tov needs to be helped and protected by his teacher, a soul in the heavenly realms. Thus, in the letter describing this experience, the Baal Shem Tov wrote: 'I asked my instructor and teacher (Rebbe) that he should go with me, for it is very dangerous to ascend to the [higher levels of] the upper worlds'.[4] Another version reads 'Also my teacher, of whom you know, was always with me'.[5]

The teacher is not identified in this text, but in other Hasidic works, in what seems to be a reliable tradition, he is described as the biblical figure Ahiyah the Shilonite, from 1 Kings 11. The Baal Shem Tov felt that the spiritual presence of Ahiyah would help him ascend to higher levels in the spiritual realms, even when this was otherwise dangerous. It was important for the Baal Shem Tov that his teacher should be accompanying him.

---

1   See Louis Jacobs, *Hasidic Prayer* (London 1972) and his works mentioned in notes 29 and 31 below.

2   See Rachel Elior, *The Paradoxical Ascent to G-d: The Kabbalistic Theosophy of Habad Hasidism*, trans. Jeffrey M. Green (Albany, N.Y. 1993).

3   See Joseph Dan, 'Hasidism: The Third Century' in A. Rapoport-Albert (ed.), *Hasidism Reappraised* (London 1996), 424–5.

4   *Keter Shem Tov* (Brooklyn 1973), 2a.

5   Y. Mondshine, *Migdal Oz* (Kfar Chabad 1980), 123.

In the most publicized version of the letter[6] — from 1781 onwards — we also see the Baal Shem Tov himself functioning as a help to other souls which were seeking to ascend higher among the spiritual realms. It seems from this version that some of these souls were of the dead while others were of the living. The Baal Shem Tov writes 'they all begged me ... please ascend with us, so that you can help us'.

Our suggestion is that an important aspect of the Hasidic Rebbe is that he functions as a 'spiritual help', as Ahiyah the Shilonite did for the Baal Shem Tov, and the Baal Shem Tov did for other souls, both of the dead and of the living. His spiritual links with the souls of other Jews, mapped out by Rabbi Elimelekh of Lizhensk (d. 1786), and also his teachings, which themselves were seen as drawn from heavenly realms, have the effect of providing this spiritual access and aid. In Habad, as in most schools of Hasidism, the aim is not that the Hasidic follower should himself or herself acquire the art of travelling in higher spiritual realms: rather, of connecting with the spiritual and drawing its radiance into the world, through prayer, Torah study and the Mitzvot of the Torah. Yet in this process the role of the Rebbe is to open the spiritual channels, to invite and to give aid.

Now, another element in the accounts of the Baal Shem Tov's ascents of the soul is his attempt to protect the Jewish people from persecution, which links too with the famous theme of the blessing given by the Hasidic Rebbe, bringing help to the living in a tangible form: miraculously healing the sick, or enabling a barren woman to bear a child. This further aspect of the Rebbe will be considered in a few moments. At this point we are focusing on this role as helping the individual to gain access to spiritual realms and draw Divine radiance into the world.

Moshe Idel quotes an interesting tradition of a path of intense Hasidic prayer which was believed to be passed down from Ahiyah the Shilonite, to the Baal Shem Tov, to his disciple the Maggid of Mezeritch, to his disciple Rabbi Levi Yitzhak of Berdichev, to his disciple Rabbi Aharon of Zhitomir (d. 1815).[7] The idea of a chain of transmission is particularly important for contemporary Habad. While in some sense here too the line begins with Ahiyah the Shilonite, the Baal Shem Tov and the Maggid, its real distinctive beginning as the Habad School is with the disciple of the Maggid, Rabbi Shneur Zalman of Liadi, founder of Habad. Then it proceeds through

---

6   This is the version printed by Rabbi Yakov Yosef of Polonoye at the end of his *Ben Porat Yosef* (1781) and subsequently reprinted at *the beginning* of *Keter Shem Tov* (1794).

7   R. Yehoshua Abraham ben Yisrael, *Ge'ulat Yisrael*, 1, fol. 17c, Appendix 1, translated in Idel, *Hasidism: Between Ecstasy and Magic* (New York 1995), 177.

his son and a chain of Habad leaders of whom the late Rabbi Menahem Schneerson, who died in 1994, was the seventh.

For the Habad Hasidic follower who engages in mystical contemplative prayer, he feels a door is being opened by this chain of spiritual guides. Through their teachings and their advice, and also simply through a sense of spiritual connection with them, and particularly through his 'own' teacher, entry is permitted to realms which might otherwise be out of bounds. For the scholar investigating the phenomenon of Habad Hasidic prayer the most obvious aspect is the structure of ideas, the 'philosophy'. However, viewing the Habad Rebbe through the model of Ahiyah the Shilonite, we see another important aspect of his role. He is indeed the author of inspiring tracts. Yet in a more mystical way he also grants permission to the Hasidic follower to study those tracts and use them in his or her own spiritual exploration and task. Sometimes his teachings speak of mystical levels which hitherto were considered out of reach, as in the case of Rabbi Dov Ber of Lubavitch (d. 1827), the son of Rabbi Shneur Zalman. In general, the connection of the hasid with the Rebbe acts as a mystical 'key' to gain access to upper realms, and draw Divine radiance into the details of one's own personal life in the world.[8]

Apart from studying the teachings of the Rebbe, the key moment for the special mystical interaction with him is that of *yehidut*, being alone with the Rebbe in private audience. In early Braslav Hasidism this sometimes took the form of a confession of one's sins, as Ada Rapoport-Albert has described.[9] In all Hasidic groups it is seen as an occasion for intimate contact of souls. Zalman Shachter has tried to explore this experience in terms of transaction analysis.[10] In terms of our Ahiyah the Shilonite model for the Hasidic Rebbe one could suggest that this is the moment of bonding in which the Rebbe is able to open doors for the Hasidic follower. The *yehidut* can be a transformative, redemptive experience, and also sometimes the source of special empowerment. Habad traditions describe the Hasid preparing for the *yehidut*, fasting that day, going to the mikveh, saying Psalms. *Yehidut* with the Seventh Lubavitcher Rebbe would generally take place late at night or in the early hours of the morning. Access to *yehidut* was greatly restricted: for a time it was possible once a year, on

---

8   Note the focus in Habad on the 'Lower Unity' — drawing radiance *into* the world, rather than only the 'Higher Unity' cleaving to the Divine beyond this world. See Rabbi Shneur Zalman's *Likutei Amarim – Tanya* (bilingual edition, London 1981), 287 (76b), 309–11 (82a–b).

9   See her 'Confession in the Circle of R. Nahman of Braslav' in *Bulletin of the Institute of Jewish Studies* 1 (1973–5), 65–96.

10 See Zalman Schachter, 'The Dynamics of the Yehidut Transaction', *Journal of Psychology and Judaism* 3:1 (1978), 7–21.

one's birthday, or, as bride and groom, before announcing one's engagement. Later it was restricted to special guests, and for visitors who had come from overseas, and appointments for *yehidut* were made months in advance.

However, the traditional form of *yehidut* ceased in the early 1980s. After this there was a period when 'group *yehidut*' would take place with several hundred people at a time; and then there began a new variety of spiritual interaction. Every Sunday, a long queue of men and women would form outside '770' in order to meet the Rebbe for a moment, receive a dollar from him which was intended as a spur to give charity, and sometimes to exchange a few words. For some, this signified the same kind of meeting as in the traditional *yehidut*. For others it was a new mode of contact, with a simplicity and immediacy which the traditional *yehidut* lacked. No special planning or appointment was needed. Further, it attracted a much wider circle of people, far beyond the Habad Hasidic community. For an orthodox Jew living in Brooklyn in the 1980s, a visit to 'dollars' on a Sunday morning in Crown Heights was a way of experiencing something extra in Judaism.

An example of the way in which a Hasidic Rebbe might enable his followers to gain access to spiritual levels they may not be able to achieve on their own includes the permission to wear a second pair of tefillin. In modern Hasidism these are donned briefly after the morning service for a further recital of the Shema and other texts. These are the tefillin of Rabbenu Tam, in which the passages from the Pentateuch inscribed on parchment have a different order to those in the ordinary 'Rashi' tefillin.[11]

This practice is mentioned in Rabbi Joseph Caro's *Shulhan Arukh* as being suitable only for 'one who is accepted and famous for his piety'.[12] Aaron Wertheim notes that from the early period, the ordinary members of the Hasidic movement would put on Rabbenu Tam tefillin, and that in this way the borders between the 'ordinary man' and the scholar 'famous for his piety' were blurred.[13]

In some cases there is some kind of involvement of the Rebbe in this step beyond one's spiritual station. Thus among the contemporary Viznitz Hasidim, followers of Rabbi Moshe Yehoshua Hager (b. 1916) who lives in Bnei Brak, when a young man gets married he starts to don a large Tallit for prayer, which is automatic and needs no 'permission', and in the recent past he would also ask the Viznitzer Rebbe if he could

---

11 In the 'Rabbenu Tam Tefillin' the order is : Exod. 13:1–10; Exod. 13:11–16; Deut. 11:13–21; Deut. 6:4–9. In 'Rashi Tefillin' the passages are in the order in which they appear in the Torah.

12 *Shulhan Arukh, 'Orah Hayyim*, 34:4.

13 Wertheim, *Law and Custom in Hasidism* (Jerusalem 1989), 79 (in Hebrew).

wear tefillin of Rabbenu Tam. Generally the Rebbe would say yes, but sometimes he would ask the young man to wait a few months or as much as a year after his marriage. When Rabbi Hager became more advanced in years he ceased this personal interaction. Hence, simply by virtue of being a hasid, rather than a *Litvisher* (a non-hasidic *ḥaredi*) a young man at marriage — or, in some groups, a year after marriage — will wear tefillin of Rabbenu Tam.

In the Habad community for many years special permission from the Lubavitcher Rebbe would allow an unmarried youth, or even a Barmitzvah boy (aged 13), to wear Rabbenu Tam tefillin. Thus the Rabbi of the Habad-Lubavitch community in North London, Dayan Itchie Raskin, had private audience, *yeḥidut*, with the Rebbe together with his father just after *bar mitzvah* in the winter of 1973. His father asked the Rebbe if the boy should put on tefillin of Rabbenu Tam. The Rebbe concurred, saying:

> if he will take on not to let his mind be distracted while he is wearing them. About forbidden thoughts one does not need to mention, but even permitted thoughts also not. And the advice how to do this is to look in the Siddur [while saying the Shema and other passages]. Especially since it is only ten minutes.

Two years later the same boy again visited New York and had *yeḥidut* with the Rebbe. In his *yeḥidut tsetel* (note), he wrote that the Rebbe's demand that he focus his attention while wearing Rabbenu Tam tefillin was difficult to achieve. The Rebbe answered him, in Yiddish:

> When there falls in a *maḥšabâh zarâh* (foreign thought) — you should raise your voice a little and that will drive away the *maḥšabâh zarâh*.[14]

A few months after this, on Purim in the spring of 1976, in a public talk which was broadcast through the phone system to many international centres, the Lubavitcher Rebbe stated that now people should no longer ask about the wearing of tefillin of Rabbenu Tam, everyone should from Barmitzvah on.[15] As a result, the Habad community is distinguished by the fact that from Barmitzvah, all boys wear tefillin of Rabenu Tam, unlike in other Hasidic groups where they are only worn after marriage. Who permits the young boy to make this extra step of 'holiness'? The Rebbe. Thus we see, in a contemporary form an example of how a Rebbe can give access to spirituality.

---

14   Oral communication by Dayan Itchie Raskin, London, May 1995.
15   In fact Lubavitch boys start wearing tefillin two months before Barmitzvah.

In the first generation of the Habad movement, it seems that this aspect of the Rebbe was his primary role: teacher and guide, who opens the doors to spiritual realms. A famous letter by Rabbi Shneur Zalman insists that his function is not to give blessings for material concerns; a similar letter by his older colleague and mentor Rabbi Menahem Mendel of Vitebsk states, 'the Baal Shem Tov was unique' in his power to give blessings and work miracles.[16] However, over the generations, giving blessings for the material concerns of 'children, health and sustenance' became a feature of the Habad leaders just as it was of other Hasidic Rebbeim, certainly by the time of Rabbi Yosef Yitzhak, the Sixth Habad Rebbe (d. 1950). Indeed, in the view of his son-in-law and eventual successor, Rabbi Menahem Mendel, to ask a blessing from Rabbi Yosef Yitzhak for something practical like an operation or to find a *shidduch* (marriage partner) was an important level of connection with him, for the Jew who was not a member of the Habad Hasidic group. Rabbi Menahem Mendel saw this as an initial step of relationship with Habad, which the Habad Hasidim of a city like Paris in the late 1940s should seek to engender among their acquaintances.[17]

So we see two main characteristics of the Hasidic Rebbe: he opens spiritual doors, in various ways, and brings blessing for 'children, health and sustenance'.

Now let us examine what happens when the Hasidic Rebbe passes away, especially when there is some uncertainty about his successor, or when there is clearly and adamantly no successor, as in the case of Braslav after 1810 and Habad-Lubavitch after 1994.

Connection with a Departed Zaddik

While during almost a century of scholarship as well as general Jewish communal life we have become familiar with the Hasidic movement, and regard a living Zaddik to whom people flock for spirituality and blessing as the norm, this was not always the case. Hasidism grew out of kabbalism, and for the sixteenth century kabbalists of Tsfat (Safed) in Northern Israel, the norm was to go to the grave of a departed Zaddik in order to gain important spiritual goals, or to connect with his soul even if this took

16 See Rabbi Shneur Zalman's *Litukei Amarim – Tanya* Part IV, sec. 22, and Rabbi Menachem Mendel of Vitebsk, *Pri Ha'Areṣ* (Jerusalem 1974), 8.

17 A letter of 1949, from Rabbi Menahem Mendel, to the Habad Hasidim in Paris, asks why they have not been sending any requests for blessings 'for an operation, a *shidduch*, or requests for a blessing for Rosh Hashanah' from members of the wider Jewish community (*'Iggrot Kodeš R. Menahem Mendel* III, 57). This letter presents request for a blessing as the outermost level of contact with the Rebbe.

place in one's own home. This connection is called *yiḥud*: it is a connection between souls, and also between spiritual qualities, the *Sefirot*. According to *Shaʿar Ruaḥ Haqodesh*, by Rabbi Haim Vital, one can carry out a *yiḥud* at the grave of the Zaddik, which imparts an extraordinary sense of unity between the person and the Zaddik: as if the Zaddik is now living in the body of the man who has come to his grave. Or one can achieve the *yiḥud* at home, but the main effect is the same: the bonding of one's soul with that of the departed Zaddik — '*ve-napšeka kelûlâh be-napšo*' — 'your soul will be included with his'. This connection between souls imparts a power to heal and purify one's own soul, and to raise it to exalted heights, and to achieve repentance for oneself and for others. Thus a kabbalist whose son had left Judaism was taught a *yiḥud* by Rabbi Isaac Luria, and he was able to cause his son to repent.[18]

According to this text, most Zaddikim have the ability to grant this kind of connection with their soul, with great spiritual effect, *after they have passed away*. However there are some Zaddikim who are so great that they could achieve this in their life-time as well. Rabbi Haim Vital gives a number of examples of Zaddikim on this level: they are biblical or Zoharic figures. One is Benayahu ben Yehoyadah, ben Ish Hai (2 Sam. 23:20). He is called 'ben Ish Hai'—i.e. 'living', *even* after his death, because 'even in his lifetime he would unify all worlds'.[19] It seems that here we have the source of both facets of the Hasidic movement which emerged two centuries later: firstly, the belief that the living Rebbe was able to 'join worlds' in his lifetime; secondly, the belief that the living retains his power, to a special degree, after his death.

Hence when a Rebbe passes away and, instead of appointing another Rebbe, the Hasidim continue their sense of connection with him by going to his grave, they are in a sense calling on an earlier form of kabbalism. As mentioned, the two foremost examples of this are Braslav and contemporary Habad.

Braslav

In the case of Rabbi Nahman of Braslav there is a clear statement from him, given before he passed away, that if anyone will come to his grave, read the *Tikkun Kelali*, the set of ten Psalms which he had revealed as something of great spiritual

---

18 *Shaʿar Ruah Hakodesh* (Jerusalem 1963), 75–6.

19 Haim Vital, *Shaʿar Ruah Hakodesh*, 74. Moses, Rav Hamnuna Sava and Rav Yaibey Sava are also mentioned.

significance, and give a coin to charity, then however grievous the sins of that man, Rabbi Nahman would 'try to come from the furthest reaches [of the heavens] in order to save him and give him *Tikkun*, [spiritual healing]'.[20]

Rabbi Nahman's faithful disciple Rabbi Nathan Sternhartz was with him as he passed away during the festival of Succot, 1810. Just before he died, Nathan cried out: 'Master, to whom do you leave us?'. Rabbi Nahman awoke, and turned his face towards Rabbi Nathan as if to say 'G-d forbid! I am not leaving you!'.[21] At least, this is how Rabbi Nathan interpreted his look.

After Rabbi Nahman passed away, in a process described by Ada Rapoport-Albert,[22] Rabbi Nathan first occupied himself with publishing Rabbi Nahman's books, as the living expression of the Rebbe. Then Rabbi Nathan decided to spend the first Rosh Hashana after Rabbi Nahman's death in Uman, where he was buried. Other Braslav Hasidim had the same idea, and thus began the practice of visiting the *Tziyun* (grave, lit. 'sign') at Uman, Rabbi Nahman's grave, at special times. So there developed what was long seen as a unique form of Hasidism, focusing on studying books of teachings, reciting the *Tikkun Kelali* and visits to the *Tziyun*, all powerfully guided by Rabbi Nathan and by successive generations of senior Braslav Hasidim, but without anyone being considered an actual 'successor' to Rabbi Nahman. As Arthur Green expressed it: 'The unique relationship he had with his disciples, unique in both quality and intensity, did not allow him in any way to be "replaced"'.[23] For nearly two centuries, despite opposition, for a variety of reasons, Braslav Hasidism has continued. It thrives particularly in Northern Israel, focusing on the Tsfat atmosphere and tomb of Rabbi Shimon bar Yochai. Now, after glasnost, at Uman, each year, on Rosh Hashana, thousands participate. Braslav teachings and stories have attracted the attention of poets and thinkers: Rabbi Nahman has not been replaced.

---

20 *Shivhei HaRan* (Jerusalem 1961), section *Sihot HaRan*, para. 141, 97.

21 Arthur Green, *Tormented Master: A Life of Rabbi Nahman of Bratslav* (Alabama 1979), 281, from R. Nathan's *Yemei Muharanat* (Bnei Brak 1956), 86.

22 In Ada Rapoport-Albert, *The Problem of Succession in the Hasidic Leadership, with Special Reference to the Circle of Rabbi Nahman of Braslav* Doctoral Thesis (University of London 1974), and in 'Dead Hasidim' an unpublished paper she gave in Philadelphia, April 2003.

23 *Tormented Master*, (n. 16 above), 265.

Habad

At the same period that Rabbi Nathan was creating the new Braslav movement around the books and the *Tziyun* of Rabbi Nahman, the Habad community was also going through a time of turmoil. When its founder Rabbi Shneur passed away in 1812, during the aftermath of the Napoleonic War, there were two contenders for the role of successor: Rabbi Shneur Zalman's son Rabbi Dov Ber, and his disciple Rabbi Aaron Halevi Horovitz. Both of these became leaders of Hasidic groups, in Lubavitch and Starosselye respectively. At the same time there were Hasidim who thought that no one could replace Rabbi Shneur Zalman. It is possible that for all these groups, occasional visits to his *'ohel*, which was in Haditz, in the Ukraine, about 400 miles from Lubavitch and Starosselye, and therefore necessitating a deliberate pilgrimage, had a certain spiritual role.[24] During the course of the nineteenth century the town of Lubavitch itself became the site of the graves of the third and fourth generation leaders, Rabbi Menahem Mendel the Tzemah Tzedek who died in 1866 and his successor Rabbi Shmuel who passed away in 1882.[25] How were grave visiting and the relationship with a departed Rebbe perceived by the Habad Hasidic followers?

Information on this is provided by a letter written by Rabbi Shneur Zalman, which was included by his sons in the posthumously enlarged edition of his *Tanya* printed in 1814, and by a work entitled *Kuntres HaHishtathut*, Tract on Prostration [at Graves], printed several times in the nineteenth century and again in the twentieth, sometimes attributed to Rabbi Dov Ber of Lubavitch.

Iggeret Hakodesh Chapter 27

Rabbi Shneur Zalman's letter, *Iggeret Hakodesh* Chapter 27 in the fourth part of *Tanya* (145b–147b), was written after his older colleague and mentor Rabbi Menahem Mendel of Vitebsk passed away in 1788. Rabbi Menahem Mendel had led the Hasidic migration to the Land of Israel in 1777, settling first in Safed and later in Tiberias. He retained links with the Hasidic community in Russia through his letters, although he also empowered Rabbi Shneur Zalman to function as a Hasidic leader in

---

24 There are anecdotes about Rabbi Aaron of Starosselye and Rabbi Dor Bev of Lubavitch visiting the *'ohel* in Haditz. See Hielman, *Beit Rebbe* (Berdichev 1902), 134, n. 3.

25 See Avrum Ehrlich, *Leadership in the Habad Movement* (Northvale NJ 2000), 108.

his own right. When he passed away Rabbi Shneur Zalman wrote a letter addressed to his followers in the Holy Land.

The letter focuses on a number of key concepts in the relations of a person with a departed Zaddik:

1. 'The effect of the Zaddik is life' (Prov. 10:16), that is, grants spiritual life to those who are bonded with him through bonds of love;

2. and especially, to those who walk in the pathways which he taught;

3. the concept from the Zohar, that 'a Zaddik who has passed away is found in all worlds more than in his lifetime',[26] comments Rabbi Shneur Zalman, means especially in *this* world, due to the fact that more and more people follow his spiritual teaching;

4. all this concerns spiritual effects, but as regards material well-being, the Zohar states that 'the Zaddikim protect the world more in their death than in their life' and 'were it not for the prayers of the Zaddikim in that [other] world, [our] world would not be able to exist for a moment'.[27]

A second part of the letter explains that the passing of a Zaddik enables his effect in the world to be all the greater. The main 'life' of a Zaddik consists of his faith in and awe and love of G-d. This is what he wishes to impart to others. However, while he is alive, these qualities are veiled by his physical body. After leaving the world, these spiritual qualities which are his true being and his true message to others, now untrammelled by the body, are able to radiate far more powerfully from his spirit in the Garden of Eden. This reaches his disciples through the channel of the love between them 'for only through great love does spirituality flow'. This kind of relationship with the Zaddik, says Rabbi Shneur Zalman, demands conscious effort on the part of the disciple. The author of the letter does not mention visiting the grave, but he is implying that the disciple makes a conscious attempt to connect spiritually with the departed Zaddik.

However, says Rabbi Shneur Zalman, there is also an unconscious form of relationship of a Zaddik for all those whom his teachings have affected. As the soul of the Zaddik ascends higher in spiritual realms, it transmits inspirations and thoughts of repentance to this wider group, just as the effulgence of Moses inspires the entire Jewish people through the generations, for they all have a connection with his teachings through the Torah. Thus many people who may hardly be aware of the Zaddik receive spiritual benefit form him.

---

26 Zohar, III, 71b.

27 Ibid., see also Zohar, II, 16b.

If we compare these ideas with their kabbalistic sources we see the process of Hasidism as deconstructive, removing barriers and giving access. Rabbi Haim Vital's depiction of carrying out a kabbalistic *yiḥud* at the grave of a Zaddik demanded implicitly that the person attempting this be on a high spiritual level himself, with the ability to pierce through the objective reality of the grave and reach the spiritual Zaddik within. Then came Hasidism, revealing a tangible Zaddik of flesh and blood, who could relate to simple people and their lives. The Hasidic community became a deconstructed form of the small Lurianic mystic circle, focusing on the central figure of Rabbi Isaac Luria, who mediated *yiḥud* relationships with the departed Zaddikim buried in and around the ancient city of Safed.

However, with the death of the Zaddik, in this case Rabbi Menahem Mendel of Vitebsk, bridging the second and third generations of Hasidism, a new form of relationship is described. By studying and following the teachings of the Zaddik one has a connection with him: this might be a *conscious* connection, in which the person feels he is a 'disciple' or 'follower' of that Zaddik, or it might even be an unconscious connection. In either case, although to varying degrees, the effect of the Zaddik is described as bringing spiritual encouragement and inspiration to others, on wider and wider levels.[28]

All this is without mentioning actually visiting the grave of the Zaddik. This is probably because Rabbi Shneur was partly addressing his words to the Eastern European Hasidic community, whom he saw as 'disciples' of Rabbi Menahem Mendel of Vitebsk, and, of course, unable to reach his grave unless they travelled to the Holy Land.

The second text, *Tract on Prostration* [*at Graves*] fills that gap. It is not clear when it was first published, and to what extent it was available in manuscript before it was printed. It has certain stylistic qualities reminiscent of Rabbi Dov Ber, the son of Rabbi Shneur Zalman[29] and in some printed texts and manuscripts this attribution is made explicitly.[30] It may have been written by Rabbi Dov Ber after the passing of his father, but not printed, simply because he was himself functioning as the living

---

28 This mirrors a claim made in Rabbi Shneur Zalman's *Tanya*, Part I, chapter 2, written in the shadow of the fierce opposition of the *mitnagdim* to the Hasidic movement, that even people who oppose the Zaddik are given spiritual input by him.

29 Namely, the abbreviation meaning 'and sufficient for the wise' *vd''l* which concludes many paragraphs in the tract. Also, the division into five ascending levels is reminiscent of Rabbi Dov Ber's *Tract on Ecstasy*, translated by Louis Jacobs (London 1963).

30 See *Sefer HaHishtathut* (Brooklyn 1996), 35, and *Ma'amarei Admur HaEmtza'i Kuntreisim* (Brooklyn 1991), 31.

successor to his father, and his followers were invited to come to him and hear *his* discourses of Hasidic teachings rather than to focus on his father's grave in distant Haditz. Nonetheless, on visiting the grave, as we know his followers did,[31] there was a spiritual gain to be achieved, and perhaps in order to facilitate this Rabbi Dov Ber compiled the tract. Rabbi Dov Ber himself would visit his father's grave, especially at times of stress. The last year of his life, 1827, was very difficult on several counts: personal attacks against him by the opponents of Hasidism, which had led to him being arrested in a way which mirrored the arrest of his father a quarter of a century earlier; his anxiety about the Jewish community as a whole, particularly as regards the Cantonist Decree which had been feared by Jewish leaders for years and was finally promulgated in 1827, forcing Jews to enter the Russian army for long periods, with a strong conversionary intent; and failing health. Late in 1827 Rabbi Dov Ber set off to Haditz, to pray at his father's grave, but he himself died on the journey and was buried at Niezhin about 100 miles from Haditz.

With two significant Habad graves of Zaddikim in the same region, it was likely people would make the considerable journey from Lubavitch and the environs to visit them. Probably at this point the *Tract on Prostration* [*at Graves*] was printed, albeit anonymously.

This first edition of the *Tract* includes also the text of the letter by Rabbi Shneur Zalman discussed above, and, in addition, in the body of the *Tract* there is a commentary on the letter. The *Tract* presents in an accessible way the different levels of emotion that a person might feel on visiting firstly, graves of any kind, reminding one of mortality or, secondly, making one feel that this is a holy place, for there are Zaddikim buried here. The third level is when visiting the grave of one's parent or a close relative, which can open one's heart to repentance. The fourth level, is when visiting the grave of a Zaddik whom one knew. The spiritual quality of the soul of the Zaddik is present in the *Tziyun* constructed at his grave, and the person can achieve a sense of connection with the Zaddik, resulting in his own prayer becoming more spiritual. At this point comes the exposition of sections of Rabbi Shneur Zalman's letter about the connection with a Zaddik after he has passed away.

Now comes a more practical discussion by the author of one's relationship with a living Rebbe, and how one should stir oneself to go and visit him, in order to strengthen oneself, even though one can read his Hasidic teachings at home. How

---

31 So too did his rival as leader of the Habad movement, Rabbi Aaron. Concerning the latter see Louis Jacobs, *Seeker of Unity—The Life and Works of Aaron of Starosselje* (London 1966).

much more so when the Zaddik has left the world! Due to the pressures of daily life the sense of connection with the Zaddik is weakened, so certainly one should embark on the journey to his grave: indeed, the journey itself has spiritual value. Then at the grave, one's prayers are able to rise, because they are lifted by the soul of the Zaddik. Even those who have never seen the Zaddik, but who study his teachings, gain a spiritual uplift by coming to his grave. The fact that they study the teachings of the Zaddik gives them the ability to glimpse something of his spiritual greatness, without harm.[32]

Finally, the tract ends with a brief exposition of the fifth level, the mystical level described by the kabbalists, whereby through *yiḥudim* as described by Rabbi Isaac Luria one reaches exalted levels of understanding of Torah, and *Rûaḥ Ha-Qodeš*. This final level is not the focus of the work: that is presented as being on a level beyond the intended reader, but perhaps tells us something further about Rabbi Dov Ber's relationship with his own father after the latter had passed away. As described in some interesting texts, Rabbi Dov Ber would enter a kind of trance-like state in which the soul of his father would come to teach him mystical teachings of Torah.[33] The focus of the tract is rather the fourth stage, the idea of maintaining a relationship with a Hasidic Rebbe by means of study of his teachings and making the journey to get to his grave, even if one has never seen him.

The Twentieth Century

This leads us to the twentieth century. When Rabbi Yosef Yitzhak Schneersohn, the Sixth Lubavitcher Rebbe, passed away in Brooklyn in 1950, his son-in-law Rabbi Menahem Mendel Schneerson had no children, and his wife, the younger daughter of Rabbi Yosef Yitzhak, was nearly 50 years old. There was another son-in-law, Rabbi Shemaryahu Gurari, who did have a son, and perhaps the fact that he himself would not have a successor prevented Rabbi Menahem Mendel from accepting leadership of the Lubavitch Hasidic following for some time. However, as a result of a campaign by certain leading Hasidim, after a year Rabbi Menahem Mendel seemingly accepted the role of Rebbe, although in an unusual way.

---

32 This is phrased in terms of T.B. Baba Metzia 85b. A scholar was taught by Elijah how to see the souls of the departed Sages. However, his eyes were burnt by looking at Rabbi Hiya's canopy. To cure himself he went to his grave and studied his teachings.

33 See G. Nigal (ed.), Y. Kaidaner, *Sippurim Noraim* (Jerusalem 1992), 93.

One distinctive feature of his leadership was that he did not refer to himself as Rebbe. In the thousands of pages of his talks his deceased father-in-law Rabbi Yosef Yitzhak is the Rebbe, the leader of the generation. This was seen by his followers simply as an expression of humility. However, in an even more unusual way, throughout his active life as Hasidic leader, Rabbi Menachem Mendel presented an example of maintaining a relationship with a deceased Rebbe, namely the Sixth Rebbe, by means of visiting his grave, the *'ohel*. In the earlier years he would visit the grave twice a month. This gradually increased, to once a week and, in his final years, to several times a week. As discussed above, a Hasidic Rebbe receives requests for blessings, in the form of letters, *tsetlakh*. If the request came by 'phone, it would be written down. These letters would be taken by the Rebbe to the *'ohel* of Rabbi Yosef Yitzhak and he would read them there, spending hours standing alone at the grave. When someone asked for a blessing, for a business venture, for an operation, for a new Habad House, the customary formulations through which Rabbi Menachem Mendel expressed approval and signified that a blessing would be given was with the words '*azkir al ha-Tziyun*', 'I will mention it at the *Tziyun* (grave)'.

What are the implications of this? Why did the Seventh Lubavitcher Rebbe resist the role of Rebbe in his own right, like the Belzer, Bobover, Satmarer, Viznitzer or any other Rebbe of the post-Holocaust period?

It is interesting that according to an informant close to the inner circle of Lubavitch, when Rabbi Yosef Yitzhak passed away, Rabbi Menahem Mendel asked an acquaintance of his, a prominent Braslaver named Rosenfeld, to bring him Braslav material on visiting graves. Does this mean that Rabbi Menahem Mendel saw Rabbi Yosef Yitzhak as someone who could not ever be 'replaced'? Or, as was suggested by a leading Habad figure, Rabbi Itchie Meir Kagan, does it mean that Rabbi Menahem Mendel was, from the start, trying to provide a pattern for his followers after his *own* demise?

He knew that he and his wife Chaya Mushka would not have children. His role as Rebbe emerged from his marriage to her, so to marry another woman under any circumstances was unthinkable. Further, for the most part, the Hasidic movement had abandoned the idea of transmission of leadership to a prominent disciple. So, as seen by Rabbi Menahem Mendel, there were two remaining options: the coming of the Messiah, or the establishment of the *'ohel* into a potential central focus for the Habad movement. He indeed tried to bring the Messiah, in the ways that he understood as possible, and, in 1992, after the Gulf War, expressed his disappointment that the

Messiah had not come. At the same time he presented a concept of a *Rebbistve*, a mode of being Rebbe, in which the *'ohel* was the focal point.

During Rabbi Menahem Mendel's lifetime, once or twice a year the local Hasidim too might visit the *'ohel* where Rabbi Yosef Yitzhak was buried. When Rabbi Menahem Mendel became ill, there were visits to the *'ohel* to ask for blessings that he be healed.

Now, however, the sixth and seventh Habad Leaders are buried side by side. Visiting their grave, saying Psalms or reciting the *Maaneh Lashon* is a significant element in Habad Hasidic life. The *Maaneh Lashon* was first published in Prague, 1610, and was reprinted many times for recital at the graves of Zaddikim. The version used by the Habad Hasidim was edited by Rabbi Yosef Yitzhak in 1912 for use when visiting Rabbi Shneur Zalman's grave at Haditz.[34] In 1950 there was a new edition, inserting Rabbi Yosef Yitzhak's name in the *Yehî Raṣôn* at the end, and in 1994 a further edition with the addition of Rabbi Menahem Mendel's name. Further editions, with English translation, introduction and notes followed.

Apart from briefly greeting the Zaddikim at the beginning, in general, the text throughout is careful to address G-d as the focus of one's prayer. At a certain point one reads one's *tsetel* and then tears it up and throws it into the top of the grave. Then there are Psalms and a long passage from the Zohar about the power of the departed Zaddikim to help this world.[35] At the end is a *Yehî Raṣôn* asking G-d to grant life 'and all the requests of our heart, by the merit of the Tannaim and Amoraim ... and by the merit of the Zaddikim who are buried here, and especially by the merit of...' — and here the names of Rabbi Yosef Yitzhak and Rabbi Menahem Mendel are inserted.

The *tsetel*, the typical text of a person's letter to the *'ohel* might read, addressed to the Rebbe: 'please arouse great mercy for me, from the source of *Raḥamim*, for success in material and spiritual matters ...'. One would add the specific points which are an issue at the moment in one's life, and give one's Jewish name, when known, and mother's name. Following the practice from the life-time of the Rebbe, in the case of asking a blessing for a non-Jew, one gives the name of the person and his or her father's name.

The writing of the *tsetel*, as in the days when the Rebbe was alive, is itself seen as a significant activity. A person asks himself or herself: What are the important things in my life?

---

34 It is based on a version compiled by Rabbi Dov Ber for recitation at Haditz.
35 Zohar, III, 70b–71b.

The effect of a visit to the *'ohel* is seen as similar to *yeḥîdut*: a connection of soul with soul, a sense of access to spirituality and empowerment. There is also a sense of joining worlds. A woman described it to me as like childbirth: the sense of a soul coming from one world into another, or like witnessing the moment of death, when a soul moves from this world to another. Yet at the *'ohel* both worlds are there at the same time.

The Lubavitch *'ohel*, in Queens, New York, is run by a young British Rabbi from Leeds and his wife. There is a Beit Hamedrash, and a place to sit and write one's *tsetel*.

Before the *'ohel*, for a man, there is the mikveh, and a modern one has been built nearby. The Hasidim do not eat a meal before going to the *'ohel*, although they do drink. Hence there is refreshment available after being at the *'ohel*. There are special arrangements for Cohanim to walk to the *'ohel*: a long-standing tradition declares that the graves of the Zaddikim are not impure. However, the roof of the *'ohel* is open, and a Cohen does not stretch his hand over the grave.

Apart from visiting the *'ohel* in person, men and women might send in a letter by hand, by fax or even e-mail, generally asking the attendant Rabbi to read it at the *'ohel*. These requests come almost continually from round the world.

Just as there are miracle stories about Hasidic leaders, there are miracle stories about the *'ohel*. The blessing asked at the *'ohel* which was miraculously effective, the way that something that happened at the *'ohel* helped a person make up his mind that this is, indeed, the girl he should marry, and similar.

The *'ohel* is always open. It seems that at any time, day or night, there are likely to be visitors. In the course of an ordinary week, hundreds come. At special times, thousands. The high point of the Conferences of Lubavitch Shluchim and Shluchot, the male and female emissaries round the world, held in the winter and early spring respectively, is a group visit to the *'ohel*. Packed inside and crowded outside, a group *tsetel* is read by a senior figure. The content, naturally enough, is peace in Israel, success in one's *shelichut*, health, finding *shidduchim* for children, the advent of the Messiah. With the Rebbe holding the door open to upper worlds, the Hasidim ask for blessings of mercy, from G-d, the source of mercy.